MERRY CHRISTMAS 1993

STEVEN,

THE HOCKEY NEWS PUBLISHED THE FIFTY BEST PLAYERS OF ALL TIME. THIS BOOK IS A RECAP, AS YOU HAVE NOTICED, I GUESS IT COULD BE USED AS A CONVERSATION OR ARGUEMENT STARTER.

BROTHER OLIVER.

IT WAS A LITTLE DIFFICULT TO GET THE PRICE OFF THIS ONE. [SEE JACKET] ALSO, I SEE TODD GILL'S NAME HAS CONSPICOUSLY BEEN LEFT OFF THE LIST.

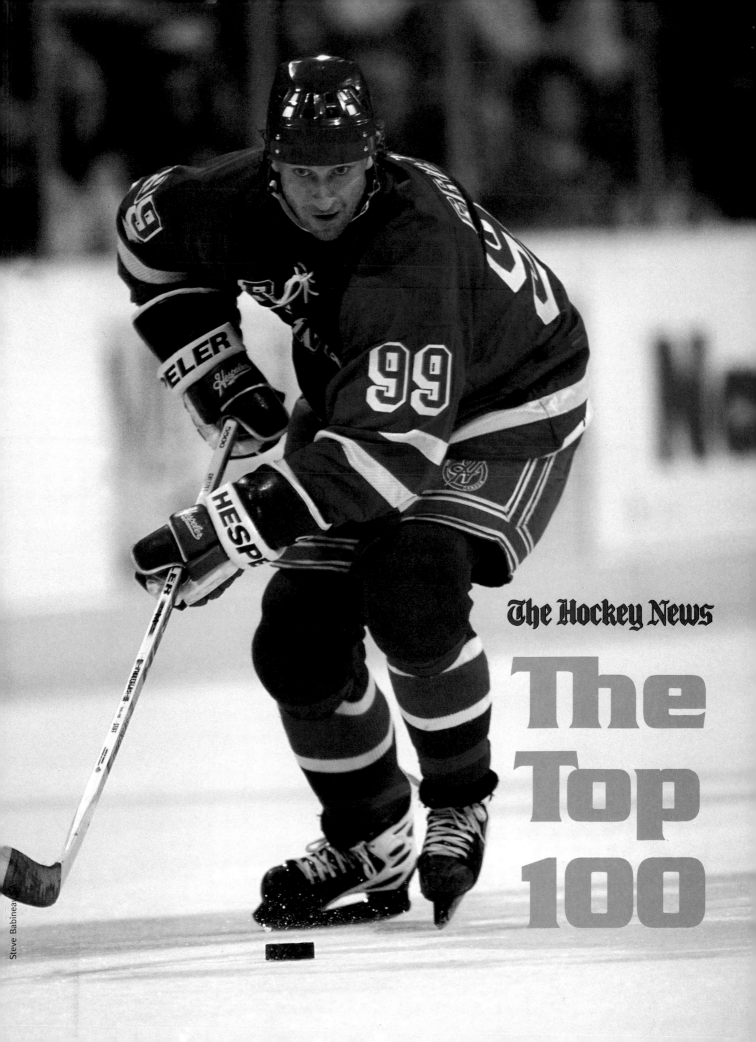

The Hockey News

The Top 100

Foreword by **Wayne Gretzky** • Edited by **Steve Dryden** • Principal Writer **Michael Ulmer**

The Hockey News

The Top 100

NHL HOCKEY PLAYERS OF ALL TIME

M&S

CONTENTS

Foreword
by Wayne Gretzky / 6

Habs Dominate
Top 100 Players / 8

No Higher Level
by Steve Dryden / 9

Canadian Cataloguing in Publication Data

Main entry under title:

The top 100: NHL players of all time

ISBN 0-7710-4175-6

1. Hockey players – Biography. 2. National Hockey
League – Biography. I. Dryden, Steve, 1957– .

CB848.5.A1T66 1998   796.962'092'2   C98-931297-6

We acknowledge the financial support of the
Government of Canada through the Book Publishing
Industry Development Program for our publishing
activities. We further acknowledge the support of
the Canada Council for the Arts and the Ontario Arts
Council for our publishing program.

Design concept developed by *ICE*
Typeset by *The Hockey News* and M&S, Toronto
Printed and bound in Canada

McClelland & Stewart Inc.
The Canadian Publishers
481 University Avenue
Toronto, Ontario
M5G 2E9

1   2   3   4   5   6   03   02   01   00   99   98

Foreword

By Wayne Gretzky

I recall so vividly riding home in my father's car, still in uniform, after having played an exhibition hockey game that followed our regular season and playoffs. I was nine years old and as I gazed out the window my mind was fixed on the pitcher's mound at Brant Park, where I was due to pitch the next day in a Little League game.

We had been soundly defeated in the hockey game and, looking back, my mind was probably on baseball even when I was on the ice. My dad went to great lengths during the drive home to explain that many people had gone to the arena that day to watch our team play. Although he didn't say that I quit on my teammates and myself, he did say I hadn't put in the effort I should have, regardless of the game's relative insignificance.

He was absolutely correct.

Some 28 years later, after spending nearly three decades following my dad's advice, I have been asked to comment on what it means to top The Hockey News' list of the best players in NHL history.

It is that work ethic, instilled by Walter Gretzky, that has served me so well.

Like so many youngsters, I grew up reading The Hockey News. The first time my name appeared in that paper, I felt a sense of amazement. Dick Duff, Frank Mahovlich, Henri Richard, and me, Wayne Gretzky—all in the same publication. Another treasured memory is the first time my picture appeared on the cover–Oct. 27, 1978, in an Indianapolis Racers' jersey.

I have had the good fortune to be surrounded by great players in more than the paper. I have been lucky to be in the right place at the right time throughout my NHL career. I got off to a good start in Edmonton, which instilled confidence and was a building block to early successes. At the same time, under the guidance of Glen Sather, our Oiler teams became adept at generating speed, developing finesse, and learning a transition game with strong European influences. We also benefited from a select group of physical players who understood and relished their roles. They made my work much easier each night.

I am told frequently by fans that hockey players are generally approachable, humble, and accommodating. The tough physical nature of our sport on the ice masks the congeniality of players off the ice. I maintain that there exists a quiet police force of active and former players who don't hesitate to give subtle, or direct, advice to wayward newcomers.

The old adage, "Let your stick and skates do the talking," has been handed down to many an NHL rookie by older, wiser veterans. Over the next decade, the people skills of professional hockey players will be even more recognized and appreciated.

On the ice, our sport is poised for growth and acceptance like never before. During my early years in pro hockey I recall the occasional player who emerged from what seemed like the outer limits of the hockey world—Nova Scotia, British Columbia, Minnesota, Massachusetts. Today, the NHL is blessed with Czechs, Slovaks, Swedes, Russians and Finns, among others. Soon, we will see hockey stars coming from such places as California, Florida and Georgia—whose idea of an outdoor rink is a roller hockey facility, complete with fast food restaurant and apparel store.

Nevertheless, the game is still the same: the marvel of a goalie's glove save on a 100-mph slapshot...The focus of a player's eyes still riveted on the puck, his hands still on the stick, after being hit low and legs sent flying above his waist...The courage of a defenseman, dropping down at the perfect moment to block a frozen puck, knowing a mistiming could mean injury to his face, head or throat...Or the exhilaration of walking that walk, from the dressing room to the player's bench, and then dashing onto the clean, fresh ice.

Today when I see my sons, Ty and Trevor, walk that walk (even when they disappear from sight, bobbing along the bench before stepping out onto the ice), I know they are feeling the same joy I have felt night after night. Another game! Let's go!

So what does it mean to be recognized as a pretty good hockey player? It means that I have made my dad proud. I listened and I learned. It means my childhood idol, Gordie Howe, indeed taught me to accept success with thanks, and never forget that hockey is a team game. It means that the smell of wet skates, whether those of my sons and their friends, or those of my New York Ranger teammates, still reminds me that hockey is all about camaraderie.

And it means that the tradition I have chosen to follow–that of the Appses, the Conachers, the Cooks and the Bentleys and the hundreds of others before me–will undoubtedly be followed in the 21st century by young men who will also spend countless hours perfecting their skills with the same passion, the same commitment and the same love of hockey.

I know I speak for every NHL player who has proudly laced up his skates in saying, "Thanks for being a fan of hockey—we all are."

Wayne Gretzky
with mom Phyllis,
dad Walter, and
the first pair of
skates he wore
in the NHL

Dan Hamilton/VPS

WAYNE GRETZKY
THE NO. 1 NHL PLAYER OF ALL-TIME
AS CHOSEN BY THE HOCKEY NEWS TOP 50 SELECTION COMMITTEE
JANUARY 9, 1998

Habs Dominate Top 100 Players

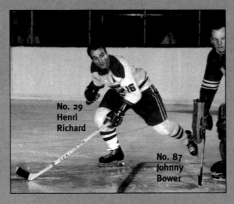

No. 29 Henri Richard

No. 87 Johnny Bower

Nearly one-quarter of the Top 100 players in NHL history recorded their greatest triumphs with the Montreal Canadiens.

With 24 representatives, the league's most storied franchise with 23 Stanley Cups has one member of the Top 100 for every Cup, plus one more for good measure. Three of the top 10 and six of the first 15 are ex-Canadiens' superstars, including Maurice (Rocket) Richard at No. 5.

Players are associated with the team with which they achieved prominence.

Team	No.		Team	No.
1. Mtl. Canadiens	24		10. Ottawa	3
2. Toronto	16		11. Quebec/Colorado	2
3. Chicago	10		12. Buffalo	2
4. Boston	9		13. Pittsburgh	2
5. Detroit	9		14. Mtl. Maroons	1
6. N.Y. Rangers	6		15. Washington	1
7. Edmonton	5		16. Los Angeles	1
8. N.Y. Islanders	4		17. St. Louis	1
9. Philadelphia	3		18. N.Y. Americans	1

No. 1 - 20

1. **Wayne Gretzky** — Edmonton Oilers
2. **Bobby Orr** — Boston Bruins
3. **Gordie Howe** — Detroit Red Wings
4. **Mario Lemieux** — Pittsburgh Penguins
5. **Maurice Richard** — Montreal Canadiens
6. **Doug Harvey** — Montreal Canadiens
7. **Jean Beliveau** — Montreal Canadiens
8. **Bobby Hull** — Chicago Black Hawks
9. **Terry Sawchuk** — Detroit Red Wings
10. **Eddie Shore** — Boston Bruins
11. **Guy Lafleur** — Montreal Canadiens
12. **Mark Messier** — Edmonton Oilers
13. **Jacques Plante** — Montreal Canadiens
14. **Ray Bourque** — Boston Bruins
15. **Howie Morenz** — Montreal Canadiens
16. **Glenn Hall** — Chicago Black Hawks
17. **Stan Mikita** — Chicago Black Hawks
18. **Phil Esposito** — Boston Bruins
19. **Denis Potvin** — New York Islanders
20. **Mike Bossy** — New York Islanders

No. 21 - 40

21. **Ted Lindsay** — Detroit Red Wings
22. **Red Kelly** — Detroit Red Wings
23. **Bobby Clarke** — Philadelphia Flyers
24. **Larry Robinson** — Montreal Canadiens
25. **Ken Dryden** — Montreal Canadiens
26. **Frank Mahovlich** — Toronto Maple Leafs
27. **Milt Schmidt** — Boston Bruins
28. **Paul Coffey** — Edmonton Oilers
29. **Henri Richard** — Montreal Canadiens
30. **Bryan Trottier** — New York Islanders
31. **Dickie Moore** — Montreal Canadiens
32. **Newsy Lalonde** — Montreal Canadiens
33. **Syl Apps** — Toronto Maple Leafs
34. **Bill Durnan** — Montreal Canadiens
35. **Patrick Roy** — Montreal Canadiens
36. **Charlie Conacher** — Toronto Maple Leafs
37. **Jaromir Jagr** — Pittsburgh Penguins
38. **Marcel Dionne** — Los Angeles Kings
39. **Joe Malone** — Montreal Canadiens
40. **Chris Chelios** — Chicago Black Hawks

No. 41 - 60

41. **Dit Clapper** — Boston Bruins
42. **Bernie Geoffrion** — Montreal Canadiens
43. **Tim Horton** — Toronto Maple Leafs
44. **Bill Cook** — New York Rangers
45. **Johnny Bucyk** — Boston Bruins
46. **George Hainsworth** — Montreal Canadiens
47. **Gilbert Perreault** — Buffalo Sabres
48. **Max Bentley** — Chicago Black Hawks
49. **Brad Park** — New York Rangers
50. **Jari Kurri** — Edmonton Oilers
51. **Nels Stewart** — Montreal Maroons
52. **King Clancy** — Toronto Maple Leafs
53. **Bill Cowley** — Boston Bruins
54. **Eric Lindros** — Philadelphia Flyers
55. **Harvey Jackson** — Toronto Maple Leafs
56. **Peter Stastny** — Quebec Nordiques
57. **Ted Kennedy** — Toronto Maple Leafs
58. **Andy Bathgate** — New York Rangers
59. **Pierre Pilote** — Chicago Black Hawks
60. **Turk Broda** — Toronto Maple Leafs

No. 61 - 80

61. **Frank Boucher** — New York Rangers
62. **Cy Denneny** — Ottawa Senators
63. **Bernie Parent** — Philadelphia Flyers
64. **Brett Hull** — St. Louis Blues
65. **Aurel Joliat** — Montreal Canadiens
66. **Toe Blake** — Montreal Canadiens
67. **Frank Brimsek** — Boston Bruins
68. **Elmer Lach** — Montreal Canadiens
69. **Dave Keon** — Toronto Maple Leafs
70. **Grant Fuhr** — Edmonton Oilers
71. **Brian Leetch** — New York Rangers
72. **Earl Seibert** — Chicago Black Hawks
73. **Doug Bentley** — Chicago Black Hawks
74. **Borje Salming** — Toronto Maple Leafs
75. **Georges Vezina** — Montreal Canadiens
76. **Charlie Gardiner** — Chicago Black Hawks
77. **Clint Benedict** — Ottawa Senators
78. **Steve Yzerman** — Detroit Red Wings
79. **Tony Esposito** — Chicago Black Hawks
80. **Billy Smith** — New York Islanders

No. 81 - 100

81. **Serge Savard** — Montreal Canadiens
82. **Alex Delvecchio** — Detroit Red Wings
83. **Babe Dye** — Toronto Maple Leafs
84. **Lorne Chabot** — Toronto Maple Leafs
85. **Sid Abel** — Detroit Red Wings
86. **Bob Gainey** — Montreal Canadiens
87. **Johnny Bower** — Toronto Maple Leafs
88. **Sprague Cleghorn** — Montreal Canadiens
89. **Mike Gartner** — Washington Capitals
90. **Norm Ullman** — Detroit Red Wings
91. **Sweeney Schriner** — New York Americans
92. **Joe Primeau** — Toronto Maple Leafs
93. **Darryl Sittler** — Toronto Maple Leafs
94. **Joe Sakic** — Colorado Avalanche
95. **Dominik Hasek** — Buffalo Sabres
96. **Babe Pratt** — Toronto Maple Leafs
97. **Jack Stewart** — Detroit Red Wings
98. **Yvan Cournoyer** — Montreal Canadiens
99. **Bill Gadsby** — New York Rangers
100. **Frank Nighbor** — Ottawa Senators

No Higher Level

BY STEVE DRYDEN

Ten thousand feet in the air, Wayne Gretzky is on top of the world.

The best player in NHL history is flying in an eight-seat aircraft with the greatest of ease, carrying his newest title with customary dignity. He has been crowned a Stanley Cup champion, a scoring champion, an MVP champion and, now, he is a champion among champions.

Gretzky has been voted the best of more than 3,500 players to play in the NHL. It is Jan. 9, 1998, and Gretzky is en route from a press conference at New York's Madison Square Garden to another at the Hockey Hall of Fame in Toronto.

Below him is New York State, Lake Ontario and every other player in NHL history. Yet the only airs about him during a 70-minute flight are those that fill the sky. He hands out sandwiches, flips through the magazine that declares him the No. 1 player during the nine decades of NHL history, trades stories with travelling companions and takes credit for a safe landing with a wink and a grin.

Awaiting him in Toronto is a crush of admirers. Journalists are trained to separate feeling from fact, but a warmth and fuzziness drenches the Bell Great Hall, on whose walls rest likenesses of the sport's greatest players.

"It was difficult not to feel a little lump in the throat, a little mist around the eyes when Wayne Gretzky was ushered into the room," wrote Cam Cole of the *Edmonton Journal.*

The scene is rich in Canadiana and, in hindsight, a rare moment of triumph during a trying season for the country that gave hockey and the best-ever player to the world.

In little more than a month, Canada would finish a deeply disappointing fourth at the Olympic Games; it would be represented by only one player–who else but Gretzky?–among the top five scorers in the 1997-98 NHL scoring race; and it would finish off a year that began with humiliation at the World Junior Championship with more failure at the World Championship. On this day, 46 of the 50 play-

9

ers voted the best in NHL history are Canadian. Forty-five of the 50 more that make up the The Hockey News Top 100 are Canadian, bringing the total to 91. It is a snapshot in time, the results of a vote conducted before the 1996-97 Stanley Cup playoffs to mark The Hockey News' 50th anniversary. Fifty experts were asked to rank the best players over 80 seasons in the NHL.

When the next generation of experts is asked to name the best players of all-time, it will not be such a celebration of hockey's roots. It will, though, most surely be a celebration of 'The Greatest One.' They say records are made to be broken.

Oilers, Los Angeles Kings, St. Louis Blues and the New York Rangers, his current club.

The 50 voters chosen by The Hockey News to determine the top players in NHL history acknowledged that circumstance by making Gretzky the No. 1 choice. He collected 2,726 voting points, 13 more than runner-up Orr (2,713) and 45 more than Howe (2,681). Both Gretzky and Orr had 18 first-place votes. Gretzky earned No. 1 status on the strength of secondary support. He had 50 per-cent more second-place votes than Orr (18-12), the point equivalent of two first-place votes. Howe received 11 first-place votes and 14 sec-

they're the players I looked up to growing up."

Pittsburgh Penguins' center Mario Lemieux was a close fourth in voting (2,308), joining the trio as separate and distinct from the pack. Lemieux reached single-season statistical heights exceeded only by Gretzky. Montreal Canadiens' legendary right winger Maurice (Rocket) Richard collected 2,142 points to complete the all-time top five.

The Selection Committee was composed of ex-NHL players, current and past coaches, GMs, league executives, journalists and hockey historians. All eras and aspects of NHL history were represented. Voters were

Wayne Gretzky   Gordie Howe   Ken Dryden

Most of Wayne Gretzky's 60-plus NHL marks won't be surpassed. And it seems impossible he will ever be supplanted as the NHL's premier player.

Gretzky triumphed in the closest race of his career to earn the ultimate designation: No. 1 NHL player of all-time. Gretzky, who has won 10 NHL scoring titles, never by fewer than 10 points and once by 79, narrowly outpolled Boston Bruins' defenseman Bobby Orr and Detroit Red Wings' right winger Gordie Howe in voting by The Hockey News Selection Committee.

No. 99, a hockey icon, has fashioned an unparalleled career with the Edmonton

onds. Fewer than two per cent in voting points separated all three.

The results speak eloquently about the respect accorded the three players. Gretzky, the smartest player in the history of the game, Orr, the most dynamic three-zone player, and Howe, the ultimate symbol of enduring excellence, represent the holy trinity of hockey greats. They are Nos. 1, 1a and 1b in the pantheon of legends.

"If I was voting," Gretzky said, "I would have voted for Gordie Howe and Bobby Orr and would have been happy with third place. I say that in all sincerity because

asked to slot players, regardless of position or era, from No. 1 through No. 50.

Enormous debate greeted announcement of The Hockey News Top 50, much of it centering on Gretzky's selection over Orr—whose legend has grown, not diminished, since chronic knee injuries forced him to retire in the fall of 1978.

"When I look at a hockey player, and I mean a complete hockey player," said Don Cherry, a voter, former Bruins' coach and Hockey Night in Canada broadcaster, "I look at a guy who can score goals, make plays, block shots, hit and, god forbid—I know this is going into The Hockey

News–fight. And Bobby Orr was the most complete player I have ever seen."

Orr was a gracious second-place finisher and said, out of respect for Howe, "If I can't be No. 1, can you make me No. 3?" Orr is the only defenseman ever to win a scoring championship–he did it twice–and revolutionized the game. Defensemen were freed from the shackles of the blueline after his emergence in 1966. Orr recorded six straight 100-point seasons, a mark shared by five others and exceeded only by Gretzky (13).

Howe, whose career spanned an amazing five decades, earned the nickname 'Mr. Hockey' and berths on a record 21 all-star teams. Red Wings' coach Scotty Bowman, a member of the Selection Committee, had Howe No. 1 on his ballot.

"Gordie played the longest," Bowman said. "He was the toughest player of his era, he could shoot left or right, he could play all forward positions and defense, too. If I could make a mould for a player, it would be Gordie."

The THN vote firmly establishes Howe as the league's best player from the pre-expansion era. He won six scoring championships and six MVP awards, totals eclipsed only by Gretzky, who completed a quadruple jump past Howe in 1997 with the 1,851st assist of his career, one more than Howe had total points. Gretzky previously passed Howe in career goals, assists and points.

"Hey I'm in the money," Howe said. "Win, place, show. When I heard about this, I knew exactly how it was going to end up and I called it. I should be a scout."

The closeness of the vote brings into sharp focus a long simmering Gretzky-Orr debate. With the utmost respect for Orr, step back for a moment from the entirety of Gretzky's career and compare the two legends over a similar time frame. Orr played nine full seasons with the Bruins before knee problems did what no team could–stop him in his tracks.

Gretzky played precisely the same number of seasons with the Oilers before the trade of the century sent him to Los Angeles. Compare their achievements over

the same period, a level playing field because those seasons covered ages 18 to 27 for both, and the similarities are striking.

Each defied the laws of statistical gravity. Gretzky won 17 major individual awards, Orr, 15; both were on nine all-star teams; and both won two Conn Smythe Trophies. Gretzky won two more Stanley Cups (4-2), but the greatest difference is in MVP honors. Gretzky won eight and Orr earned three. Gretzky added a ninth in his 10th season to complete the most dominating individual run in North American major pro sports history.

Kareem-Abdul Jabbar was named National Basketball Association MVP six times (equalling Howe in the NHL). Nobody but Gretzky has won his sport's top award nine times.

It stands as a monument to Gretzky's career and a reminder to those who have witnessed a natural decline in productivity that, no matter how overwhelming today's career numbers are, the single-season numbers from the first half of Gretzky's career surpass them.

Among them are most goals (92), assists (163) and points (215) in a season. Those and a host of others will be chased–but likely never caught–for generations to come. "Gretzky's records transcend sports," said voter Kevin Allen of USA Today. "He has gone beyond the scope of a normal human being."

Gretzky has proved time and again that hockey played at its highest level is a victory of mind over matter. He had elite-level quickness during most of his career–and remains nimble to this day–but possesses little else physically that distinguishes him as special.

In the wake of Gretzky's coronation as the best player in NHL history, the Brantford (Ont.) Expositor recalled one local hockey man remarking of the home-town prodigy, a spindly-legged superstar not yet 10 years old: "If you wrapped him in a fur coat, you could use him as a pipe cleaner."

The weight of his accomplishments so many years later represents the heaviest imprint ever left on the game.

No. 1 | Center | Wayne Gretzky

Don Dixon

THE GREATES ONE BAR NONE

"He is great who is what he is from nature,
and who never reminds us of others."

Ralph Waldo Emerson, *Uses of Great Men*

Inside the New York Rangers' dressing room at the Playland Rink in Rye, N.Y., on this cold and drizzly Saturday morning, Wayne Gretzky, dressed in a white crew-neck T-shirt, black pants, black socks and brown Gucci horsebit buckle loafers, leans back in an overstuffed chair and, in answer to a writer's question, contemplates the pantheon of 20th Century sports immortals.

"Let's see...Muhammad Ali is pretty special...then there's Michael Jordan for what he's done for basketball..." He mentions Joe DiMaggio and Babe Ruth and then stops. "I'd be honored to be anywhere in the top 10," he says. "I think I'd vote for Ali."

And this is where Wayne Gretzky has brought us in the 20 years he has played hockey for a living. That he is the greatest hockey player of all-time is a given, merely affirmed–not decided–by the voting of The Hockey News' 50-member committee. "How Great is Gretzky?" says committee member and Edmonton Oilers' president and general manager Glen Sather, who coached Gretzky for 10 seasons. "There aren't enough adjectives. Just look at his records and longevity."

By
Jack
Falla

13

Gretzky's 62 NHL scoring records–and the sheer enormity of some of those numbers–make him the most statistically dominant athlete ever in North American team sports. And as Gretzky, now in the November of his career, rises above the worthy likes of Gordie Howe and Mario Lemieux, and inches past the once seemingly incomparable Bobby Orr, he draws ever nearer to Ali, Jordan, Pele and that elite handful of others who make up the sporting patriciate of our fast passing century.

Congratulated on his election as the greatest hockey player ever, Gretzky at first slips into media interview auto pilot–yes, it's "a great honor because of all the other great players" blah, blah, blah–and then, as he often does after he gets beyond the first draft drift of his mind, he supplies a more thoughtful and revealing reaction. "As I get older I savor these things more. I enjoy the moment more. When I was younger things were happening so fast I hardly knew what I was doing."

It is a thought he will express in similar words the next night at Madison Square Garden though his enjoyment of that moment will be so obvious as to require no further expression. On his first shift in the third period of a game against the Mighty Ducks of Anaheim, Gretzky takes a pass from linemate Niklas Sundstrom and feeds Ulf Samuelsson, who scores, thus giving Gretzky his 1,851st assist or one more assist than second all-time scoring leader Gordie Howe has goals and assists combined. In the second period, Gretzky had tied the record, setting off a two-minute standing ovation. "Gret-SKI, Gret-SKI," they chanted, the accent on the wrong syllable, the sentiment on the right man, while on the Rangers' bench Gretzky

smiled, waved a quick self-conscious acknowledgement and twice indulged in long cheek-puffing thank-God-that's-over exhalations. But now with the new standard set, the ovation is more restrained–not quite loud or long enough to drown out 2 Unlimited's "You All Ready 4 This?" pulsing out of the Garden's sound system. Yes, Gretzky is ready for this...

With the record not just equalled but broken, Gretzky grins broadly, waves more enthusiastically and this time mouths a "thank you" and when that brings up the volume of the ovation, he smiles again. This time it is the smile the writer has not

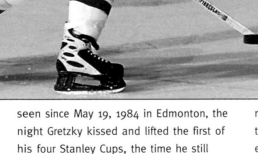

seen since May 19, 1984 in Edmonton, the night Gretzky kissed and lifted the first of his four Stanley Cups, the time he still calls, "my sweetest moment in hockey."

Now, in Manhattan, Wayne Gretzky is savoring the moment in which he pushed back one of hockey's last statistical frontiers. If the man never scored a goal he would still be the NHL's all-time leading scorer. It is almost unimaginable, as are so many of Gretzky's records because he does not merely extend by small increments the limits of what was once proven possible, but instead makes irrelevant previous standards, putting up numbers that belong on a pinball machine–NHL career

records in goals, assists and points. The philosopher Emerson wrote "great men exist that there be greater men," but it seems unlikely that some of Gretzky's marks will ever be equalled. A few may not even be approached.

The day before ringing up assist No. 1,851, Gretzky reflected on some of his more compelling statistics.

"I think 163 assists in a season will be hard to beat. That and 215 points in a season," he says. He set both marks with Edmonton in 1985-86. "And the 51-game scoring streak will stand for awhile," the reference being to the 1983-84 feat that had sportswriters across North America comparing Gretzky's accomplishment to DiMaggio's 56-game hitting streak. Reminded of his 50 goals in 39 games, Gretzky says, "I almost forgot about that one. Yeah. A guy could have forty-five goals in thirty-five games and he'd still have to average better than a goal a game to beat it." He breaks into a bemused smile at the thought.

Indeed, of all Gretzky's records, scoring 50 goals in 39 games may be the most otherworldly. Fifty goals in 50 games had been one of hockey's mythical barriers since Maurice Richard set that standard in 1945. Mike Bossy equalled the mark in 1981. Then Gretzky simply destroyed it. It would be as if Roger Maris had not broken Babe Ruth's record of 60 home runs in a season by hitting 61, but had instead hit 73. Incomprehensible. Or if Roger Bannister had run the first sub four-minute mile not in 3:59.4, breaking the existing record by eight-tenths of a second, but had instead broken it by, say, four seconds. To find statistical comparisons to Gretzky, it is necessary to turn to rare events in other sports, to Bob Beamon breaking the world long jump record by nearly two feet at the

Mexico City Olympics, to Secretariat, Ron Turcotte up, winning the 1973 Belmont by a super-equine 31 lengths, to Babe Ruth hitting a "dead ball era" baseball 579 feet in a 1919 spring training game in Tampa. Gretzky gave the NHL record book a torching that conjures up the memory of rocker Jerry Lee Lewis closing a set by playing "Great Balls of Fire" with his elbows and feet before setting his piano on fire with lighter fluid, walking off the stage and saying to the next act, "Top that." Were any of us ready for this?

Yet it is ironic that the top goal-scorer of all time thinks it is his most famous record–92 goals in a season–that is most vulnerable. "Ninety-two goals can fall," he says of the record he set in 1981-82. Asked who among current players could do it, Gretzky says, "Paul Kariya. He takes a lot of shots....yeah, if a guy stays healthy and he's on the right team he could break that one."

But the operative phrase is "if a guy stays healthy," a difficult thing to do in a game played by athletes who are bigger, stronger and faster than ever. Staying healthy is one of Gretzky's more remarkable achievements and likely the key to his selection as the No. 1 hockey player ever. Put it this way: if Gretzky were a mountain range he would not only be as high as the Himalayas, he would be as long as the Rockies. It is the heights he has reached that separate him from Howe, and it is the length of time he has occupied those heights (Gretzky has a league record 15 seasons with 100-or-more points and four seasons with 200-or-more) that separates him from the star-crossed Orr and Lemieux. Lemieux scored virtually the same number of goals as Gretzky over the same number of games (Gretzky had 616

to Lemieux's 613) and the transcendent Bobby Orr re-invented defense and was the first player to dominate a game over three zones. Lemieux, victim of a bad back and of Hodgkin's disease, never played a complete NHL season, and Orr played most of his nine full seasons on knees surgically repaired so many times writer George Plimpton described them as "looking like a bag of handkerchiefs."

WAYNE GRETZKY	1979-present	
Born: Jan. 26, 1961 Brantford, Ont.		
Teams: Edmonton, Los Angeles, St. Louis, Rangers		
NHL	Regular	Playoffs
Seasons	19	16
Games	1,417	208
Goals	885	122
Assists	1,910	260
Points	2,795	382
Penalties	563	66
All-Star: 15 (First-8, Second-7)		
Trophies: 25 (Hart-9, Ross-10, Smythe-2, Byng-4)		
Stanley Cup Championships	4	

"I've stayed healthy because I'm not a banger and a crasher," Gretzky says. "Guys who bang and crash wear down and I think the body can't keep repairing itself."

Early in his career Gretzky refused to follow off-ice weight training programs, sometimes glibly offering the non-sequitur, "Show me a weight that ever scored a goal and I'll start lifting." That has changed.

"I train harder in the off-season now," he says. "Since I turned 28 or 29 I lift and work out about two hours a day in the summer. My No. 1 obligation is to be ready to play hockey." The weight work has re-shaped him slightly. Striding across the Rangers' Madison Square Garden dressing room after a post-game shower and wearing only a towel, Gretzky reveals the trim lean body of a swimmer.

He appears to be slightly bigger through the chest and shoulders than he was in his Edmonton heyday. But back at the practice rink your eyes are drawn to the pipe cleaner thinness of his arms and the smallness of the most gifted hands the game has ever seen. With his blond hair longer than he wore it last year and now swept back in a mane falling to mid-neck, Gretzky looks more like a dancer or rock singer than professional athlete in a contact sport. Ask him for insight to his game and he doesn't talk of quickness (which he has in abundance) or his ability to know where the puck is going (a pre-science acquired from his father, Walter, on the family's backyard rink in Brantford, Ont. ("don't go where the puck is; go where it's going to be") or of unusual peripheral vision (a canard disproved early in his career by vision tests given to all Oilers' players). He talks of love.

"I still really, really love this game," he says. "I like playing it. I even like getting on the bus and talking about it."

And he loves talking about his children

playing it. In a long conversation with Gretzky, nothing lights him up as much as the chance to talk about the three children he has had with his wife, actress Janet Jones. "The two guys (Ty, 8, and Trevor, 6) play on the same team. Mike Richter's wife Veronica is the assistant coach." Ask him their positions and he looks at you incredulously. "Oh, they're both forwards. The little guy patterns himself after me, but Ty is more of a bull. He

likes the physical contact. We don't push them, but they both just love the game. I guess it'll be harder on them as they get older." Then he laughs and says, "I hope they'll both be baseball players."

Gretzky's daughter, Paulina, 10, doesn't play hockey. "She's into piano and ballet. Just got accepted to the American Ballet Theater School. I guess that's like making an all-star team," he says. Paulina may be the hardest hitter in the Gretzky family.

When the Philadelphia Flyers eliminated the Rangers from the 1996-97 playoffs and her father returned to the family's East Side Manhattan apartment, Gretzky recalls that "Paulina said I shouldn't worry about the loss. I said, 'Why shouldn't I worry about it?' She said, 'Because the Flyers are so young and you guys are so old.'" (Give her an extra two minutes for intent to injure.)

That summer Gretzky sent his sons to

California where his father, Walter, now retired from Bell Canada and fully recovered from a brain aneurism suffered in 1992, runs a hockey camp. "They thought they were going to spend a nice week with Grandpa. Hah! Grandpa skated them into the ground."

Gretzky calls Walter and Glen Sather the two most important influences in his development as a hockey player. "It's as if my father raised me until age 17, then turned me over to Slats and said, 'You take him from here.' The one thing they had in common," says Gretzky, "is that they both pushed me. If I got 80 goals, Slats would tell me I could've had 85." Says Sather: "It would be a crime to have the God-given talent he has and not make the most of it because you didn't push hard enough." Sather's pushing caused some iciness between the two men during Gretzky's career in Edmonton, but Gretzky says that's meltwater under an old bridge. "No. We're fine. The best thing about Slats is that he always had faith in me."

Indeed, Sather may have the best understanding of the Gretzkian genius: "He does everything in the sweet spot," says Sather. "He's like the best golfers or tennis players or like Mickey Mantle. Every pass and every shot, right on the sweet spot."

Others can appreciate, but not comprehend. Says Boston GM Harry Sinden: "Gretzky sees a picture out there that no one else sees. It's difficult to describe because I've never seen the game he's looking at."

There is an almost Jesuitical quality—a confidence born of faith, works and insight—in Gretzky's game. "When he makes a pass you can't explain how he makes it," says Rangers' coach Colin Campbell, who played briefly with Gretzky in 1979 in Edmonton. "It's not a Mark

Messier pass or a Gil Perreault pass; it flutters over, under and around things and lands on the right stick blade too many times for it to be an accident. And he masquerades his intentions so well he mesmerizes everyone on the ice."

Not even Gretzky could argue that he's past his physical peak but, as Campbell says, "That's like saying my Rolls Royce is five years old. It's still a Rolls and it's still worth a lot."

There were whispers of the Rolls not being shipped to Nagano, Japan for the Olympics last year, but Gretzky's strong play during the season, not just his reputation, earned him a spot. Gretzky's presence at the Olympics, World Cup, Canada Cup or any special event is hockey's gain because he is the world's greatest ambassador for his sport, its most recognized, promotable and evangelistic athlete. It is a role he takes seriously and that he credits to Gordie Howe. "Growing up, my player role model was always Gordie. Later, as I got to know him, I noticed how he always had time for everyone. He'd go out of his way to talk to kids about the game. He told me it was a responsibility and an obligation. It's not a problem for me. It's part of my hockey schedule."

❑ ❑ ❑ ❑

Back at Madison Square Garden, it is now about 20 minutes after the game in which Gretzky recorded his 1,851st assist and a group of writers and broadcasters have gathered in a corridor outside the Rangers' dressing room where Colin Campbell is holding an impromptu press conference. He is struggling to explain Gretzky's latest achievement. "How many assists is 1,851?" he asks rhetorically. "You can't even think of it. It's mind boggling. It's like how many stars are in the sky."

No it isn't, Colin. There are billions of stars in the sky; but Gretzky is more like the sun. And when the sun shines, the stars disappear.

THN's All-Time NHL All-Star Teams

According to The Hockey News panel of experts, the all-time NHL first all-star team consists of goalie Terry Sawchuk, defensemen Bobby Orr and Doug Harvey, left winger Bobby Hull, center Wayne Gretzky and right winger Gordie Howe. Here are the first, second and third teams. Listed are the teams with which they are most closely associated and, in parentheses, their THN all-time rank. The Montreal Canadiens lead with five representatives on the three teams. The Detroit Red Wings have four reps and three of the six defensemen are Boston Bruins.

FIRST TEAM	SECOND TEAM	THIRD TEAM
Goalie	**Goalie**	**Goalie**
Terry Sawchuk (No. 9), Detroit	Jacques Plante (No. 13), Montreal	Glenn Hall (No. 16), Chicago
Defensemen	**Defensemen**	**Defensemen**
Bobby Orr (No. 2), Boston	Eddie Shore (No. 10), Boston	Denis Potvin (No. 19), Islanders
Doug Harvey (No. 6), Montreal	Ray Bourque (No. 14), Boston	Red Kelly (No. 22), Detroit
Left Winger	**Left Winger**	**Left Winger**
Bobby Hull (No. 8), Chicago	Ted Lindsay (No. 21), Detroit	Frank Mahovlich (No. 26), Toronto
Center	**Center**	**Center**
Wayne Gretzky (No. 1), Edmonton	Mario Lemieux (No. 4), Pittsburgh	Jean Beliveau (No. 7), Montreal
Right Winger	**Right Winger**	**Right Winger**
Gordie Howe (No. 3), Detroit	Maurice Richard (No. 5), Montreal	Guy Lafleur (No. 11), Montreal

Don Dixon

Vital Statistics

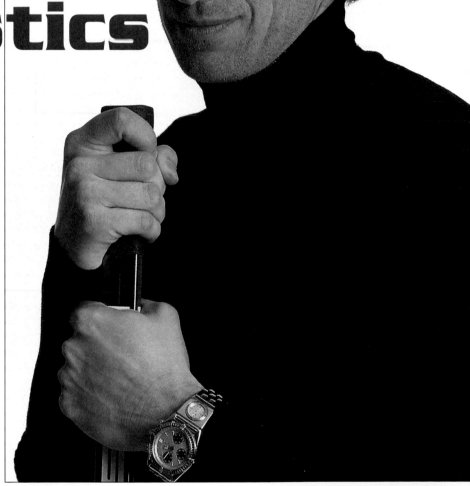

Wayne Gretzky and Bobby Orr not only changed the game, they changed the way we add in the NHL. Hockey fans had to throw away their abacusses and buy calculators to keep track of Nos. 4 and 99. Both changed league standards, rendering existing measures of excellence obsolete. Gretzky, Orr and Gordie Howe finished neck-and-neck-and-neck in voting for The Hockey News all-time No. 1 player. Howe was a fabulous player over an unfathomable period of time, but it was Orr and Gretzky who re-defined NHL math.

Orr's star-crossed career has elevated him to cult status. We all wonder what might have been had he been healthy. How long would he have played? How many more scoring titles would he have won? How many Norris Trophies would he have accumulated? There are no such questions with Gretzky. Nothing has been left to the imagination. One result of Gretzky playing so long—he is in his 20th NHL season—is that his career averages have declined. Mario Lemieux, for instance, is listed ahead of Gretzky in career goals-per-game average (.823 to .625) and points-per-game (2.01 to 1.97) in the 1998-99 NHL Official Guide and Record Book. But Gretzky's averages covered nearly twice as many games' work. He actually scored three more goals than Lemieux, 616-613, over the same number of games.

Listed at right are some vital stats assembled by Gretzky and Orr. For comparison purposes, we have not listed Gretzky's career stats, but those from the first nine seasons of his career, the same number of full seasons played by Orr. Not included are the bits of three seasons—including two with Chicago Black Hawks—Orr played while he tried valiantly to play in spite of debilitating knee injuries.

Don Dixon

99 vs. 4: By The Numbers

Comparing the first nine seasons of Wayne Gretzky's and Bobby Orr's careers is more appropriate than some would think. The Great One played exactly nine seasons in Edmonton before being traded to Los Angeles. Orr left Boston for Chicago after nine full seasons and an injury-shortened 10-game 10th season. Below left are the two megastars' totals after nine seasons each, including games, maximum number of games each could have played and what percentage that represents. Below right are the seminal regular season standards set over that time. Only Orr's record for goals by a defenseman has been eclipsed. Paul Coffey holds that mark of 47. Listed are their record totals, the previous high recorded by any player but themselves, the total increase and the percentage increase that represents. Legend: Hart, MVP; Conn Smythe, playoff MVP; Art Ross, scoring title; Norris, best defenseman.

Category	Gretzky	Orr
Seasons	1979-88	1966-75
Games/NHL	696/720	621/688
Games Pct.	97%	90%
Hart Trophy	8	3
Smythe Trophy	2	2
Ross Trophy	7	2
Norris Trophy	–	8
Stanley Cup	4	2
First All-Star	7	8
Second All-Star	2	1

Gretzky's Regular Season Records

Category	Record	Previous	Inc.	Pct.
Goals	92	76	16	21%
Assists	163	102	61	60%
Points	215	152	63	41%

Orr's Regular Season Defenseman Records

Category	Record	Previous	Inc.	Pct.
Goals	46	24	22	92%
Assists	102	52	50	96%
Points	139	63	80	121%

THE KILLER 'B'

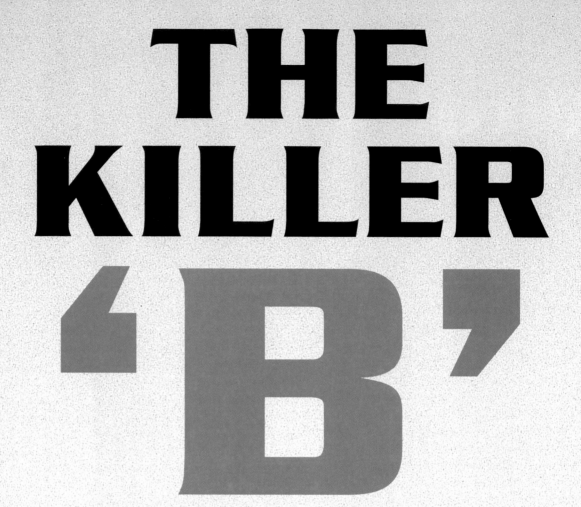

By
Michael
Ulmer

Forty years ago in a Northern Ontario dressing room, a minor hockey coach called for his team's attention and held up a piece of paper.

"Look at this scrawl, look at the way he signs his name," the coach bellowed about one of the opposing players. "He can't even write properly. How can a kid who can't even sign his name play hockey? He can't, that's what, he can't."

But he could. When the game started, eight-year-old Bobby Orr blasted down the ice, banked into the tight turn he would make famous, straddled the blueline and ripped a wrist shot over the goalie's shoulder.

Through his youth, minor, junior and then nine NHL seasons, the gap between Orr and his contemporaries never closed.

No one ever caught up.

Bobby Orr is the consensus choice as the greatest defenseman in NHL history, a prodigy who rocketed past even the most glowing projections, a player whose ascent only stopped when incendiary desire and ability burned through the body that carried them.

"My favorite as the No. 1 player of all-time would be Bobby Orr," Gordie Howe said. "I loved the way he played the game, I loved the way he changed the game and the quickness he had."

No. 2 Defenseman Bobby Orr

Don Dixon

"All Bobby did," said longtime Boston Bruins' teammate Phil Esposito, "was change the face of hockey all by himself."

Orr's impact can be measured by the scores of next-generation imitators he spawned. Orr begat Paul Coffey, who begat Brian Leetch who begat Bryan Berard, a one-year-old when Orr retired.

"What a legacy to have," said *Hockey Night in Canada* analyst Harry Neale. "People who never saw Bobby Orr want to play like him. They want to be like the players who wanted to be like Orr."

The immortal Jacques Plante, the greatest innovator ever among NHL goalies, considered Orr the best player ever and if further proof is needed, it can be easily rendered with a look at the highlight

videos of some of Orr's greatest plays. The superb unfolded at a languid pace from Bobby Orr. Usually, the foray started with a few steps toward his defense part-

BOBBY ORR		1966-1978
Born: March 20, 1948 Parry Sound, Ont.		
Teams: Boston, Chicago		
NHL	**Regular**	**Playoffs**
Seasons	9	8
Games	657	74
Goals	270	26
Assists	645	66
Points	915	92
Penalties	953	107
All-Star: 9 (First–8, Second–1)		
Trophies: 16 (Hart-3, Ross-2, Norris-8, Smythe-2, Calder-1)		
Stanley Cup Championships	2	

ner, Dallas Smith, before Orr would veer around in an impossibly tight circle and begin the attack.

Waves of forecheckers and backcheckers were left to look as if they had taken root in the ice as Orr began to accelerate. The checkers flashed different colors and hair styles, but forwards and defensemen, journeymen and stars, were united in failure by Orr. Once, while killing a penalty against the Atlanta Flames, Orr lugged the puck for 21 straight seconds. He could have gone longer, but they had to stop the clock when he scored.

Of all the prodigious talents allotted Orr, the greatest was skating. "Bobby," Johnny Bucyk said, "has 16 levels of fast."

His was the platinum combination of

skating gifts, breakaway speed, devastating acceleration and a powerful stride.

His skating was so magnificent, the geometry of the game altered at his whim. Fail-safe angles and positioning NHL defensemen used to ride out and cut off every other player were rendered ludicrously ineffective by Orr. Playing him as you would play anyone else left you only close enough to catch his breeze and the silent sound his sweater made as he went by.

"What's his best move?" Howe once said. "Putting on his (expletive deleted) skates." The highlights all ended the same, with a prone goalie and one arm lifted in respectful victory.

An Orr celebration was preserved forever when he lifted the Bruins to the 1970 Stanley Cup an instant before being knocked to the ice by St. Louis Blues' defenseman Noel Picard, but his post-goal moments were usually studies in anti-climax. He raised an arm and looked for a teammate to tousle his hair. No wind-milling or punching of air, just a tap on the bum from a Bruin as he skated resolutely back to his podium along the blueline. When you author the impossible so often, to you it becomes commonplace.

The Bruins found him in 1960, a 5-foot-2, 110-pound peewee from Parry Sound, Ont., playing in an All-Ontario bantam tournament. Immediately, the club invested $1,000 to sponsor his team and earn his rights. Becoming Bruins' property earned Orr a few hundred dollars, a new coat of stucco for the house in Parry Sound and some new clothes.

Orr streaked through minor hockey and set a new record for points by a defenseman with the Ontario League's Oshawa Generals. He hit the NHL at 18, but changed the rules even before he arrived. Before Orr, the best NHL salary a rookie could hope to garner was $8,000. Orr's negotiations were handled by a brash Toronto lawyer named Alan Eagleson. To land him in time for the 1966-67 season, the Bruins coughed up $25,000.

Only his first season came in the six-team NHL, but the Original Six mentality never left his game. He scored 13 goals and outslugged the league's toughest hardrocks, among them the New York Rangers' Vic Hadfield and Reggie Fleming and Ted Harris of the Montreal Canadiens, in that rookie season. "People are crazy if they want to fight him," said Bruins' coach Harry Sinden. "He has got about the fastest hands in hockey."

He scored 13 goals and notched 41 points while winning the Calder Trophy. Pierre Pilote of the Chicago Black Hawks, an 11-year NHLer, was the only defenseman to score more points. Harry Howell, the Rangers' genial defenseman, won the Norris Trophy and delivered one of the most prophetic and oft-repeated quotes in league history. "I'm glad I won it now," Howell said, "because it's going to belong to Orr from now on."

Orr won the Norris the next eight seasons.

There had been no precedent for Orr. Yes, there had been mobile defensemen. Orr's predecessor, Eddie Shore, was the best offensive rearguard of his generation. Flash Hollett of the Detroit Red Wings scored 20 goals. Wings' great Red Kelly was a superb offensive defenseman who hit double figures in goals nine consecutive years. Montreal defender Doug Harvey, a gifted all-around player and tactician had, until Orr, held the throttle on the pace of the game more tightly than any defenseman had before.

But when most of those players attacked, a forward hung back to defend. Hollett, Kelly and the rest were more like defensemen who took an occasional turn at center. Orr was a center who played defense. He could lose a gamble on a pinch and skate back into the play so quickly, the game rotated around him, even when he didn't do the right thing. He was not another star. He was a new sun.

"The guy always had (the puck)," said Vic Hadfield, "and when he had it, there wasn't a thing we could do about it."

But late in his rookie season, Orr injured his left knee when Detroit defenseman Marcel Pronovost pinned him into the boards. That August, Orr underwent his first knee operation,

Don Dixon

another came three months later, then in 1972 and twice more in 1975. Each time, bone chips or cartilage were removed. By the mid 1970s, his left knee had been effectively gutted.

In 1970, Orr had become the only defenseman to win a scoring championship and repeated the trick in 1975. En route to the Bruins' 1970 championship, Orr became the first defenseman and only the fourth player to crack the 100-point barrier thanks to a 33-goal, 87-assist season. The next year, an even more jaw-dropping total: 37 goals and 102 assists for 139 points. Paul Coffey is the only defenseman to score more goals in a regular season. No defenseman has recorded more points or piled up 100 assists.

Orr recorded six consecutive seasons of more than 100 points. During that string, he missed hitting the 30-goal mark once—by one goal. It took Harvey 18 seasons to set the record for assists by a defenseman. Orr broke Harvey's mark of 452 in seven-and-a-half.

"In many ways," said Philadelphia Flyers' captain Bobby Clarke, "Orr was actually too good for the rest of us in the NHL."

Fran Rosa, longstanding hockey writer for the Boston *Globe*, tells a story in which a New York *Times* reporter watched Orr and cornered a colleague from the *Globe*. "I counted six things Orr did tonight that I've never seen in a hockey game. Is that about right?" "I really couldn't say," came the answer. "We stopped counting about four years ago."

Orr won the Conn Smythe Trophy as the Bruins triumphed in 1970 and 1972 and became the league's first NHLer to sign a million-dollar contract.

Thanks to Orr, the Bruins became a better draw than the Boston Celtics, but his knees imploded after his greatest goal-

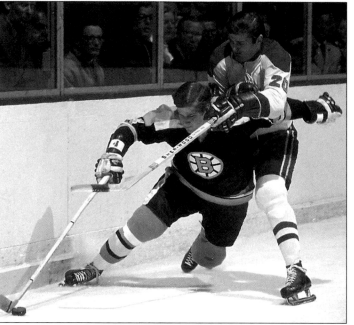

scoring year, the 46-goal 1974-75 campaign. The next season, injuries limited him to 10 games. Then came a protracted and fruitless salary dispute with the Bruins. Finally, Orr accepted a free agent offer to move to Chicago.

Orr's final greatness was played out at the 1976 Canada Cup where, playing on intelligence and barren knees, he still emerged as Canada's best player. He played 26 games over two seasons with the Black Hawks before leaving at 31 the game he had so dominated. "Losing Bobby," said Gordie Howe, "was the biggest blow the NHL has ever suffered."

It was, at least in the early years, an agonizing retirement. Orr tried his hand as an assistant coach with the Black Hawks, as a broadcaster and as a personal assistant to NHL president John Ziegler, but those jobs were short-lived fixes.

He could find nothing inside the game that gave him a fraction of the satisfaction of playing. After a public divorce from Eagleson, he made what would be an ultimately successful transition to the business world as a corporate spokesman. Orr now works as a Boston-based player agent.

But the drive, that which made him grab his head after making a mistake on a rush, never left. Orr's desire to play was as prodigious as his talent. He was always first at the rink, playing gin with Bruins' trainer Frosty Forristall, always inventing new ways to shine.

Nobody wanted to play more than Orr. In 1976, on the brink of retirement, he even talked about the possible use of an experimental man-made joint with doctors at the Mayo Clinic.

"If they invented an artificial knee that would withstand the contact of hockey, yes I'd have the operation tomorrow," he once told an interviewer.

"I'd give anything to play again. Anything. I loved it so much."

Left Wingers No Centers Of Attention

Left wingers have every right to feel left out of The Hockey News Top 50 Players.

Left wing is the most under-represented position. Only five left wingers were picked, three or four fewer than what you'd expect if all positions were represented in proportion to their place on the ice. Projecting a normal lineup of one goalie, two defensemen, one left winger, one center and one right winger over 50 players, there should be eight or nine at each position and 17 defensemen.

The breakdown is as follows: Goalies–7; Defensemen–12; Left Wingers–5; Centers–17; and Right Wingers–9. *(See pg. 14 for All-Star Teams.)*

Centers are over-represented almost 2-to-1, which is no surprise because the best players have traditionally gravitated to center ice. Not included is superstar defenseman Red Kelly, who played center after leaving Detroit for Toronto. Mark Messier, one of only two players in history to earn all-star status at two positions–center and left wing, is listed at center. Dit Clapper, the other player to earn all-star honors at two positions is slotted as a defenseman.

Mr. Hockey

By Michael Ulmer

When the Detroit Red Wings honored Gordie Howe for his 25th NHL campaign, they included a quote from an unidentified rival player in the evening's program.

"He is everything you expect an ideal athlete to be," said the unknown NHL soldier. "He is soft-spoken, self-deprecating and thoughtful. He is also one of the most vicious, cruel and mean men I have ever met in a hockey game."

While there is a compelling argument to be made that Bobby Orr changed the game more than Gordie Howe, (Orr is Howe's choice as the number one player of all-time), hockey's unmatched blend of staggering skill and often chilling violence was showcased at its best and for the longest by Gordie Howe.

They don't call him Mr. Hockey for nothing.

Howe played 33 pro seasons, one as a 17-year-old with Omaha in the United States Hockey League, 25 with the Red Wings, six in the World Hockey Association and one final NHL campaign as a 52-year-old Hartford Whaler.

Wayne Gretzky has bested his career marks for NHL goals and points—and even earned more assists than Howe's 1,850

points—but Howe's sheer dominance over several hockey lifetimes makes him the most distinctive NHL player ever. For 20 straight seasons, from 1949-50 through 1968-69, Howe finished among the top five scorers in the NHL.

Indeed, Howe considers that unprecedented run his crowning statistical achievement, more so even than six Hart Trophies as league MVP and six Art Ross Trophies as league scoring champion.

In his fourth NHL season, 1949-50, Howe began one of hockey's most amazing streaks. For 22 years in a row, he never scored fewer than 23 goals. The owner of 801 career goals, Howe scored more NHL goals after his 30th birthday than before. As a 41-year-old in 1968-69, he scored 44 goals. In 1970-71, his last year with the Red Wings, his 23 goals were second-most on the team. At 43, he had slowed all the way down to the level of his peers.

After an unhappy two-year retirement, Howe, along with sons Mark and Marty, signed with the WHA's Houston Aeros and turned in an MVP, 31-goal, 100-point campaign as a 46-year-old reborn rookie. He spent six years in the WHA before turning in one final NHL tour of duty as a 15-goal scorer for the Hartford Whalers at 52.

Forged in the heat and squalor of the Depression, Howe was the product of hard times. Born 18 months before the stock market crash, he was one of nine children produced by Ab Howe, a laborer, and his wife, Kate. In Gordie's first year, the family moved from a shack in what was then the village of Floral, Sask., into nearby Saskatoon, where Ab Howe worked as a laborer. While he still occasionally received relief to ensure his family was fed, Ab's only break from working for the City of Saskatoon came in late summer when he booked time off to make extra money bringing in the harvest.

Kate Howe was every bit as resilient. She bore three of her nine children when her husband was away working. Always taller and stronger than the rest, Gordie suffered from a mild case of dyslexia. Reading was virtually impossible for him and, because he was bigger than the rest, his classmates called him 'Dough-head' and 'Dummy.'

"Kids, you know, can be cruel as hell," said Howe, "but when I got bigger I made sure it stopped." Howe would, indeed, later use his size to fight back, but as a young boy, the lack of success in school and the taunts those failures provoked were devastating. "I could remember quite often I

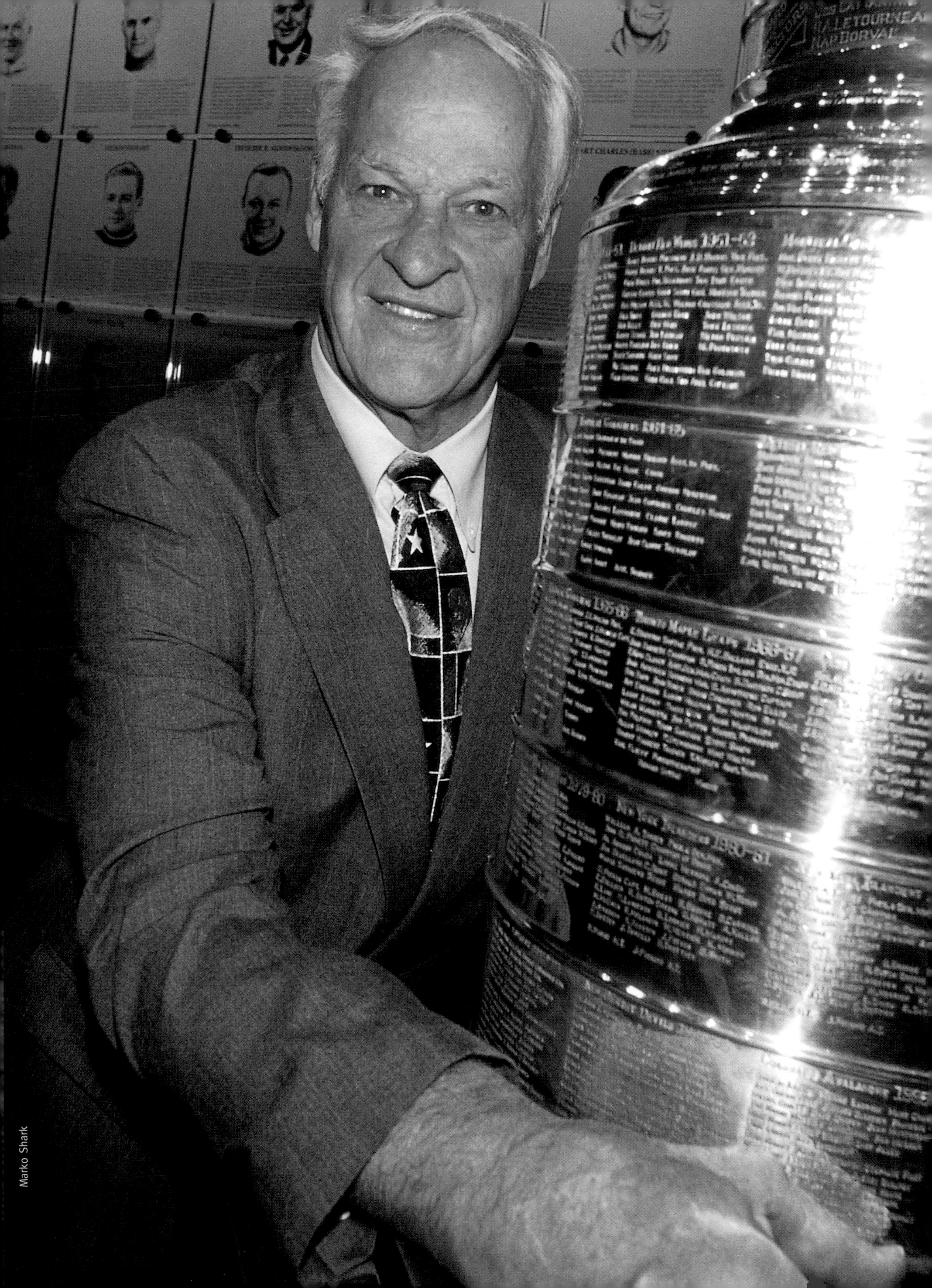

Marko Shark

would bring back my report card, which was just horrible, you know, to my Mom and I'd be crying, and she'd put me on her lap," Howe said.

Howe worshipped his mother. As a boy, he circled items in the catalogue he would buy for her when he became a successful hockey player. One day, he decided to perfect his autograph and asked his mother which version of his name she preferred. She liked the one that read 'Gordon Howe.' Howe signs every autograph that way, as a tribute to his mother.

From his mother came the calm and compassion that has defined his life. Bobby Hull has always claimed an incident at Maple Leaf Gardens, in which Howe obligingly signed an autograph for him, was the example he'd use in always making time for his public. Howe's gentle nature never changed, his ease with children and fans never wavered. Nor did the wit he inherited from his mother. Once, while appearing on the Dick Cavett Show, Howe was asked why he wouldn't cover his head with a helmet, but nonetheless wore a protective cup. "You can always get somebody to do your thinking for you," smiled Gordie Howe.

The Howes were too poor to afford frills like skates, but when a woman came by the house selling her possessions to buy food during the worst of the Depression, Kate Howe managed to scrounge a couple of dollars from around the house.

The bag was dropped onto the kitchen floor and two shopworn men's hockey skates thudded into Howe's life.

While he found unconditional love from his mother, he learned a flinty self-reliance at the hands of his father. A rugged, powerful man, Ab Howe preferred the company of Gordie's oldest brother, Vern. If he was lucky during a job, Gordie got to pass the tools to the elder males.

Ab Howe, himself a devastating fighter, couldn't understand why his soft-natured

son took abuse from the other children.

"I told him that he should never take dirt from anybody because if he did, they'd keep throwing it on him," Ab Howe told an interviewer when Howe was playing his last NHL season. "He was clumsy and backward and bashful. That's why I thought he would never amount to anything."

Longtime linemate Ted Lindsay said even at the peak of his stardom, Howe

feared he would lose his position to a rookie. On the ice, he never forgot a slight and held as gospel his Dad's warning about retaliating against wrongs. Once, he waited nearly a year to flatten Canadiens' defenseman J.C. Tremblay with a vicious elbow for calling him a dummy during an off-season card game.

While he did not play organized hockey until he was eight, Howe quickly proved himself a hockey prodigy. He was six feet by his mid-teens, but he grew so quickly doctors were concerned he had a calcium deficiency and prescribed chin-ups to strengthen his spine. Howe exercised relentlessly and, thanks to summers spent working construction with his father, fashioned a powerful physique that gave him the strength of a man while still a boy.

Howe was first noticed by a Rangers' scout when he was 15, but a tryout in Winnipeg failed, largely because of Howe's homesickness. A year later, Detroit scout Fred Pinckney signed him.

School ended for Howe at 16. He was moved to the Red Wings' Galt, Ont. junior team, but the Wings chose to develop older players. Because of a quota on the number of players from Western Canada the team could ice, Howe could only practice in Galt.

A shy boy, Howe couldn't bear the social process of school. Intending to take three high school classes, he stood around before the first bell, saw somebody he knew vaguely and handed him his textbooks. "I walked up the railroad track and the first sign I saw was for the Galt Metal Industry. I walked in and asked for a job."

In addition to his obvious skating and shooting skills, Howe polished another vital element of his game in Galt. He fought, early, often and passionately and it was duly noted by the organization.

The next season, Howe was promoted to Omaha of the United States League and scored 22 goals as a 17-yearold, but it would be in Omaha that Howe would nearly get away.

Frank Selke, then an assistant to Maple Leafs' president Conn Smythe, scouted Howe in Omaha and found that because of a clerical error, the teenager wasn't registered as Red Wings' property. Selke and Jack Adams, the Red Wings' coach and GM were friends, and in the clubby atmosphere that was the NHL at that time, Selke felt Adams should be told. The train back to Toronto stopped in Detroit, Selke got off, walked to the Olympia and told Adams he should put his greatest prospect back on the protected list.

Adams made Howe his most lasting work. When Howe started the 1946-47 season as an 18-year-old rookie, he fought twice in his first two games, scored once and felt he was on his way to establishing himself as an NHL player.

"My thinking was if fighting was what I had to do to be an NHLer, then why not? I never saw the ice for about 15 games. Finally he called me over and said, 'Young man, I know you can fight. Now can you show me you can play hockey.' He told me, 'Don't forget this. Don't ever turn your back on a fight, but don't go looking for one.' "

well, Howe and Lindsay were excellent defensive players.

Howe soaked up the strategy sessions convened on every train ride by Abel and worked relentlessly to improve his game. It was part of his ritual to shoot pucks for 30 minutes, usually into the top of the net, after even the most gruelling practice. "Once in Boston, he skated in against the goaltender, feinted and deliberately tried to put the puck in the top of the net,"

Cups in six seasons, three with the great Terry Sawchuk in goal. Lindsay, Abel and Howe finished one-two-three in league scoring in 1949-50.

Sandwiched in all the winning was Howe's worst injury. During the 1950 play-offs against Toronto, he veered toward Leafs' captain Ted Kennedy. Kennedy and Howe still disagree on what happened next. Kennedy said Howe missed him and crashed into the boards. Howe feels

Howe had made another decision that would define him in his first year. A lower uniform number guaranteed a lower berth on the interminable train rides that made up the life of NHLers. Howe opted for number nine because it made for a more comfortable ride. Howe, and later Maurice Richard and Bobby Hull, would make number 9 the symbol of hockey royalty.

Teamed with Lindsay and Sid Abel, Howe became the driving force behind the 'Production Line,' one of the the NHL's all-time great units.

The strength of the unit lay in the versatility of its members. While Abel was the best playmaker, Howe and Lindsay were accurate and instinctive passers. All three had excellent scoring skills and Howe and Lindsay were formidable in the corners. As

Abel said. "He shot it right over the goal. He went behind the net, dug it out, came back, gave the goalie a different feint and put it up top for the goal. Then he came over to Lindsay and me and said, 'That's where the first one was supposed to be.' "

Howe was 21 when he met 17-year-old Colleen Joffa at a Detroit bowling alley. They began to date steadily, but Howe was so tongue-tied, one of the first clues of his affection came when he blurted out, "Hey, how old does a person have to be to get married?" after a movie. It took two years for Gordie to muster up the courage to say he loved her. After a four-year courtship, they married in 1953.

The late 1940s and into the middle of the next decade were the glory years for the Red Wings. Detroit won four Stanley

Kennedy, a rugged but honorable player, accidentally high-sticked him.

Howe had a fractured skull and required emergency surgery to relieve the pressure building on his brain. Despite the injury, he would return the next season, play all 70 games and win the scoring championship by a gaudy 20 points over Maurice Richard.

The 1955 regular season championship was the Red Wings' seventh. They would qualify for the league finals five more times, but never repeat. Adams traded Lindsay and future Hall of Fame goalie Glenn Hall to squash a players' union drive in 1957. That, along with the emergence of the Canadiens and later, the Maple Leafs, would keep Howe from lifting a Stanley Cup again.

Howe, however, remained as constant and dominant a figure as always.

He was 30 when he fought his last fight of consequence, a battle against up-and-coming Rangers' tough guy Lou Fontinato at Madison Square Garden in 1959.

Howe was looking for Fontinato when a skirmish broke up and saw the Ranger forward steaming in on him from the side. "Gordie's wrist went whomp, whomp whomp to Fontinato's head," said Jack McIntyre, one of the players surrounding the fight. "It sounded just like an axe chopping wood." The fight broke Fontinato's nose and the young Ranger's mystique. Howe would never again be challenged so openly in a fight.

Howe, however, perfected the art of delivering an elbow. He almost never threw an obvious elbow, instead he incorporated an exaggerated arm swing into his skating style, left foot forward, right elbow back, right foot forward, left elbow back. All perfectly above board, *Sports Illustrated* once observed, "except the natural rhythm of a skater does not call for elbows at ear level."

Never a strong proponent of weight-training or off-ice conditioning, Howe was nonetheless gifted with ideal genetics and a superhuman tolerance for pain.

Lloyd Percival, the early guru of hockey conditioning and tactics, tested Howe's flexibility, mobility, skating muscles, strength and shooting muscles.

Only one athlete, boxer Sugar Ray Robinson, had ever scored as high on Percival's test as Howe.

Howe was never a man to waste energy. "I don't hold with futile rushing about," he said. "In hockey, when I'm beaten on a play I relax and wait for the next time. If a guy has a 20-foot head start on me down 200 feet of ice, I'm dead from the word go

and I don't go chasing after the impossible." From the midway point of his career on, Howe made it a practice never to eat anything later than noon.

Howe was a perpetual motion machine into his 40s. At 40 he scored a career-high 103 points with 44 goals, the most he had scored in 12 years.

But while Howe's game continued to endure, his relationship with the Red Wings became fractious. He was devastat-

ed to learn he was the third-highest paid Red Wing in 1969 and, while owner Bruce Norris increased his salary from $45,000 to $100,000, Norris sneered that Colleen was behind the salary demand.

By now, Colleen Howe had become the financial mastermind of the Howe family, a move that chafed at Norris.

Tired of the constant losing and the poisonous attitude that permeated the Red Wings, Howe retired as a player in 1971.

The Red Wings promised a vice-president's job, but as his arch-rival Richard learned a decade earlier, a player's on-ice exploits carried little weight when the athlete moved to the boardroom.

Colleen was also representing Mark Howe, a highly-rated prospect when the WHA came into being in 1973. The prospect of returning to the ice to play with his children proved an irresistible lure for Howe. All three Howes signed on with the Aeros and the elder Howe turned in an MVP season.

"When we talk about the joys of my whole career, that was in Houston," said Howe. "If it wasn't for the kids I would never have come back. They put fun back in the game."

Howe ploughed through six WHA campaigns, averaging 29 goals and 84 points before returning to the NHL with the Hartford Whalers, for one final victory lap.

The only father to play professional hockey with his sons, Howe finally retired in 1980 with 801 NHL goals and another 174 in the WHA.

While his longevity began to take on the look of a sideshow in October of 1997, when he returned for one shift with the International League's Detroit Vipers, Howe had, nevertheless, established himself as the most durable athlete in North American team sports history.

GORDIE HOWE		1946-80
Born: March 31,1928 Floral, Sask.		
Teams: Detroit, Hartford		
NHL	Regular	Playoffs
Seasons	26	20
Games	1,767	157
Goals	801	68
Assists	1049	92
Points	1,850	160
Penalties	1,685	220
All-Star: 21 (First–12, Second–9)		
Trophies: 12 (Hart–6, Ross–6)		
Stanley Cup Championships		4

Greatest Physical Talent Ever

The portents of Mario Lemieux's greatness were everywhere, not the least of which a record 133-goal, 282-point 1983-84 season in his final year of junior hockey with the Laval Voisins.

His reach, shot, skating and vision were obvious at a glance. Scotty Bowman, who coached Lemieux with the Pittsburgh Penguins, watched him play minor hockey in Montreal. "You always knew," Bowman said, "even when he was 13. He was the best I ever saw at that age."

But there were doubts. Lemieux had flunked out at the Memorial Cup and was roundly criticized in the conservative hockey world for refusing to go to the Penguins' table or wear their sweater when he was drafted first overall in the 1984 NHL entry draft.

"There's a difference between being the most talented player and becoming the best player," an NHL scout told THN in 1984. "I think it will be boom or bust with Mario."

Thirteen years later, as Lemieux faced retirement, no less an authority than Bobby Orr pronounced Lemieux the most talented player in NHL history–if not necessarily the best. "What he can do, I couldn't do," Orr said. "He can do more things than any player I've seen. When he wants to play, he's scary." Gordie Howe is Orr's choice as best ever.

From the beginning, Lemieux was a star. Three minutes into his first NHL game, on his first shift, he stripped Boston Bruins' superstar Ray Bourque of the puck, veered in on goalie Pete Peeters and scored. He collected 100 points as a rookie and won the Calder Trophy as the league's top freshman.

Lemieux had a 141-point sophomore year, but was criticized when he refused to

play for Canada in the World Championship. Doubts about his ability to lead the Penguins to a championship flourished.

"I think he can push himself harder," observed Los Angeles Kings' star Marcel Dionne. Television analyst Bill Clement agreed Lemieux had yet to adopt the warrior mentality, but astutely foresaw something greater, an indomitable individualist.

Lemieux was a solitary figure in a team game. No wonder he found such passion in the sporting world's most solitary pursuit.

"There is something clean and bright about golf," Lemieux told an interviewer. "It is a game where you are alone and within yourself and that is something I like sometimes, to be alone and to see what is

inside myself. Sometimes with hockey, although I do not try to let it be so, there is not time for reflection."

As Lemieux entered his mid 20s, his control and understanding of the pace of the game was so pronounced he seemed as unaffected in the heat of a game as he would be in measuring a putt.

"When I'm going good, everything seems to slow down, and I'm seeing everyone on the ice," he said. "Every time I get the puck, I see the whole ice; who is open, who's not. It doesn't happen often, but if I'm playing real well, I can go four or five games like that." While he was a phenomenal playmaker, Lemieux was, first and foremost, a scorer, the most potent the NHL has ever seen. John Vanbiesbrouck was victimized 30 times by Lemieux, the most of any NHL goalie, and could never come to terms with his goal-scoring arsenal.

"He has got the wing span of an albatross," Vanbiesbrouck said. "For a big man, it's amazing how quickly he can react. But he also trusts his shot more than anybody in the league. One time, he shot from the corner to my right and put it between my pads."

No one will ever forget Lemieux's brilliant end-to-end effort against the Minnesota North Stars in Game 2 of the 1991 Stanley Cup finals.

Dan Hamilton/VPS

The best a defenseman could do was pick his poison against Lemieux "If you go at Mario like a madman, he'll make you look like a complete idiot," confided one high-profile defenseman who begged for anonymity. "He just holds the puck out there on his forehand and dares you to commit yourself. If you do, he slips it past you and, if you don't, he controls the blueline and has time to make the play."

The emerging maturity in Lemieux was apparent in 1987 when he scored 11 goals, nine on assists from Wayne Gretzky, as Canada won the Canada Cup in a thrilling three-game final over the Soviet Union. Gretzky fed Lemieux for the winning goal and in doing so passed the baton from the world's greatest player to his heir apparent.

As if to prove his virtuosity, on New Year's Eve, 1988, Lemieux became the first NHL player to score five different types of goals–power play, even strength, shorthanded, penalty shot and empty net–in the same game. He finished that season with 85 goals and 199 points.

Only back pain forced Lemieux to end a 46-game point streak Feb. 14, 1990, and ended his pursuit of Gretzky's record 51-game streak.

In May, 1991, nine months after a back injury and deep infection forced him into hospital, Lemieux won the Conn Smythe Trophy and lifted his first Stanley Cup. The injury had knocked him out of 54 regular season games, put his career in doubt and, now, played a large part in silencing any remaining critics. "No strain at all," said Lemieux as he picked up the Cup.

That Cup completed a seven-year cycle of the Penguins' rebirth. When Lemieux arrived in town, the Penguins were averaging just over 6,000 fans a game and were outdrawn by the local indoor soccer team. The team was gushing red ink, a move to Hamilton, Ont., seemed imminent and fan morale was even worse than the ledger.

"You'd walk into the arena and there

would be 3,800 people in the place and most of them were booing," said then-marketing director Paul Steigerwald. "Some of them had bags on their heads. The team would take the ice and they'd yell obscenities. Hockey in Pittsburgh had reached the bottom, the absolute pits of professional sports."

In 1992, there was another scoring title,

MARIO LEMIEUX		1984-97
Born: Oct. 5, 1965 Montreal		
Teams: Pittsburgh		
NHL	**Regular**	**Playoffs**
Seasons	12	7
Games	745	89
Goals	613	70
Assists	881	85
Points	1,494	155
Penalties	737	83
All-Star: 8 (First–5, Second–3)		
Trophies: 13 (Hart-3, Ross-6, Smythe-2, Calder-1, Masterton-1)		
Stanley Cup Championships		2

another Conn Smythe and another Stanley Cup. Lemieux's image was now cast. He was a champion and, while he lacked the ambassadorial skills and inclinations of Gretzky, what had been construed as aloofness was now seen as elegance.

The defining moment of Lemieux's life and career came in January of 1993. Doctors found a suspicious lump in his neck during a physical and further examination revealed Hodgkin's disease.

Then came two months of radiation

therapy, a plane ride to Philadelphia after his final treatment and a one-goal, one-assist comeback performance against the Flyers.

Despite missing 23 games, Lemieux roared past Pat LaFontaine to win the scoring title. His 2.67 points per game that season was third-best in league history. More importantly, he came back to a level of stardom that usurped the trophies, even the championships.

The effects of back surgery and the lingering effects of radiation knocked Lemieux out of the 1994-95 season, but he returned for two more sterling seasons and two more scoring championships.

The individualist, however, never ebbed in Lemieux. Unwilling to fall into a less prolific version of himself and tired of the constant clutching and grabbing, he announced his retirement in the spring of 1997. He was inducted to the Hockey Hall of Fame Nov. 17, becoming only the ninth player to have the standard three-year waiting period waived and be honored immediately upon retirement

Lemieux finished his career with 613 goals and 1,494 points in 745 career games. His career points-per-game average, 2.005, is comparable to Gretzky's 2.026 (entering 1997-98), but No. 99's production has declined over time. In his first 745 games, Gretzky had 616 goals compared to Lemieux's 613 and 1,774 points compared to Lemieux's 1,494.

There was a final moment, a victory lap of the Civic Arena after scoring a late goal and being named first star in the Penguins' last playoff home game in 1997. Two nights later, the Penguins lost in Philadelphia.

Lemieux left with six scoring titles, three MVP honors and a space beside Gretzky as the only player to average more than two points a game. In leaving he did the unthinkable: he walked away from the game as its best player.

Mario Lemieux

Jaromir Jagr

Rocket Ride To Superstardom

One day in the winter of 1942, Maurice Richard lay in a Montreal hospital bed, his confidence broken more seriously than his badly fractured right ankle.

He thought about quitting.

He was 21. Trained in technical school to be a machinist, he had accrued some job experience making tanks in a local factory. Were he to work a lathe or as a riveter, there would be no coach wondering, as the Montreal Canadiens' Dick Irvin had, whether Richard was too fragile to play in the NHL. No GM, such as the Canadiens' Tommy Gorman, would venture the same thoughts.

Richard had already broken his left ankle and left wrist the previous season and the injuries had darkened his hopes for a career. Now, when he was feeling his most vulnerable, he read of his employers' doubts in the morning newspaper.

First came feelings of despair, and then, perhaps as Irvin and Gorman had expected, the white hot rage of the Rocket. "This time the depression I suffered was infinitely worse than it had been before," Richard said later. "I was a very young man starting out in hockey and, so far, very unlucky. Instead of recognizing that, the club worried publicly about whether I would be able to last in this league. Tommy Gorman never said this to me, but he did talk about it to the papers. I did not appreciate that, but I was young and he was the boss. I could say nothing."

But he could do something. And he did.

Richard returned the next season and bumped Charlie Sands off the right side of

a unit that featured Elmer Lach at center and Toe Blake on the left side. One of the NHL's best-ever lines, the 'Punch Line,' had been formed and Richard scored 32 goals that season.

The following year, 1944-45, he attained a standard that would, in time, be met by Mike Bossy, Wayne Gretzky, Mario Lemieux and Brett Hull and, yet, always remain

Richard's–50 goals in 50 games. He finished his career 15 years later as the all-time NHL leader in games and, at the time of his retirement, his 50-goal season still stood as the NHL high-water mark.

There was in Richard a natural rage, an instinctive need to overcome whatever obstacles were put in his way. He poured resentment toward his bosses into his play and regarded the shadows who followed his every move as necessary stagehands for his greatness.

The harder they worked, the harder he had to, and invariably the more he produced. Once Richard wore strapping Detroit Red Wings' defenseman Earl Seibert like a coat before scoring. Red Wings' coach Jack Adams began to berate

Seibert on the bench before Seibert held up a gloved hand.

"Mr. Adams," he said, "I'm 6-foot-2. Any man who can carry me on his back from the blueline in deserves to score."

"How do you stop Richard?" a newsman once asked a disconsolate Adams after Richard had destroyed his Red Wings.

"Shoot him," came the response.

When he retired in 1960 at 39, Joseph Henri Maurice Richard owned 17 NHL records and a stature among hockey fans in Quebec and elsewhere that has only grown with time. There have been more productive players, perhaps even a few, such as Bobby Orr and Gordie Howe, who were better loved. But Maurice Richard, minted in the foundry of the Depression, imbued with the hopes of a people, driven by a level of will as yet unrepeated, remains by far the most charismatic.

The first NHL game Richard played in was the first he had seen. There was no money for such frills growing up poor in Montreal's Bordeaux region. He spoke two words of English when he made the Canadiens: yes and no.

To French Canadians, living in a city dominated politically and economically by an English elite, he was an inherently political figure. In 1955, when NHL president Clarence Campbell suspended Richard for the remainder of the season and the playoffs for hitting a linesman, the infamous 'Richard Riot' erupted at the Forum and fans rampaged through the city's downtown.

"He was our flag," longtime Canadiens' publicity director Camil Desroches once said. Richard would fight and, there, in

those famous dark green eyes there lived not so much anger, but emptiness: no hesitation, no weakness, no fear.

"He wasn't crazy," his longtime linemate Bert Olmstead said. "He just had the fire."

Richard never analyzed his goals and, for that reason, never remembered them, even moments after scoring. He never cared about tactics.

Instead, he made himself blank. Everything came on instinct.

"To tell you the truth, I try to think of nothing," Richard once said. "I think you call it keeping your mind a blank. I find if I have a plan to fool the goaler he usually beats me. But if I don't know what I'm going to do, how can he?"

When teammate Ray Getliffe christened the young rookie, 'Rocket' Richard, he bestowed the best and most memorable nickname in hockey history. In finishing among the top five goal-scorers in 15 of his 18 years, Richard developed a familiar style.

Like a rocket, he travelled at incredible speed in a straight line to the goal. His hunger for goals never ebbed with age or injury.

One of Richard's favorite tactics was to shove a puck into a defenseman's skates and tie up the defenseman with one arm while he knocked the puck free with the other. Often he would use a defenseman as a springboard and push off him to make his escape.

Richard liked to shoot often and shoot low; he knew goalie pads took on water and weight as the game wore on while a netminder's hands were always unfettered. Often he would keep his hands higher on his stick to whip the shot on goal in much the same way Eric Lindros does today.

Video tapes show a surprisingly average sized player. Richard was 5-foot-10 and weighed only about 160 pounds when he entered the league, but he had superior first-step quickness and an excellent backhand.

Richard is believed to have scored about half his 544 career goals on the backhand.

Richard was a rarity, a left-shooting right winger, so as he cut into the middle from the right side he earned a better shooting angle than most.

"He didn't think of anything else but putting that puck in the net," said long-

time left winger Dickie Moore. "He always had that strength, that left arm out and cutting in on the right side.

"That was a great advantage because he had such great strength he was able to throw a defenseman behind him. Plus, he was so quick, three feet in front of a goaltender, he could shift gears. No one could do it like he did."

Richard, now 77 and battling a rare form of stomach cancer, embodied drama.

He is one of five players who shares the mark of five goals in one playoff game and is third in game-winning goals with 18. Richard still holds the record for career overtime goals with six.

Richard's greatest goal won the 1952 semifinal series against the Boston Bruins and enshrined on film the sheer drive

that powered him. Knocked unconscious in the first period when he hit his head against the knee of a Boston player, Richard spent most of the game on the trainer's table.

He returned to the Canadiens' bench late in the third period, but since he could not focus on the clock he had to ask Lach the score and how much time remained. With four minutes left Richard jumped over the boards, picked up a loose puck, bulled past two Bruins and beat Boston goalie Sugar Jim Henry to score the game winner.

The post-game picture of Richard, bloodied and barely conscious, shaking hands with Henry, whose eyes were blackened because of a broken nose, speaks more to the essence of Richard and the game than any picture before or since.

He went into wild convulsions in the Canadiens' dressing room and had to be sedated.

"That beautiful bastard," said Montreal *Herald* writer Elmer Ferguson, "scored semi-conscious."

Toe Blake took over for Irvin as the Canadiens' coach in 1955 and coaxed 38- and 33-goal seasons out of him, but injuries, the plague of his early career, and a new enemy, excess weight, slowly grounded the Rocket.

While he managed a respectable 19 goals in only 51 games in his last NHL season, onlookers noticed he fished the puck out of the net on his last playoff goal. That was in 1960, the year the Canadiens won their record fifth straight Cup.

Richard showed up for training camp the following season, but lasted only a few days. On Sept. 15, 1960, he retired, but not before ripping four goals past Jacques Plante in practice.

"It was," wrote Montreal newspaperman Andy O'Brien, "his way of saying goodbye to the big time."

MAURICE RICHARD		1952-74
Born: Aug. 4, 1921 Montreal		
Teams: Montreal		
NHL	Regular	Playoffs
Seasons	18	15
Games	978	133
Goals	544	82
Assists	421	44
Points	965	126
Penalties	1,285	188
All-Star: 14 (First–8, Second–6)		
Trophies: 1 (Hart)		
Stanley Cup Championships		8

Blueline Great Passing Fancy

Nat Turofsky/HHOF

Doug Harvey appraised rules and policies the way a high jumper considered the bar. He was, in the words of longtime friend, newspaperman Eddie MacCabe, "a non-conformist when conformity was the norm."

Harvey, who died Dec. 26, 1989, was a seven-time Norris Trophy winner and the triggerman for the Montreal Canadiens' 1950s brand of firewagon hockey.

He was the contrarian who found a better way and while his recklessness would darken the latter chapters of his life, Harvey did what few dare to dream—he improved the way the game of hockey was played.

When Harvey entered the league in 1947, the style of the day was to drop the forwards back in support of the two defensemen. Harvey's gifts were so unique—he was superb at stealing the puck off an attacker and even better at

keeping it—backchecking forwards were largely redundant.

Harvey instructed his forwards to stay high. When he got the puck, he refused to lug it up ice. Instead, he would drift near his own net, attracting a forechecker or two, before laying a perfect pass on the stick of a teammate to ignite a Montreal attack.

DOUG HARVEY		1947-69
Born: Dec. 19, 1924 Montreal		
Teams: Montreal, Rangers, Detroit, St. Louis		
NHL	**Regular**	**Playoffs**
Seasons	20	15
Games	1,113	137
Goals	88	8
Assists	452	64
Points	540	72
Penalties	1,216	152
All-Star: 11 (First-10, Second-1)		
Trophies: 7 (Norris-7)		
Stanley Cup Championships		6

"He had a great ability to trap the other team's forwards," remembered longtime Montreal teammate and Boston Bruins' executive Tom Johnson. "He would draw them in and then put the puck by them."

It was an heretical style. Fans and media thought Harvey looked lazy. One newspaperman dubbed him 'Dawdling Doug.' Canadiens' coach Dick Irvin constantly fretted Harvey would end up surrendering the puck near his own net, but the results were so obviously worth the risk that Harvey's way won the day.

Harvey passed with the grace of an elite forward. "He could have played center, he could have played left wing, he could have played goal," Johnson said. "There was no part of the game he couldn't do."

A 10-time first team all-star, Harvey led all defensemen in points three times and assists five times, including 1954-55 when he earned a record 43 assists.

Harvey was the backbone of a Montreal power play that was so devastating, league officials decided in 1956 to change the rules and allow a player to return to the ice if his team surrendered a power play goal.

A reckless competitor, Harvey nearly killed New York Rangers' forward Red Sullivan with a vicious spear and his stick bouts with Detroit Red Wings' star left winger Ted Lindsay were bloody and regular.

Through 14 years in Montreal, the contrarian never changed his ways. Harvey was the highest profile player to back Lindsay's ill-fated drive for a players' association.

Kind-hearted to a fault, Harvey was chronically late and stood out as one of

the Canadiens' most willing and gregarious partiers. All this made Harvey a player favorite and a management headache. In 1961, the Canadiens' shipped Harvey to New York where he could operate as player-coach.

Harvey excelled during his first year in New York, winning his seventh Norris to become the first player to win back-to-back best defenseman awards on different teams. But Harvey abhorred the wedge his coaching duties drove between him and his players. He quit coaching, saying he wanted to be able to go out with the players for a beer again after the game.

Harvey would play two more seasons with the Rangers and then begin a five-year odyssey through the minors before returning to the NHL, first with Detroit for two games in 1966-67 and then with the St. Louis Blues the following season and 1968-69 before the phone stopped ringing.

By now, drinking was taking an increasingly prominent role in Harvey's life and he worked in and out of hockey after that. He had a keen eye for talent and a strong memory for prospects, but he would rarely bother to write down the names of the players he watched.

His drinking worsened and he spent several years near the end of his life doing odd jobs and living in an old railway touring car at an Ottawa-area race track.

Harvey died of cirrhosis of the liver in Montreal General Hospital. He stopped drinking about three years before his death and to the end he was entertaining nurses and fellow patients like an old vaudevillian.

Even on the cusp of death, the contrarian dismissed any thought of repentance. "If I had to do it over again," he said, "I wouldn't have changed a thing."

'Le Gros Bill' Dignity On Ice

Howie Morenz kept the Montreal Canadiens in business during the 1920s and 1930s. Maurice Richard permanently installed the team as a pillar of Quebec culture in the 1940s and 1950s.

But no team trades on its image more than the Canadiens and it is here that Jean Beliveau has outstripped the rest. Regal on the ice, humble and diplomatic away from the rink, Beliveau made red, white and blue the colors of hockey royalty.

The embodiment of handsome athleticism, Beliveau became the blueprint for a generation of Quebec superstars. "When I was a kid, I was told that I was born 10 miles from the little town of Victoriaville,

where Jean Beliveau was raised," Rangers' Hall of Famer Rod Gilbert recalled. "For all my childhood on, I kept thinking if he comes from there and I come from there, there is a possibility that Rod Gilbert can imitate Jean Beliveau."

Buffalo Sabres' star Gilbert Perreault, a Victoriaville native, learned about stickhandling from watching Beliveau. Guy Lafleur wore Beliveau's No. 4 and it was Beliveau's admonishments that helped spur Lafleur to stardom.

Beliveau arrived in the NHL to stay in 1953 and broke through in his third NHL season, winning the 1955-56 scoring title and Hart Trophy with a 47-goal, 88-point campaign. He did it by displaying a new

level of toughness. His 143 penalty minutes incurred that year remained a club record until John Ferguson rang up 156 nine seasons later.

At 6-foot-3 and 205 pounds, Beliveau was the blueprint the hockey gods used to build another French-Canadian superstar, Mario Lemieux.

The two used their reach to equal and great effect. Lemieux, before his back injury, was probably a slightly stronger skater. Beliveau was a slightly superior stickhandler, but both thrived on an instinct that outdistanced even their reach.

"The thing about Jean was that he could size up a situation so well," said Hall of Famer Frank Mahovlich. "I remember Jean's 500th goal. We were teamed with a young player named Phil Roberto and Jean went to the net at just the right time to finish off one of the prettiest three-way passing plays you'll ever see. That was Jean Beliveau. He had that vision and he could position everybody and set everybody up."

Beliveau set the standard as the most coveted junior player ever, but he made the Canadiens wait five years before trading icon status in Quebec City as a junior and senior star for even greater fame with Montreal.

Nicknamed 'Le Gros Bill' after a French folk hero, he captained the team for 10 years and worked for the Canadiens' owner, Molson Brewery on off-days and through the summer.

He was a company man who straddled the line between player and management. Beliveau's job with the organization never compromised his standing as captain and he was a revered and much-respected leader.

"Part of your job is to listen to your teammates and help them with their problems," Beliveau said. "I always tried to solve things right in the dressing room without getting management involved."

It was Beliveau who made it a practice to carry extra money on the road for cash-strapped rookies, Beliveau who silenced Henri Richard with a squeeze of the arm when Richard blasted coach Al MacNeil for benching him in the 1971 playoffs, Beliveau who set the tempo in the dressing room and for 23 years, as an ambassador and club executive.

Beliveau was offered the figurehead position of Governor General in 1994, the only hockey player asked to serve as Canadian head of state. He turned down the offer.

He was the most successful captain of hockey's most successful team, winning five of his 10 Stanley Cups as captain. No other captain has been handed the Cup so many times. Beliveau contributed mightily to the Habs' triumphs, scoring 79 goals, the seventh-highest playoff total. He was the first winner of the Conn Smythe Trophy (1965) as playoff MVP.

When he arrived in Montreal from the New York Rangers in December of 1964, forward Dick Duff sought out Beliveau. "I asked him if there was anything special he wanted me to do," Duff said. "He smiled and said, 'Just play.' "

Beliveau would do the rest.

JEAN BELIVEAU		1953-71
Born: Aug. 31, 1931 Trois-Rivieres, Que.		
Teams: Montreal		
NHL	Regular	Playoffs
Seasons	18	17
Games	1,125	162
Goals	507	79
Assists	712	97
Points	1,219	176
Penalties	1,029	211
All-Star: 10 (First-6, Second-4)		
Trophies: 4 (Hart-2, Ross-1, Smythe-1)		
Stanley Cup Championships		10

Harold Barkley

'Golden Jet' Flew Above Rest

Bobby Hull was a force. In full stride, he skated at almost 30 miles per hour. His slapshot travelled 118 mph, 19 mph faster than the winning blast at the 1997 all-star skills competition.

The Golden Jet pushed the envelope on how fast a man could skate, how hard he could shoot, how bravely he could ask for more money and his charisma matched the power of his game. "You know," he once told his Chicago Black Hawks' coach Billy Reay, "I might want to coach some day." "Geez," Reay said, suddenly insecure, "I hope not here."

In Hull's era, no player was bigger than his sport. Today every sport is only as big as its marquee players. For hockey, one of the master architects of that change was Robert Marvin Hull.

Hull's decision to become the 34th NHL player to sign with the rival World Hockey Association was a seminal moment in NHL history. Hull's 10-year, $2.75-million contract (the $1-million signing bonus was shared by all WHA owners) let the genie out of the bottle, the going rate for NHL stars doubled and in some cases tripled.

Without Hull, the league's first MVP, the WHA may never have lasted a season. Instead it survived seven years, left a legacy with NHL teams in Winnipeg, Quebec City, Edmonton and Hartford, standardized the use of player agents in negotiations and ended

the feudal hold NHL teams held on players.

Hull was often stung by that power.

Despite his status as one of the game's premier attractions and ambassadors, he battled, frequently and publicly, with the Black Hawks for more money. Hull spoke and acted as quickly as he skated and shot. "One of these days," Hull would say after his latest imbroglio, "I'm going to learn to keep my big mouth shut."

It took a long training camp holdout to secure a $100,000 contract in 1968 and Hull missed the Hawks' first 11 games in 1969 in a battle over deferred income. The Black Hawks, knowing that Hull had lost his copy of the contract, froze out their biggest star. When Hull finally agreed to come back, the Black Hawks attached humiliating conditions. He was forced to blame his advisers for misleading him and the media for misquoting him.

When he signed with the Winnipeg Jets in 1972, the NHL sought a petty injunction to prevent him from publicly speaking about hockey.

"He's like an evangelist," an NHL lawyer said. "Children follow him around." In this they were right. Adults as well as children flocked to Hull, as obliging a superstar as the NHL has ever showcased.

His game was instant gratification on ice, speed and power without even a hint of nuance. Hull enjoyed picking the puck up in his zone and creating

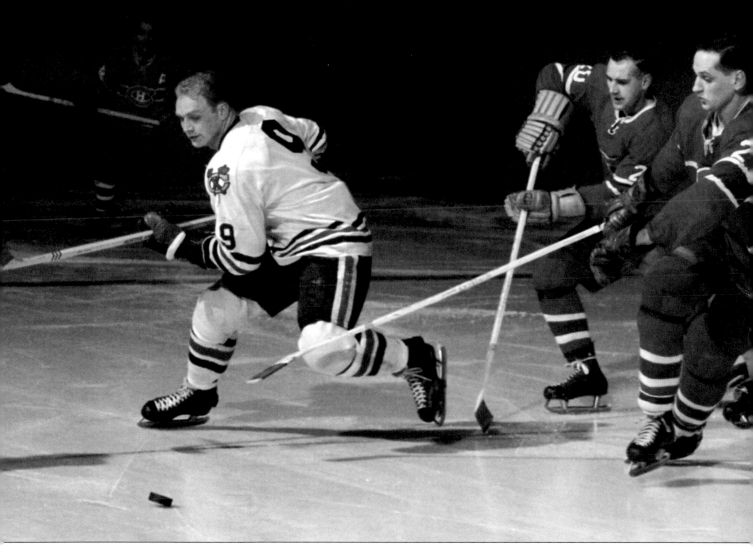

his own opportunity, the sight of Hull making a rink-length dash was the most arresting of his generation.

His shot made those of other NHLers seem comical in comparison. "You have to see it coming to really believe it," Jacques Plante once said of Hull's shot. "When it hits you, it feels like a piece of lead."

Hull led the league in goals seven times and in points on three occasions. The first player to score 50 goals more than once, he collected 610 NHL goals and 1,170 points and earned 10 first team all-star selections.

Four of the first six 50-goal seasons ever recorded in the NHL were fashioned by Hull and his 58 goals in 1968-69 represented eight more than any other player had ever scored.

It was a huge moment in 1966 when he scored his 51st goal, one more than co-recordholders Rocket Richard and Bernie Geoffrion.

Hull was often at odds with the new

league into which he had breathed life. "The idiot owners, the incompetent coaches, the inept players are dragging the game into the mud," he said during one outburst in the mid-1970s. "They're destroying it with their senseless violence. The game is no pleasure anymore, it's an ordeal."

Hull waged a sit-down strike to protest violence in the WHA and found solace on outdoor rinks in Winnipeg where he and Jets' teammate Ulf Nilsson would skate

and shoot long after the children had gone home.

For a while his tumultuous and virulent relationship with wife Joanne threatened to darken the image of the Golden Jet, but the union would ultimately produce in Brett Hull a worthy inheritor of the family's sterling scoring touch.

Bobby and Brett are the only father-son combination to win the Hart Trophy and between them have scored more than 1,100 goals.

Hull tried his hand at broadcasting but was booted off Toronto Maple Leafs' broadcasts after a typical burst of candor.

In the late 1980s, Hull along with Carl Brewer, Gordie Howe and others helped initiate a successful lawsuit that challenged the NHL's use of players' pension contributions.

The players won. Bobby Hull, as he had been about his contracts, the WHA and violence in hockey, was proven right again.

BOBBY HULL		1957-80
Born: Jan. 3, 1939 Pointe Anne, Ont.		
Teams: Chicago, Winnipeg, Hartford		
NHL	Regular	Playoffs
Seasons	16	14
Games	1,063	119
Goals	610	62
Assists	560	67
Points	1,170	129
Penalties	640	102
All-Star: 12 (First-10, Second-2)		
Trophies: 6 (Hart-2, Ross-3, Byng-1)		
Stanley Cup Championships		1

Shutout King Showdown Star

From the moment he strapped on his dead brother's pads, it seemed like Terry Sawchuk had entered into a pact with the devil.

The Winnipeg native would become one of the greatest NHL goalies of all time. Fame, money and stardom, all would be his, but it would come at the usual price.

Mike Sawchuk, Terry's older brother, was the real goalie of the family, but he died at 17, the victim of a heart ailment. It was a devastating loss for 10-year-old Terry. "I couldn't believe when it happened," he once told an interviewer. "I missed him for a long time afterwards."

When the regular goalie on Sawchuk's bantam team moved, Sawchuk strapped on his brother's pads. "The pads were there where I could always look at them," Sawchuk said. "The day they put me in the net I had a good game. I've stayed there since."

When Sawchuk's father broke his back in a fall off a scaffold, Terry was left as the family's sole breadwinner and hockey proved the family's salvation. A 17-year-old Sawchuk cashed his $2,000 signing bonus check from the Detroit Red Wings into small bills, returned to his Windsor hotel, threw the money in the air and rolled around in it. Then came a career punctuated by greatness and injury. On his 18th birthday, while playing minor pro for Omaha, Sawchuk was hit in the eye by a shot. By chance, an excellent surgeon happened to be passing through town and Sawchuk's vision was saved.

In all, he took more than 400 stitches in his face and his injury list included a herniated disk and severed wrist tendons which prevented him from closing his left hand, bone chips in his elbow and arthritis. Sawchuk's right arm was two inches shorter than his left after elbow surgery and he lost two inches in height after back surgery.

The good-natured kid from Winnipeg grew into a chain-smoking, angry adult. He lived with constant pain and poked at the scars. Sawchuk kept the teeth he lost and the

spurs surgeons took out of his elbow and even pickled his own freshly removed appendix.

"When we woke up in the morning, I would say good morning to him in both French and English," said one-time Red Wings' roommate Marcel Pronovost. "If he answered, I knew we would talk at least a little that day. But if he didn't reply, which was most days, we didn't speak the entire day."

Sawchuk's actions invariably spoke louder than words. He was a spectacular prospect who was the first player to be named rookie of the year in three leagues—the United States League, American League and NHL.

Sawchuk was a reflex goalie, putting little emphasis on angles, covering the net, instead, with explosive movements. He was considered the toughest goalie of his era to beat 1-on-1 and his record of 103 shutouts, earned in 971 games, is one of hockey's unattainable standards. Among his many achievements was a run of five years with a goals-against average of less than 2.00. Sawchuk is one of only eight goalies to earn four shutouts in a single playoff year; he did it in 1952 when the Red Wings won eight straight games to claim the Cup—one of four to Sawchuk's credit.

In 1970, Sawchuk was 40 and a shadow of the man and the goalie he had been while playing out the string with the New York Rangers. After returning home from Detroit, despondent over being unable to resurrect his failed marriage, he picked a fight with Ron Stewart, a genial man and his roommate at a Long Island cottage. The two fell over a barbecue pit and Sawchuk suffered internal injuries. Sawchuk seemed ready to recover. He absolved Stewart, who visited him in the hospital, but Sawchuk's liver was damaged and during surgery, a blood clot worked its way through an artery and stopped his heart.

A 30-year chain of events that began with a broken heart and an abandoned set of goalie pads had come to end the very same way.

TERRY SAWCHUK		1950-70
Born: Dec. 28, 1929 Winnipeg		
Teams: Detroit, Boston, Toronto, Los Angeles, Rangers		
NHL	**Regular**	**Playoffs**
Seasons	20	15
Games	971	106
W-L-T	447-330-173	54-48
W Pct.	.562	.529
GAA	2.52	2.54
Shutouts	103	12
All-Star: 7 (First-3, Second-4)		
Trophies: 5 (Calder-1, Vezina-4)		
Stanley Cup Championships		4

Shore Defined Game's Early Era

I t began for Eddie Shore, as it so often did, with a challenge. Shore and his brother, Aubrey, had graduated from a huge family farm in Saskatchewan to the Manitoba Agricultural College in Winnipeg during the early 1920s, where Aubrey, not Eddie, was the hockey player of the pair. Shore's brother, a year older, taunted him that he wasn't good enough to make the school team. Indeed, the younger Shore had played very little as a child.

Shore practised unrelentingly through a brutal Winnipeg winter and landed a spot on the team for the final three games of the season. It would have been a minor memory in Shore's life but that summer, his father, a prosperous farmer who owned 36 square miles of farmland, sold the farm, put the money into a steel business and quickly lost everything.

The boys were now recast as breadwin-

EDDIE SHORE		1926-40
Born: Nov. 25, 1902 Ft. Qu'Appelle, Sask.		
Teams: Boston, N.Y. Americans		
NHL	Regular	Playoffs
Seasons	14	11
Games	553	55
Goals	105	6
Assists	179	13
Points	284	19
Penalties	1,047	179
All-Star: 8 (First-7, Second-1)		
Trophies: 4 (Hart-4)		
Stanley Cup Championships		2

ners and in hockey, Shore found a living and a home for the singular drive that would make him one of the league's all-time great defensemen. After stints on three senior teams, Shore was sold to the Boston Bruins when the old Western League folded in 1926 and he ignited hockey interest in what had been a floundering NHL market.

Shore scored an astounding 12 goals in

his rookie season, set an NHL record for penalty minutes with 165 in 44 games and immediately became the focus for Boston hockey, the tiller of the soil Bobby Orr would harvest 40 years later.

Shore won four Hart Trophies as the league's most valuable player, one more than Orr would win, and when he picked up the puck only one of three things seemed possible, a goal, an assist or a fight.

Through tireless practice and study, Shore perfected a peculiar crouch in his skating stride that made him all but impossible to knock down.

"He was a powerhouse of a hockey player, awesome," said King Clancy, a Shore contemporary. "He was a hard man to hit because he had that weaving style of skating."

Instead of shooting at the goal, he would aim a few feet wide and charge

past a defender to pick up the puck on the carom. The best offensive defenseman of his era, Shore was even better on defense and he treated every incursion into the Bruins zone as an enemy invasion.

He fought often and viciously, collecting 978 stitches and 80 cuts, a fractured back, a fractured hip and broken collarbone, 14 broken noses, five fractured jaws and even more enemies. His left ear was almost torn off in one fight and both his eyeballs were split.

His most famous collision nearly ended the life of Toronto Maple Leaf forward Ace Bailey, whose head smashed into the ice after a check by Shore. Immediate surgery saved his life, but Bailey never played again.

Shore's combination of offensive skill and absolute brutality made him a phenomenal drawing card. Legendary American sports columnist Ring Lardner called him "the only man in hockey generally known to the people who dislike hockey."

Shore luxuriated in notoriety. For a time, the Bruins' pre-game warmup at home included the sight of Shore skating about with a cape while a small band played Hail to the Chief. Seconds before the opening whistle, a valet would appear and remove the cape.

Shore, always aware of his drawing power, was a regular holdout who commanded double the league's stated salary limit of $7,500.

How big a draw was the Bruins' star? When Shore held out in 1934-35, league president Frank Calder intervened to act as arbitrator and get Shore to sign minutes before the season's first game.

The NHL did not designate all-star teams until Shore's fifth year but he nonetheless, made the first all-star squad seven times. He was second only to King Clancy in NHL points by a defenseman and no blueliner has ever equalled his four MVP awards.

Flower Power Ruled NHL Rinks

For six of Guy Lafleur's 17 NHL seasons, every square inch of the playing surface in every NHL rink was more canvas than ice.

From 1974-75 through 1979-80, Guy Lafleur averaged 54 goals and 128 points. In the nine other seasons that he played more than 50 games, he averaged 24 goals and 61 points.

In his prime, Lafleur was as elusive and impromptu as a windblown leaf. "He's all over the ice and he doesn't have any idea what he's going to do," said his long-time Canadiens linemate Steve Shutt. "So how can I know?"

Few descriptions have been more apt. Lafleur's game was speed and passion, he a singular talent who played with a desperation that matched his skills. It often seemed he was a man among boys, inventing and reshaping a game that only he could play.

He played the game with an instinctual flair combining brilliant playmaking with superior goal-scoring and an ability to seize the moment. In the wake of the Boston Bruins' much-remembered too many men on the ice penalty in 1979, it was Lafleur who set the stage for the series-winner in overtime with a late-game tying goal. More than a quarter-century

after his rookie season, no Canadien has usurped Lafleur. He remains the last Canadien to win a scoring championship or Hart Trophy.

As a child, Lafleur loved the game so deeply he often slept in his equipment so he could get to the rink quicker in the morning. Every move up the hockey ladder was chronicled by a hockey-mad media

and when he scored 233 goals in his final two years of junior hockey and surfaced as the No. 1 choice in the 1971 amateur draft, Lafleur's destiny as the Canadiens' next great Francophone star was cast.

Then came three ordinary NHL seasons and a crossroads. The desire to succeed hadn't ebbed in Lafleur, but the understanding of how to achieve it seemed stillborn. He was a talent but not yet a man.

Beliveau, Lafleur's idol, grew distressed that his protege was missing optional practices and tampering with his gift. The message to shape up, emphatically delivered, took. Lafleur discarded his helmet and 'Le Demon Blond' was born.

The artistry Lafleur brought was the product of tireless and solitary practice. It was greatness built on his fanatical love of the game. "Any guy who would be in his hockey uniform, skates tied tight, sweater on and a stick beside him at four o'clock in the afternoon for an eight o'clock game has to be a little strange," Shutt once said.

His achievements would be monumental, including a Conn Smythe-winning performance in 1977 when Lafleur earned points on the Canadiens' final eight goals over three games.

His 26 points that spring were the second-highest total in league history to that point.

Bruce Bennett/BBS

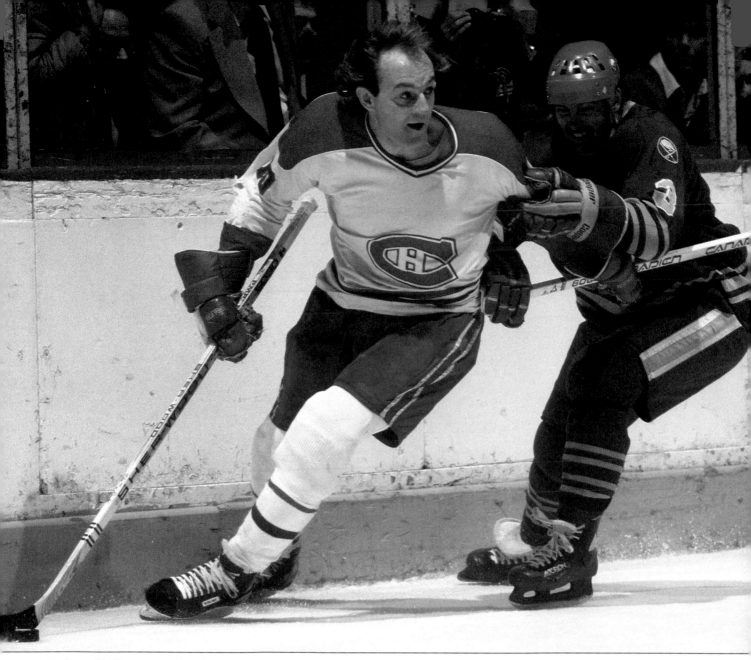

But it would all come crashing down when Lafleur returned to play too quickly after a strained knee ligament in 1980-81. Years of smoking and drinking began to catch up.

Elusive on the ice, he was as impossible to pin down in public and would change bars hourly. In March of 1981, Lafleur narrowly avoiding being decapitated when he fell asleep and drove his car off a Montreal area road on his way home after a night at the bars.

The final Montreal seasons would see Lafleur play in mounting frustration. His old linemate Jacques Lemaire, now coach, installed a defense-first system that limited Lafleur's ability to improvise. It became clear the club would not trade him. Finally,

19 games into the 1984-85 season, Lafleur retired at 33 and received a hero's send-off.

After he retired, Lafleur, who had once said that his wife and children ranked somewhere around his fans in impor-

GUY LAFLEUR		1971-91
Born: Sept. 20, 1951 Thurso, Que.		
Teams: Montreal, Rangers, Quebec		
NHL	Regular	Playoffs
Seasons	17	14
Games	1,126	128
Goals	560	58
Assists	793	76
Points	1,353	134
Penalties	399	67
All-Star: 6 (First-6)		
Trophies: 6 (Hart-2, Ross-3, Smythe-1)		
Stanley Cup Championships		5

tance–well behind hockey–found acceptance somewhere other than at the rink.

Yet, days after being selected for the Hockey Hall of Fame and four years after quitting the Canadiens, Lafleur was in the uniform of the New York Rangers, but it was a different Lafleur who came back. The mesmerizing skills were now gone, but in his dotage the mercurial artist had matured into a contented master.

Lafleur toiled happily, first in New York and then for two seasons, with the Quebec Nordiques before quitting for good at the end of the 1990-91 season.

"I know it sounds strange," Lafleur said near the end of the second phase of his NHL career, "but I made this comeback so I can have a nice retirement."

Victory: Mark of Magnificence

From the beginning, Mark Messier knew. As a Grade 1 student, he watched his father, Doug, tough out life on the minor pro circuit as a Portland Buckaroo. "I always remember the sound of the crowd, it did something for me," Messier once said. "That feeling never left me. I remember being six years old and thinking, 'I'm going to be a hockey player and that's all there is to it."

Doug Messier would be the blueprint his son used to carve out an NHL career. A hardrock defenseman, Doug was one of the toughest survivors of the old Western Pro League. "Mark," said matriarch Mary Messier, "is a reflection of what Doug was."

"I never let the kids win, even when they were small," said Doug Messier. "I don't know whether that's right or wrong, but that's just the way we are."

Mark Messier inherited the desire of a career minor leaguer but he was blessed with skating, anticipation and hand skills for which his father would have killed.

Those skills landed Messier a spot on the World Hockey Association's Indianapolis Racers as a 17-year-old, fresh from playing for the St. Albert Saints of the Alberta Junior League. He moved from the Racers to the Cincinnati Stingers five games into his first pro season.

Messier was far too green to produce

Bob Mummery

much offensively. He scored just once in 52 WHA games, but he caught the eye of Edmonton Oilers' coach Glen Sather when he beat up the Oilers' Dennis Sobchuk. The Oilers drafted him the following year for their move into the NHL and, except for four games in the minors, Messier has been a big-leaguer ever since. "Even as a 17-year-old, there was no mistaking it," Sather once said. "They talk about Maurice Richard. Well Mark has the same look."

While Wayne Gretzky would become

the greatest scorer the game has known, it fell to Messier to make the Oilers win. Never as prolific as Gretzky, he was expected to score big goals in tight games and hostile arenas. In 1983, after the New York Islanders had beaten Edmonton in the Stanley Cup final, Messier emerged wearing a towel around his waist just in time to catch a television interview in which Isles' coach Al Arbour said his team won because they had greater character.

Messier reacted like a wild west gunman. In one motion, he ripped the towel from his waist and snapped it violently at the screen. The loud crack, coupled with the sight of the suddenly naked and scowling Messier served notice that second best would not do. The next year Messier went the length of the ice to blow a goal past Islanders' goalie Billy Smith and help give the Oilers a 2-1 lead in games against the same Islanders. The rest of the series was not close and Messier earned playoff MVP honors.

The Oilers had arrived, on Gretzky's shoulders to be sure, but just as much on those of the man teammates called 'Moose.' He has always shone brightest during the playoffs and holds the NHL record for most post-season games, as well as trailing only Gretzky in goals, assists and points.

"We've got the best player in the world out," Sather once said when Gretzky was hurt, "and the second best plays like he's the best."

Messier would lead the Oilers to five Stanley Cups, including a dramatic 1990 title after Gretzky was traded to the Los Angeles Kings. In the opening game in Edmonton, Messier levelled Gretzky against the boards with a firm, clean hit. "It was one of the hardest things I ever had to do," Messier said, "But you've got to be able to separate friendship from business."

Business called again in 1991 when Messier, the only player ever to be named a first team all-star at two positions (left wing and center), unsuccessfully pressed the Oilers to double his $1-million salary. Unwilling or unable to

satisfy Messier's financial demands, the Oilers packaged him to the New York Rangers.

If Edmonton would provide Messier the stage to establish his formidable reputation as a winner, New York would give him the chance to immortalize it. He moved to fill what had been a huge

MARK MESSIER	1979-present	
Born: Jan. 18, 1961 Edmonton		
Teams: Edmonton, Rangers, Vancouver		
NHL	Regular	Playoffs
Seasons	19	17
Games	1,354	236
Goals	597	109
Assists	1,015	186
Points	1,612	295
Penalties	1,654	244
All-Star: 5 (First-4, Second-1)		
Trophies: 3 (Hart-2, Smythe-1)		
Stanley Cup Championships		6

leadership void in the Rangers' dressing room and played a role in a player revolt that cost coach Roger Neilson his job. Messier challenged Neilson's successor Mike Keenan after he benched a host of stars in losing a semi-final game to the Devils and told him to stick to basic coaching. Messier then guaranteed a victory in Game 6 against the Devils and delivered a hat trick.

In leading the Rangers to their first Stanley Cup in 54 years, Messier became the first man to captain two different championship teams and a New York icon. The Buckaroo's Boy had become Manhattan's favorite son. Messier would remain so until the summer of 1997 when he joined the Vancouver Canucks as an unrestricted free agent.

Man Of Vision
Solitary Figure

In 1971, the producers of a hockey movie named *Face Off* were shooting a sequence at Maple Leaf Gardens that involved Jacques Plante.

The script called for Toronto's Mike Walton to break in alone on Plante, a teammate decked out in opposition colors for the shoot, and coolly score the winning goal.

After the requisite tinkering with camera angles and lights, Walton, on cue, burst in. Plante stopped him. Another orchestrated breakaway, another impromptu save.

After a lengthy argument between extra and director, a compromise was found. "Mr. Plante has consented to allow the puck to enter the net," Gardens public address announcer Paul Morris intoned to the extras, actors and crew. Finally, Walton skated in...

Plante stopped him again.

Plante, who died on Feb. 26, 1986 of stomach cancer in Switzerland at 57, was one of the most singular people to play hockey's loneliest position. He cared little for protocol or other people's plans. Plante took every goal against, even the scripted version, as an insult. So deep-seated was his disgust for surrendering a goal, he viewed his own defensemen with distrust and opposing shooters with outright loathing.

"No, I never make friends, not in hockey not elsewhere, not since I was a teenager," he said. "What for? If you are close to someone you must be scheduling yourself to please them."

Plante never socialized with his teammates, even on the bus he sat in the front seat, left-hand side, far away from the back and the safety of the group. While teammates went out on the town on the road, Plante stayed in his hotel room, knitted and answered his fan mail.

Plante said some hotels bothered his asthma more than others, used a disinfectant spray to purge germs from his hotel rooms and sometimes cited the asthma in determining whether he was ready to play. Teammates and opponents often considered him selfish and said he chose to play only in games he could win.

But Plante's prideful obstinacy, the bane of coaches and teammates, made him the game's greatest innovator. With the sanction of his coach Toe Blake, Plante began the practice of leaving the crease to corral loose pucks and setting the puck up for defensemen on shoot-ins. He was the first goalie to dive out of the net to smother loose pucks.

Blake was far less tolerant of Plante's greatest innovation. A fractured cheekbone and facial cuts had prompted him to devise and use a face mask for practice. When he tripped the Rangers' Andy Bathgate in a game in 1959, Bathgate retaliated by deliberately hitting Plante in the face with a shot. Plante would only return to the net with the mask, the Canadiens won the game and embarked

JACQUES PLANTE	1953-73	
Born: Jan. 17, 1929 Mont Carmel, Que.		
Teams: Montreal, Rangers, St. Louis, Toronto, Boston		
NHL	Regular	Playoffs
Seasons	17	16
Games	837	112
W-L-T	434-246-147	71-37
W Pct.	.614	.657
GAA	2.38	2.17
Shutouts	82	14
All-Star: 7 (First-3, Second-4)		
Trophies: 8 (Hart-1, Vezina-7)		
Stanley Cup Championships	6	

on an 18-game unbeaten string. Plante
would continue to tinker with masks and
eventually had a hand in the design of
virtually all those worn by NHL goalies
during his time.

Like any great innovator, Plante borrowed liberally from the strengths of others to find a better way. Chuck Rayner's
stand-up style, Terry Sawchuk's balanced
crouch and Johnny Bower's obsession over
maintaining the correct angle all went into
Plante's technique.

The result was a remarkable career.
Between 1956 and 1960, 'Jake the Snake'
won five consecutive Vezina Trophies. He
won seven in all, more than any other
goalie and fashioned a 2.23 goals against
average in his 11 seasons with Montreal.
Plante compiled a 2.13 goals against average in post-season play for the Canadiens,
claimed six Stanley Cups and was named
the league's first team all-star goalie three
times.

Plante recorded a record three 40-or-
more win seasons en route to 434 career
wins, second-most in NHL history, behind
Terry Sawchuk's 447. Nonetheless, Blake
tired of Plante's melodramatics in 1963
and dispatched him to New York. Plante
endured two miserable years in New York,
retired and began playing for a Canadiens'
oldtimers team.

Then came expansion and a seller's
market for goalies. Over the protests of
St. Louis Blues' coach Scotty Bowman,
owner Sid Solomon signed the veteran
Plante, 40, and teamed him with 38-year-
old Glenn Hall. They shared the Vezina in
1969. Plante went on to play with the
Maple Leafs, for whom he recorded the
second-best goals-against average (1.88)
of his career at 44, and the Boston
Bruins.

Even as his skills diminished with age,
the hubris that comes with genius never
did. At 46, Plante retired from the World
Hockey Association's Edmonton Oilers. "I
wanted to go out," Plante said, "while I
was still on top."

Ice Craftsman Of Highest Order

One day, in the early fall of 1979, the general manager of the Boston Bruins sat watching a training camp practice, his eyes drawn to the movements of a rookie defenseman.

"Who are you looking at?" a writer asked Harry Sinden.

"His name is Raymond Bourque," answered Sinden, "and he's sending chills down my spine."

And so it would be for 20 years and counting. After the Calder Trophy, five Norris Trophies and 12 selections to the NHL's first all-star team, Bourque is not just the dominant Bruin of his generation, like Eddie Shore and Bobby Orr, he is his generation of the Bruins.

"Everyone wants you to compare players from different eras," said Bruins vice-president Tom Johnson, who played with Doug Harvey with Montreal and was an executive with the Bruins during the Bobby Orr era. "But it's very, very difficult because they never played against each other. All you can do is be the best in your era. And Ray has done that."

"Ray Bourque," said kingpin Chicago Black Hawks' defenseman Chris Chelios, "is the best defenseman I've ever seen."

Bourque may or may not be the pre-eminent all-purpose defenseman of all-time, but this much is sure: no defenseman did as many things as well for as long as Bourque. An excellent passer, his defensive reads and instinct for joining the rush are the standard for modern day defensemen. Almost impossible to knock off the puck, he handles the spade work in front of the net and in the corners willingly and remains one of the best skating defensemen in the NHL. Extraordinarily durable, Bourque will have played well over twice as many games as Bobby Orr by the time he retires.

In this, the era of the one-way power forward and power play quarterback, it's the thoroughness of Bourque's game that endures. Even as the years and miles begin to erode the individual elements of his performance, the weight of all the things Bourque does well has kept him among the elite.

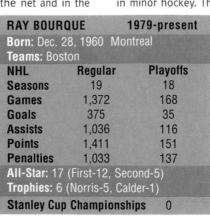

It is a fitting reward for one of the game's most gifted craftsman. "I'm a perfectionist, and I want to do well all the time," Bourque said. "No matter what, you can always be better. Some nights I might get a goal or a couple of points and people say I played well, but I keep looking for perfection."

Bourque, a quiet man, has had the perfect temperament for his time and place. The craftsman is by nature self-sustaining; while the artist looks for expression, the craftsman seeks perfection. The artist needs recognition, the craftsman, only tools and a place to work. Through the early years of his career Bourque was regularly overlooked for the Norris Trophy in favor of flashier but more limited players such as Paul Coffey (the only other defenseman to have 1,000 assists), Rod Langway, Doug Wilson or Randy Carlyle. He didn't win his first Norris until he was 26. He scored 31 goals and recorded 96 points in 1983-84 yet didn't even earn runner-up status.

Bourque's 17 straight all-star selections is an NHL record as is his defenseman standard of nine 20-goal seasons (first established by Denis Potvin). Only Gordie Howe, an all-star 21 times, has more all-star team selections than Bourque. Even Gretzky has only 15.

Much of Bourque's stardom came during an era when the Boston Celtics' Larry Bird owned the town. All of it was spent playing a position indelibly defined by Orr.

Bourque, 38, grew up in Montreal watching the Canadiens roll to championships but he has never won a league championship, even in minor hockey. The Bruins still look far removed from a Stanley Cup title and Bourque, for all his greatness, seems destined to become one of the best players in NHL history to never win a championship.

With hockey's holy grail potentially unreachable, Bourque continues to do what he always has, spend each night in a valiant but ultimately failed search for perfection. Tom Johnson is right, there is no profit in competing with ghosts. All you can do is be the best of your era. All you can do, everything you can do, is what Ray Bourque has done.

RAY BOURQUE	1979-present	
Born: Dec. 28, 1960 Montreal		
Teams: Boston		
NHL	Regular	Playoffs
Seasons	19	18
Games	1,372	168
Goals	375	35
Assists	1,036	116
Points	1,411	151
Penalties	1,033	137
All-Star: 17 (First-12, Second-5)		
Trophies: 6 (Norris-5, Calder-1)		
Stanley Cup Championships	0	

Steve Babineau/SA

The Legend Has Never Died

His story is so laden with myth, the man himself has long since been lost. How to appraise Howie Morenz, the man many believe died rather than stop playing for the Montreal Canadiens?

Start with the fact that when he crumbled into the south boards of the Forum in late January, 1937, Morenz, 34, was the NHL's all-time leading point-getter. Next, consider a goals-per-game average (.49) better than that of Gordie Howe, Frank Mahovlich and Jean Beliveau.

Consider how journalists strained for new monikers–he was called the 'Stratford Streak,' the 'Mitchell Meteor,' the 'Hurtling Habitant'–and weigh the words of those who saw him play and said his greatness would transcend any era. King Clancy, who first broke a sweat in the NHL in 1921, said Morenz was the best player he ever saw.

"There's nobody in the league today who is as good a skater," Clancy said in the 1980s. "He could start on a dime and hit full speed within a couple of strides. He had wide shoulders, thin hips and about the strongest legs I've ever see on a hockey player."

But inevitably, you return to the story.

Morenz, re-acquired by the Canadiens after desultory campaigns with the Chicago Black Hawks and New York Rangers, had broken through the Chicago defense and was after a loose puck at the end boards when Chicago defenseman Earl Seibert reached out to collar him.

Off-balance, Morenz fell feet first into the boards. His skate dug into the wood and snapped the bone in his left leg. A little more than a month later, Morenz was dead.

The doctors said he was killed by an embolism. Romantics said he died of a broken heart. Morenz told his longtime linemate, Aurel Joliat, he would never play again and, gesturing skyward, said he would watch the Habs from the next world. "I think Howie died of a broken heart," said Joliat.

His injury would not have necessarily ended his career, doctors thought he could play the following season. But Morenz was profoundly depressed, the media was told he suffered a nervous breakdown a few days before his death and required a straitjacket.

There were titanic drinking binges in his room at St. Luke's hospital (the whiskey was on the counter, the beer was under the bed, said one visitor).

"People say I killed him but that isn't really true," Seibert later said. "I hit him with a check and he broke his leg and I take the full blame for that, but it was his friends coming into the hospital and bringing him drinks. They're the ones who killed him."

Forty thousand people sauntered past his body at centre ice at the Forum and his funeral was the most widely attended in Canadian history.

Long ago enshrined in hockey lore were his reluctance to play for the Canadiens (he cried and begged manager Leo Dandurand to allow him to return to Stratford and play senior) and his influence on the game (after seeing Morenz play, Tex Rickard, one of the NHL's pioneers was so impressed he bought into the league and founded the New York Americans).

Morenz won three Hart Trophies and two scoring championships and was named player of the half-century by Canadian Press 13 years after his death.

But lost in the canonization of a hockey player were the small elements of a man's life. Morenz loved to dress well, he sometimes changed his clothes three times a day. He was a relentless roamer who paced before games, walked deserted city streets after losses and wandered around the ice largely oblivious to his position.

And though the cause of his death has long since passed into mystery, doctors who attended to him said on the night of March 8, 1937, Howie Morenz simply ate a light meal, closed his eyes and got his wish.

HOWIE MORENZ		1923-37
Born: June 21, 1902 Mitchell, Ont.		
Teams: Montreal, Chicago, Rangers		
NHL	**Regular**	**Playoffs**
Seasons	14	11
Games	550	47
Goals	270	21
Assists	197	11
Points	467	32
Penalties	563	68
All-Star: 3 (First-2, Second-1)		
Trophies: 5 (Hart-3, Ross-2)		
Stanley Cup Championships		3

La Presse

Floating Like A Butterfly

The Butterfly, like the man who borrowed from it, is at once languid and anxious, skittish and resolute; both are moved by subtle jetstreams only they can feel.

At 67, Glenn Hall, the father of the butterfly style of goaltending, is a genial Alberta farmer who reads William Wordsworth and Robert Service.

The butterfly is above all unpredictable. Hall, deferential and soft-spoken, defied Jack Adams when the despotic Detroit Red Wings' general manager was at the height of his power. Hall's pre-game nervousness was legendary. He threw up regularly before games and between periods ("Someday, Hall's bucket should be in the Hall of Fame," a teammate once cracked), but he proved unbelievably durable. His regular season consecutive games streak of 502 contests is an unassailable goaltending record and one of the prime contributors to his longstanding nickname: Mr. Goalie.

Hall's technique was based on necessity. As a young goalie he frequently found himself beaten by shots between his legs. Because he lacked the arm strength to keep his stick firmly on the ice, he began tinkering with the idea of digging his toes into the ice and dropping to his knees to maximize the amount of ice covered by his pads.

Shooters intent on beating Hall high had to overcome rapier-like reflexes. Hall's hand speed was considered superior to that of Jacques Plante and Terry Sawchuk.

Hall was a smalltown boy. He grew up in Humboldt, Sask., the son of a Canadian Pacific Railway engineer who often took his son on rides in the train cab. At 10, he was the captain and manager of his elementary school's hockey team and donned the pads when nobody else would.

The path to the NHL began with a gift. At 17, a junior teammate named Bob Parker was sitting next to Hall on a bus ride back to Humboldt. Parker, already invited to a tryout with the Red Wings in Saskatoon, Sask., gave one of his extra forms to Hall, who would play his way onto the Wings' protected list.

After an eight-year apprenticeship in junior and minor pro, Hall reached the NHL for good in 1955 when Adams, mindful of his trump card, dealt Sawchuk to the Boston Bruins.

Hall would capture the Calder Trophy for the league's top rookie and star for two seasons with the Red Wings, but in 1957, when Adams traded Ted Lindsay to Chicago for instigating a players' association, he included Hall, a union sympathizer who refused to distance himself from Lindsay.

Hall took a streak of 140 straight games to Chicago and played in every Hawks' game for the next five seasons. His streak, begun in 1955, ended in the 13th game of the 1962-63 season, the result of a pulled back muscle sustained while attaching a toe strap.

Hall, who played barefaced most of his career because he thought a mask compromised his vision, stopped 16,000 shots in the run and led the Hawks to their 1961 Stanley Cup victory. After a decade in Chicago, the seven-time first team all-star who led the league in shutouts six times, spent four years with the St. Louis Blues. There, he cemented his place among the game's greats with a Conn Smythe Trophy performance against Boston in 1968. On retirement, Hall held the NHL record for most playoff games by a goalie (115).

Those extended seasons, however, were often followed by extended off-seasons. His holdouts were rites of fall; each year he would stay home as long as possible, declaring he had to "paint the barn."

"All I want to do when the season is over," Hall once said, "is stand in the quarter-section I've got near Edmonton and holler, 'Damn you, damn you, damn you.'"

GLENN HALL		1955-71
Born: Oct. 3, 1931 Humboldt, Sask.		
Teams: Detroit, Chicago, St. Louis		
NHL	**Regular**	**Playoffs**
Seasons	16	15
Games	906	115
W-L-T	407-327-163	49-65
W. Pct.	.545	.430
GAA	2.51	2.79
Shutouts	84	6
All-Star: 11 (First-7, Second-4)		
Trophies: 5 (Smythe-1, Calder-1, Vezina-3)		
Stanley Cup Championships		1

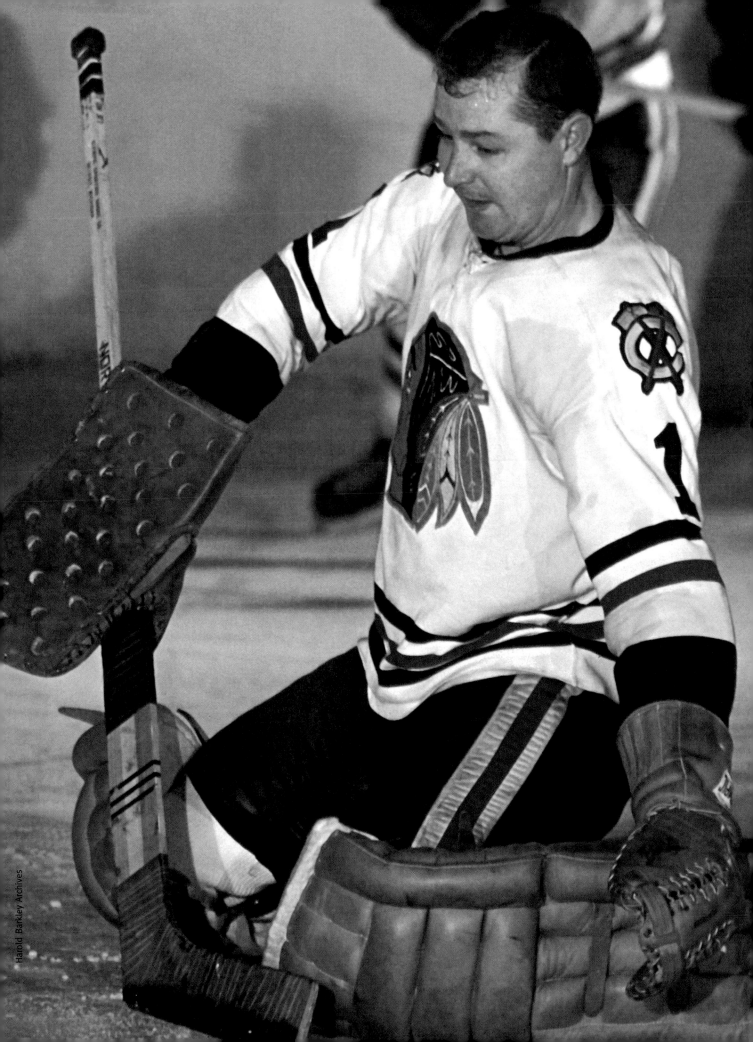

Change Of Heart To Hart Trophy

His name was Stanislav Gvoth and he was an eight-year-old boy who would pay the price for being born in the wrong place, at the wrong time.

In 1948, Communist Russia installed a puppet satellite in Czechoslovakia and Stanislav Gvoth's parents did what must have seemed unimaginable. Just before the Iron Curtain was drawn closed, they bundled up their son and sent him from Sokolov, a small town in the western part of the country, to relatives in Canada.

The little boy with the Slavic features spoke no English. His schoolmates taunted him and called him the worst racial epithet of the day: 'DP' (Displaced Person).

Stan Mikita took his uncle and aunt's surname and quickly learned to fight back. By his mid-teens, he was a ducktailed small town tough guy with an anger that only grew when he strapped on skates.

"I was basically hostile and so I was rough and often downright mean," Mikita said. "It helped in one way because I always believed that, being a so-called DP, somebody people picked on and looked down on, I could only succeed by being better than everybody else. As a hockey player, I always tried that much harder."

His abrasiveness as well as a natural athleticism made Mikita a prized hockey

prospect. The St. Catharines junior team was owned and operated by future Chicago Black Hawks' coach Rudy Pilous and Mikita's snarl and skill landed him with the NHL team as a regular at 19. But first he was named the Ontario Hockey Association MVP in 1958-59.

Mikita was obviously skilled enough to play in the NHL. The childhood taunts and fights had given way to punches and bully tactics. Mikita, well-versed in hitting back or hitting first, never shied away.

"That's the way it started, the chippiness, the fighting," he said. "When I got to the NHL, it continued. They weren't going to push me around. So I fought them. It was something I believed in."

Mikita averaged nearly 100 penalty minutes over his first seven NHL seasons. And then, with time and a family of his own, Mikita found a new way.

"I came home from a game one night and my daughter Meg was still up, after watching it on television. She asked me why I spent almost the whole game sitting down while the other players were out on the ice skating around. Right then I woke up to reality. If a two-year-old could see there was something wrong, why couldn't a supposedly intelligent 26-year-old figure it out."

Mikita slashed his penalty minutes to 58 from 154 in 1965-66. The next season he cut his total to 12. "It was," one writer

STAN MIKITA	1959-80	
Born: May 20, 1940 Sokolov, Czech.		
Teams: Chicago		
NHL	**Regular**	**Playoffs**
Seasons	21	18
Games	1,394	155
Goals	541	59
Assists	926	91
Points	1,467	150
Penalties	1,270	169
All-Star: 8 (First-6, Second-2)		
Trophies: 8 (Hart-2, Ross-4, Byng-2)		
Stanley Cup Championships	1	

remarked, "like Attila the Hun refusing to sack Rome."

"I got married, raised a family. I figured we were all out there trying to make a living, so why try to kill someone," Mikita said. "I thought, I'll try to beat the other guy with my skills instead of knocking his head off."

Mikita, who won the Lady Byng Trophy as the NHL's most gentlemanly player twice, anchored the 'Scooter Line' with Kenny Wharram and Doug Mohns. He would win the scoring title four times in five years and, in 1967, became the first player to win three major trophies when he won the Art Ross, Hart and Lady Byng. He repeated the feat in 1968.

Twice, Mikita fell just short of the 100-

point plateau and he seemed destined to be the first NHLer to break the 100-point plateau until he was crosschecked from behind by the Canadiens' Jacques Lemaire and Ted Harris in 1969. "I felt something snap," Mikita said. "No vertebrae were broken or damaged, apparently. There's no specific term for the injury I suffered. I can describe it though, if anyone is interested. It's plain hell."

Mikita would spend the rest of his career battling another virulent enemy, the pain in his lower back. He was given regular cortisone and struggled most mornings just to get out of bed. Still, he would play 20 full seasons and parts of two more before retiring in 1980 at 39 as the Black Hawks' all-time leader in games, assists

and points. He scored 541 NHL goals, averaged more than a point a game and became an enduring example of tenacity combined with clean play.

While he never spent a day as the league's top skater, shooter or stickhandler–Mikita was, however, its top playmaker four times–he consistently delivered every element, every night. "Stan Mikita," Hawks' coach Billy Reay once said, "has done more with what he's got than any other player I've seen."

Global events had shaped his life, but in the end Stan Mikita became the man he wanted to be. In doing so, he won a triumph many never could. The man, Stan Mikita proved, did not have to follow the path set by the boy.

Star Hot Shot From The Slot

P hil Esposito was an original, 205 pounds of superstition, theatrics, ego and courage piled 6-foot-1 high.

Like all great goal-scorers, Esposito had the gift of mastering time and space. He was an awkward skater, but in the instant Esposito had the puck in the slot, the plough horse showed the finish of a thoroughbred. Esposito didn't just wait for the puck and shoot. Lost in the volume of close-in, 'garbage goals' was a canny craftsmanship and imagination that produced five consecutive seasons of 55 or more goals and six 100-plus point campaigns.

"Why learn Esposito's tricks," Jacques Plante once said. "By the time you do, he'll have new ones."

Esposito played for the Black Hawks and New York Rangers, but in his heyday with the Boston Bruins, he often took three-minute shifts, wearing out smaller men assigned to check him.

"What Esposito has," said Vancouver Canucks' coach Hal Laycoe, "is an amazing ability to slow the game down to a scoring pace. So many goals are missed because the forwards are going too fast. He dictates the speed of the game better than any offensive player I have ever seen."

Esposito grew up in Sault Ste. Marie, Ont., and like most hockey stars, his background was working class. His father, Pat, was a nickel miner. That did not mean Esposito attacked hockey with a singular passion. At 12, he failed to make his local

minor bantam team. By virtue of a sponsorship agreement, the Chicago Black hawks owned Esposito's NHL rights, but even though he advanced to the Hawks' St. Catharines junior team, he was not a standout.

"Phil wasn't very serious as a junior," recalls Ken Hodge, who played with him. "All he thought about was going back to the Soo and driving a truck. I don't believe he had any serious hockey ambitions, but when he went to St. Louis (in the Central League) and started to play well he realized he had a career."

Esposito certainly could clutter an opposing crease and he had an instinctive knack for passing. Locked in the big body were the skills and vision of a 5-foot-10 center. The Black Hawks installed him as Bobby Hull's set-up man in 1965, but Esposito's salvation came in a trade to the Bruins two years later. Chicago deemed him expendable after Esposito failed to earn a single point in a 1967 semifinal series loss to the Toronto Maple Leafs.

Esposito would prove a revelation in Boston. In his second season as a Bruin, he became the league's first-ever 100-point player and shattered Hull's record for most goals in a season by 18 with a stunning 76-goal season in 1970-71.

That same season, Esposito took an incredible 550 shots on goal to set a record nobody has approached or likely ever will. He is runner-up to himself (426 the following season) and Bobby Hull's 414 in 1968-69 is the next highest total.

PHIL ESPOSITO		1963-81
Born: Feb. 20, 1942 Sault Ste. Marie, Ont.		
Teams: Chicago, Boston, Rangers		
NHL	**Regular**	**Playoffs**
Seasons	18	15
Games	1,282	130
Goals	717	61
Assists	873	76
Points	1,590	137
Penalties	910	138
All-Star: 8 (First-6, Second-2)		
Trophies: 7 (Hart-2, Ross-5)		
Stanley Cup Championships		2

Esposito would win two Stanley Cups and claim five Art Ross Trophies with the Bruins, but his finest moments were rendered in the 1972 Summit Series against the Soviets. Originally, Esposito didn't want to play.

When pressed by the media he said he had commitments to his summer hockey school and feared a career-ending injury, but feeling coerced by the media and pressured by fans, he went to camp.

When he scolded the nation on television for booing Team Canada after the team badly lost its final home game, Esposito's grip on the team's leadership became unshakeable.

Esposito courted drama. When he fell during introductions for the first game in Moscow, he got up on one knee and delivered a grand bow. Then he stood up and played the best hockey of his life in the historic series.

A loud, boisterous personality, Esposito commandeered a dressing room. His locker was a shrine to superstitions, plastered with clovers, amulets and pictures of opposing players hung upside down to ensure their own bad luck.

But it was the strength of his personality that eventually forced him out of Boston.

Bruins' general manager Harry Sinden knew Esposito would never accept the incursions into his role that would come with age and in November of 1975, shipped the 33-year-old star to New York in a deal that brought Brad Park to Boston.

"The coaches and management were under his power too," Sinden said later. "We always felt we had to use him in most situations. His presence became overwhelming."

Maybe, but the heartbeat of the most rollicking era of Bruins' hockey had been stilled.

"Phil Esposito," said his one-time Bruin teammate Walt McKechnie, "is the best team leader I ever played with. He took me and made me feel as important as Bobby Orr."

An Islander Unto Himself

Because his middle-class family in Ottawa included two older brothers, Denis Potvin had to make do with third-hand hockey equipment. Maybe that's why from the moment he stepped into the NHL, Potvin wanted to be front and center.

Potvin battled New York Islanders' coach Al Arbour over his playing style, distanced himself from teammates and flouted the demands of diplomacy. "I'm going to stir up people's emotions one way or the other," he said.

Alternately egotistical and insecure, Potvin's growth as a person and a player mirrored that of the Islanders from sad sack expansionists to four-time Stanley Cup champions.

Potvin, a three-time Norris Trophy winner and five-time first team all-star, was the linchpin of the Islanders' power play and a gifted offensive defenseman who broke the 20-goal standard nine times—sharing a record with Ray Bourque—and recorded three seasons of 30 or more goals.

Only seven defenseman have scored as many as 30 goals in a season. He was a magnificent force in the playoffs; only Paul Coffey has accumulated more points among defensemen.

Like Bourque, Potvin delivered a complete game. "He's the closest thing I've seen to Doug Harvey," Scotty Bowman once said. "He doesn't rush the puck all the time, he's a beautiful passer and he can be a mean son-of-a-gun."

Rock solid at 6 feet and 205 pounds, Potvin was a devastating hip checker. "Absolutely one of the strongest men I have ever seen," said longtime Islanders' teammate Ken Morrow. "He didn't just hit guys, he devastated them."

That Potvin is remembered for a superbly well-rounded game is largely a tribute to Arbour, himself a stay-at-home NHL defenseman for 14 seasons. Potvin broke Bobby Orr's scoring records while playing for the Ontario Hockey Association's Ottawa 67's. Like Orr before him, he played in the OHA as a 14-year-old.

When he joined the Islanders, and for years after, he saw himself largely as an offensive defenseman. Arbour, on the other hand, wanted Potvin to dominate by joining the play, not by leading it.

"Al Arbour and I have fought from the first day I came here," Potvin said. " My argument was that if I took off with the puck, someone else should drop back to cover. Al's argument was that if you're in good position defensively, you'll be in good position offensively."

Arbour once observed that half his job involved coaching his star defenseman, but the arranged marriage prospered.

Potvin led the play a little more than Arbour liked and stayed in the background far more than he would have liked. "Denis would challenge you," said Islanders' general manager Bill Torrey, "but once he understood what you were doing, he would never second-guess you."

By the time Potvin began playing defense in the NHL, Orr had defined the position and any compliments were the hockey equivalent of hand-me-downs. Unwilling to suffer in silence at what he considered a snub, Potvin went public with his feelings that he had outplayed Orr at the 1976 Canada Cup, only to see the great Boston Bruins' star awarded the tournament MVP award.

"Is Bobby Orr only going to have to play to be known as the best defenseman or is he going to have to prove it?" Potvin said in a Canadian newsmagazine.

As Potvin matured, he began to see the hurdles placed before him for what they were—incentives for greatness. Arbour's confines made him a superb all-around defenseman.

Orr, meanwhile, gave him a prodigious standard to strive for.

"It might have been the best thing for me, having a living legend six years ahead of me, the hound chasing the rabbit," Potvin said. "Sometimes I felt that my middle name should be Bobby."

DENIS POTVIN		1973-88
Born: Oct. 29, 1953 Ottawa		
Teams: Islanders		
NHL	**Regular**	**Playoffs**
Seasons	15	14
Games	1,060	185
Goals	310	56
Assists	742	108
Points	1,052	164
Penalties	1,354	253
All-Star: 7 (First-5, Second-2)		
Trophies: 4 (Norris-3, Calder-1)		
Stanley Cup Championships		4

Bruce Bennett/BBS

More Magician Than Marksman

I t was always, with Mike Bossy, about magic.

First, the wondrous apparition: time and time again Bossy seemed to materialize, unchecked, in scoring position with the puck on his stick.

Then came the sleight of hand. "When he shoots," said Al Arbour, Bossy's coach with the New York Islanders for all but one season, "it doesn't even look like he touches the puck."

Poof. Red light. Like magic.

Every magician's trick, of course, is fuelled by the assumptions. The audience can't see or even feel the slight taper on a deck of cards or the false panel that frees the damsel long before she is cut in half.

Bossy was the first rookie to score 50 goals. Five times he hit the 60 mark and his nine consecutive 50-goal seasons is an NHL standard. Bossy thrived by turning assumptions around. He didn't worry about fear of failure; instead he concentrated on remaining unafraid of succeeding.

"I think the biggest asset of successful people is that they are not afraid of success," Bossy once said.

"There are so many people who are

afraid of having success for fear of having to repeat their successful ways. It's so easy to see that in people. I'll read quotes in the newspaper and I can tell people who are afraid to be good."

Bossy, an articulate and thoughtful man, used human nature. He thrived on other players' beliefs that he was tied up, that the penalty was almost over, that the period would play out uneventfully.

In 1980-81, Bossy seemed destined to fall two goals short of being the first NHL player to tie Maurice Richard's record of 50 goals in 50 games.

Then, in a game against the Quebec

Nordiques, Bossy scored twice in the last four minutes to earn a piece of Richard's mark. Like magic.

"A lot of times players look up at the clock and say to themselves, 'Well it's too late to score,'" explained Bill Torrey, the Islanders' longtime general manager. "It was never, ever, too late for Mike Bossy to score."

The devastating marksman behind the Islanders' four Stanley Cups, Bossy's 85 career playoff goals represent the fifth-highest total in playoff history and his .66 goals-per-game average is fourth-best. He scored two Cup-winning goals, the only player to do so in back-to-back seasons, and won the Conn Smythe Trophy (1982).

Bossy grew up the fifth of 10 children in the Montreal suburb of Laval. It remains one of hockey's mysteries how Mike Bossy lasted so long in the 1977 amateur draft. He scored a phenomenal 308 goals in just 260 Quebec League major junior games with Laval, but Bossy wasn't selected until 15th overall by the Islanders.

Despite his obvious athletic grace, there was little ease about him as a young man. Sensitive and thin-skinned, he was a regular target of Islander veterans who exploited his fretfulness. "I used to be needled unbelievably and I couldn't take it," Bossy recalled. "Someone would needle me and right away I'd be in an argument. I bet I was in one every day back then."

He smoked a pack of cigarettes a day for 10 years, obsessed when he couldn't balance the family checkbook to the penny and often stayed up until dawn, fretting about lost scoring chances. Next time, he vowed, he would welcome success.

Invariably, Bossy did. No one scored more goals during his NHL tenure and with adulthood, marriage and children came an ease and even a willingness to laugh at himself.

Today, Bossy is a Montreal stock broker after a stint as a radio personality.

Bossy's particular brand of on-ice magic was stilled in 1986. He bent over to catch his breath at training camp, straightened up and felt a sharp pain along the left side of his back.

It was the beginning of the end, probably the result of receiving a decade's worth of crosschecks.

He played through increasing pain and still managed 38 goals—it was the only season that he did not score 50—but the pain kept him sidelined through the entire 1987-88 season.

At 32, he retired officially. With the suddenness and speed that had been his trademark, one of the NHL's premier goal scoring wizards was gone.

MIKE BOSSY		1977-87
Born: Jan. 22, 1957 Montreal		
Teams: Islanders		
NHL	Regular	Playoffs
Seasons	10	10
Games	752	129
Goals	573	85
Assists	553	75
Points	1,126	160
Penalties	210	38
All-Star: 8 (First-5, Second-3)		
Trophies: 5 (Smythe-1, Calder-1, Byng-3)		
Stanley Cup Championships		4

Spirit Could Not Be Broken

To 'Terrible' Ted Lindsay there were no strangers, only players he hadn't fought yet.

In 1965, Lindsay retired not only as the NHL's all-time penalty king, but also the catalyst of a Detroit Red Wings' dynasty that saw the club claim four Stanley Cups and eight league titles. The Production Line, one of the greatest units of all time, was powered by Gordie Howe, steered by veteran center Sid Abel and sparked by Ted Lindsay.

Lindsay, who played at 5-foot-8 and 160 pounds, was always the runt of the litter. He was the youngest of nine children and when the Kirkland Lake, Ont., native starred at Toronto's St. Michael's College, his destiny as a Maple Leaf seemed assured.

But a knee injury soured the Leafs on Lindsay, who recovered and signed instead with Detroit. Lindsay, a relentless competitor on the ice and off, refused to sign with the Red Wings without a guarantee that he couldn't be sent to the minors and he never forgot a snub. Some of his greatest scoring and bloodletting came at the expense of the Maple Leafs. Once he garnered a 10-day suspension for filleting a Toronto fan with his stick.

Another time, under the weight of a death threat, he scored the winning goal against the Leafs, tucked the blade of his stick under his shoulder and picked off Gardens' patrons in pantomime. "Against any other club, I'd want to get paid, but

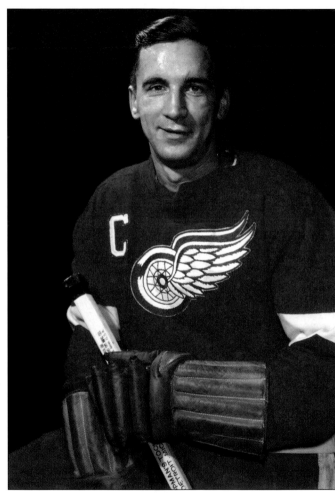

when the other team is Toronto, I'd do it for free," Lindsay told a newspaperman. "And I hope you tell them that."

The only thing worse than Lindsay's stick was his tongue. Maurice Richard was among the stars who, even after retirement, refused to forgive Lindsay's verbal abuse, but to Lindsay, any weapon left unused was a waste. "Different people have different ethics and beliefs," said teammate Glenn Hall. "Ted Lindsay was full out, all the time. He would do anything to win."

Lindsay wielded his stick like a scythe and opponents responded in kind. Lindsay took over 700 stitches in his face and earned the nickname 'Scarface' in the toughest corners of every NHL rink.

Lindsay's greatest fight was one of the few he lost. Tired of being rebuffed when he asked about the players' share of the contributions to the NHL pension plan, Lindsay and longtime nemesis Doug Harvey of the Montreal Canadiens became the ringleaders of the NHL's first players' association. Adams crushed the association and traded Lindsay, his captain and a player coming off his most productive season, to the lowly Chicago Black Hawks in 1957.

"When I got caught up in this, I was so grateful to the game for all it had done for me," Lindsay said, "but it was a dictatorship on the part of the owners, who didn't realize any of us had a brain. There we were sitting there in 1956, these dumb hockey players and we were going to ruin their game?"

'Terrible Ted' played three seasons with the Black Hawks, but never moved his family from Detroit. After a four-year retirement, Lindsay returned to the Red Wings at 39 for a one-season swan song in 1964-65. He scored 14 goals and, as if to prove he hadn't gone soft, registered 173 penalty minutes, his second-highest total.

Retirement meant Lindsay stopped playing, but he never stopped fighting. He

refused to attend his induction into the Hockey Hall of Fame because the event was a stag affair. "I'm not trying to be obstinate," he told Hall officials, "but my wife and children sacrificed a lot during my career and they deserve the honor as much as I do."

Lindsay was lured out of retirement to be the Red Wings' general manager in 1977, but chafed against the realities of the day. Lindsay resented Bobby Hull because Hull kept the World Hockey Association afloat and weakened the NHL's talent pool. He said contractual restrictions on how players could be sent to the minor leagues were heavy-handed.

But Lindsay was well-regarded by players, and if there is a constant in Lindsay's story it is this: the battles obscured the brilliance.

TED LINDSAY	1944-65	
Born: July 29, 1925 Renfrew, Ont.		
Teams: Detroit, Chicago		
NHL	**Regular**	**Playoffs**
Seasons	17	16
Games	1,068	133
Goals	379	47
Assists	472	49
Points	851	96
Penalties	1,808	194
All-Star: 9 (First-8, Second-1)		
Trophies: 1 (Ross-1)		
Stanley Cup Championships	4	

He was a terrific hockey player, his totals of 379 goals (including 57 game winners) and 851 points were the highest career totals for a left winger when he quit in 1965. He was an eight-time first team all-star and Art Ross Trophy winner in 1949-50.

Lindsay was the first player to lead the NHL in goals (1947-48), assists (1949-50, 1956-57), points (1949-50) and penalty minutes (1959-60).

Since Lindsay's retirement, nearly 40 players have topped his career penalty minutes mark.

Only one, Pat Verbeek, has scored more goals.

A Championship
Two-Way Force

In the center of the rabble that was the great Detroit Red Wings teams of the late 1940s and early 1950s stood Red Kelly, gentleman tobacco farmer from Simcoe, Ont.

Surrounded by hockey roughnecks typified by captain Ted Linsday, Kelly didn't smoke, never swore and rarely drank ('bring me the first beer you find', he would tell a waiter on his few tavern excursions).

The ways of the farmer never left Kelly. Unflappable and resilient, he was a stubborn workhorse who fashioned himself into a hockey player. The Red Wings selected him for their protected list from the St. Michael's College juniors, only because the Boston Bruins had drafted several members of the championship team and Detroit scout Carson Cooper didn't want his employers to think he wasn't paying attention.

An excellent skater, Kelly turned himself into a sterling defenseman. He was sure-handed in his own end, daring with the puck and extraordinarily adept at controlling the puck in a crowd or on the boards with his skates.

New York Rangers' general manager Frank Boucher ventured during the Red Wings glory days of the mid-1950s that it was Kelly, not Gordie Howe, who accelerated the hard-driving Wings. Kelly scored 162 goals, almost entirely as a defenseman (he played some forward in 1955-56

and on the power play), more than Bill Gadsby and Doug Harvey, his only real offensively gifted contemporaries, combined. He led NHL defensemen in goals eight times, assists three times and points five times. Kelly was the first defenseman

to score 10 or more goals in nine straight seasons.

"The Redhead," said Boucher, "attacks like a great forward and defends like an even greater defenseman. There's nobody like him for taking the pressure off his own team and in a few seconds applying it on the other guys."

Kelly's play actually helped spur the league to introduce the Norris Trophy, which honors the game's best defenseman. He was the first winner, in 1954.

There was a surprising contrariness in Kelly. He seethed when constantly stirred and his resolve toughened under a challenge. Maple Leafs' scout Squib Walker was among those who underestimated Kelly. He bet Cooper that Kelly's placid demeanor would limit him to no more than 20 NHL games. Kelly played 20 years.

Kelly, a light heavyweight boxing champ in his undergraduate days, rarely retaliated for opposition muggings (he won the Lady Byng Trophy four times and remains the last defenseman to earn the honor), but it was well-known in the six-team league that, if provoked, he was a devastating fighter.

Along with Howe, Kelly was one of the key figures in the Red Wing players' decision to back down from forming a players' association in 1957. But trading Lindsay to the Chicago Black Hawks and installing

RED KELLY		1947-67
Born: July 9, 1927 Simcoe, Ont.		
Teams: Detroit, Toronto		
NHL	**Regular**	**Playoffs**
Seasons	20	19
Games	1,316	164
Goals	281	33
Assists	542	59
Points	823	92
Penalties	327	51
All-Star: 8 (First-6, Second-2)		
Trophies: 5 (Norris-1, Byng-4)		
Stanley Cup Championships	8	

Kelly as captain did not, as Wings' general manager Jack Adams hoped, end the players' rebellion to his arbitrary rule. Kelly brought the Wings' grievances to an increasingly angry Adams.

"I felt it was my duty as a captain," Kelly said. He lasted two seasons with the 'C' and was replaced as captain by Howe.

In February of 1960, angry at Kelly for telling a reporter he had pressured him to play with a broken ankle, Adams traded his six-time first team all-star defenseman to New York along with forward Bill McNeil for Gadsby and forward Eddie Shack.

And then Red Kelly did what few if any NHL players had ever done. He refused to report.

The Red Wings and Rangers, accustomed to placid acquiescence by players, were flabbergasted. Maple Leafs' general manager Punch Imlach moved to break a week-long stalemate and stole Kelly in a deal for a journeyman defenseman named Marc Reaume.

Kelly arrived in Toronto out of game shape and volunteered to play center in his first appearance to minimize the impact of any errors he might make. While the Leafs lost to Montreal, Kelly neutralized his check, Jean Beliveau, all night long. He was a center forevermore.

Kelly won four Stanley Cups in Detroit and added another four in Toronto. No player, other than those who performed for the Montreal Canadiens, won as many Cups as Kelly, who extended his winning streak outside the rink and won election as a hockey-playing politician. Elected in 1962, Kelly served until 1965 as a Liberal MP for a Toronto riding.

Most games were on weekends, so he would practise with the Leafs, fly to Ottawa to spend a day in the House of Commons and then fly back to Toronto to sleep and prepare for the next day's grind.

"Sometimes I thought I wouldn't get through the day," Kelly said. "Then I'd remember times back on the farm when I was sure I'd never reach the end of a row. You live through those things somehow."

Broad Street's Leader Of The Puck

Bobby Clarke wasn't the perfect hockey player, not even close. At 5-foot-10, and 185 pounds he was blessed with average size and a good but not outstanding package of NHL skills.

Clarke's gift, and it was a prodigious one, was one of hockey in character, a sublime blend of virtue and malevolence, perfect for the sport he played.

There is ample nobility in Clarke's career. The son of a miner and a department store cashier from Flin Flon, Man., Clarke's middle class work ethic and small-town values have never left him.

"In Flin Flon, you either play hockey or work in the mines," said Clarke, who had been underground often. "There's no way I wanted to work in those mines."

A diabetic since he was 15, he hated talking about his disease for fear it would be used to set him apart. He was easily the best junior of his 1969 draft year, but concern about his medical condition left Clarke undrafted until the Philadelphia Flyers' turn in the second round. "You have to take him, you have to take him," Flyers' scout Gerry Melnyk shouted at president Ed Snider at the draft table. Snider did, and the championship direction of the club was set.

At 23, Clarke shared the team captaincy with Ed Van Impe and one year later went solo. "The perfect captain," coach Fred Shero called him. "I had minor league

clubs at Omaha and Buffalo that had more real ability than this one," Shero said of his 1974 championship Flyers, "but I never had a team with this much courage and discipline and spirit. Most of it comes from Clarke."

A three-time Hart Trophy winner, Clarke

was the moral nucleus of the franchise. He volunteered to take struggling players on his line and billeted rookies at his home. Once, Shero devised an inane drill that sent players skidding into each other. Clarke ignored Shero's instructions for the drill. "Do it my way," bellowed Shero. "Your way," Clarke shouted back, "is wrong."

Clarke was more than a force of sheer willpower, though. He had three 100-point seasons and led the league in assists twice.

His overtime goal in Game 2 of the 1974 Stanley Cup final gave the Flyers a 3-2 win over the Boston Bruins and is considered one of the most important in team history. It evened the series at 1-1 and propelled Philadelphia to the first Cup victory by an expansion team.

Virtuous to the point of naive, Clarke was at first unwilling to enlist an agent and, in 1972, shook hands with Snider on a contract for $120,000 a year. Before the paperwork had been initiated, the World Hockey Association took wing, instantly and radically inflating the going rate for talent. Clarke was now worth at least twice what he said he would play for, but honorbound by the handshake, he played for $120,000.

But the road out of a small town wasn't just built on virtue; Clarke's game had a chilling ruthlessness. In the 1972 Summit Series, he watched from the bench as Soviet star Valery Kharlamov overwhelmed

BOBBY CLARKE	1969-84	
Born: Aug. 13, 1949 Flin Flon, Man.		
Teams: Philadelphia		
NHL	**Regular**	**Playoffs**
Seasons	15	13
Games	1,144	136
Goals	358	42
Assists	852	77
Points	1,210	119
Penalties	1,453	152
All-Star: 4 (First-2, Second-2)		
Trophies: 5 (Hart-3, Selke-1, Masterton-1)		
Stanley Cup Championships	2	

Bruce Bennett/BBS

Team Canada. "Somebody's got to stop that guy," said Team Canada assistant coach John Ferguson on the bench. Clarke delivered a two-handed slash to Kharlamov's ankle that effectively ended the superlative left winger's series.

"It's not something I'm really proud of," Clarke has said, "but I can't say I was ashamed to do it."

Clarke's choirboy features obscured an often unconscionable viciousness. He was reckless with his stick, and because the Flyers were top-heavy with fighters, Clarke often dodged retribution for his actions.

He was unapologetic.

"People who think I'm a dirty player should go home with my body for a night," he said.

In a sport whose culture considers penalty minutes a positive statistic, Clarke's blend of loyalty, industry and on-ice cruelty was the best of all possible combinations and easily obscured his weak shot and mediocre skating.

In one poll, Clarke was the choice of NHL coaches as the league's best penalty killer, checker, faceoff man, hardest worker and best leader.

Even while his Flyers were engaged in a reign of terror in the league, Clarke added one more honor. The same coaches voted him the player they would like most to have on their team.

Imposing Control in Game

It is a trickle now, but once there was a flow of players from farms and small towns across Canada who brought with them a rural ethos that would shape the NHL.

Eddie Shore walked off the farm in Ft. Qu' Appelle, Sask., towards stardom and the Boston Bruins. Floral, Sask. gave the world Gordie Howe, Bobby Hull was the product of tiny Pt. Anne, Ont.

Like them, Larry Robinson was a rural kid. Big, tough and a little slow to ripen. The Montreal Canadiens' Hall of Fame defenseman grew up on a dairy farm in Marvelville, Ont., near Ottawa and over 20 NHL seasons, 17 in Montreal, pieced together a game born of the earth: resolute, relentless and powerful.

While Robinson's contributions far outstripped the statistical, his 958 points nonetheless remains the seventh-best total among NHL defensemen.

He skated almost as early as he could walk, but didn't play organized hockey until he was eight. It was a leisurely introduction to the game and for Robinson, the perfect one. "I have parents tell me they have kids who are eight years old and play 120 games a year," Robinson said.

"The kid loses the love of the game. The most fun you can have as a kid is throwing the puck on the ice and having a little game of shinny, not getting up at six in the morning to go to practise for six or seven hours skating through pylons."

As rural kids often do, Robinson married young. He already had a son while playing junior in Kitchener and his prospects for providing for his family seemed to darken when he was drafted 20th overall by the Canadiens in 1971. The Habs were the reigning Stanley Cup champs and were well-stocked on the blueline for years to come.

It would take a star to earn a spot in Montreal, and Robinson, gifted with decent skills and excellent size, would be turned into one, largely by his first pro coach, Al MacNeil of the American League's Nova Scotia Voyageurs.

"After our first few games I remember him calling me into his office and almost reading me the riot act," said Robinson. "I was 6-4 and 190 pounds, but he told me that either I change my style of play or there wouldn't be a place on the team for me."

Robinson listened and added a physical dimension to his burgeoning offensive skills that would see him step in as one of the Canadiens' Big Three: Guy Lapointe, Serge Savard and Robinson. His devastat-

LARRY ROBINSON	1972-92	
Born: June 2, 1951 Winchester, Ont.		
Teams: Montreal, Los Angeles		
NHL	**Regular**	**Playoffs**
Seasons	20	20
Games	1,384	227
Goals	208	28
Assists	750	116
Points	958	144
Penalties	793	211
All-Star: 6 (First-3, Second-3)		
Trophies: 3 (Norris-2, Smythe-1)		
Stanley Cup Championships	6	

Denis Brodeur

76

ing bodycheck of Philadelphia Flyers' hardrock Gary Dornhoefer in the 1976 finals was recognized as the pivotal spiritual moment in the Canadiens' elimination of the Flyers and ascendancy to four consecutive Stanley Cups during the late 1970s.

Robinson's 20 consecutive years in the playoffs are an NHL record and only Mark Messier has appeared in more post-season games. Robinson, a two-time Norris Trophy winner, would come to exude presence.

"There have been many tough guys in the NHL who could stamp out trouble, but usually they had to beat up somebody to

do it," Scotty Bowman said. "In Larry's case, he would just skate into the middle of any trouble or confusion on the ice and things would straighten out automatically. He always was able to take control of most situations."

While he would become a polo-playing millionaire, Robinson never lost the humility and stolidness of his roots. Once, when told he had been named player of the week, he asked of the media: "What happened, was Wayne Gretzky sick?"

Robinson had just been told he had won a car as MVP of the 1976 Stanley Cup playoffs, while at the other end of the

training table, Mario Tremblay, Montreal's 19-year-old winger, was embracing the Stanley Cup for the first time. Tremblay was sobbing quietly, tears running down his cheeks.

"That's what it's all about," Robinson said, nodding toward Tremblay, "Not winning a car. A car you can buy...you can't buy that."

Then he went over and wrapped his arm around Tremblay's shoulder.

"Whatdyasay Mario. She's a beauty isn't she," said the boy from Marvelville as he pointed to a blank spot on the cup. "Your name will go right about here."

Choosing A Path Less Travelled

Immune to the sway of pressure or precedent and unaffected by the self-destructiveness that often claims original thinkers, Ken Dryden was the most formidable rebel the NHL has ever known.

Dryden was the product of the baby-boomer, post-secondary education system. The Hamilton native spent four years in the Ivy League at Cornell University and graduated with a pre-law degree. His studies separated him from previous generations of poorly educated players who depended on hockey as their sole chance for a career.

Nor was he a member of the generation of NHLers who would be offered the equivalent of a lifetime's wage for a season of NHL labor.

The combination of those two factors, and Dryden's ability to understand them, created what, up to then, had been a rare scenario: the Montreal Canadiens needed a player more than a player needed the Canadiens.

Even before Montreal, Dryden had followed his own path, eschewing the major junior Peterborough Petes for Grade 13 and then attending Cornell. Upon graduation, he spurned the Canadiens in favor of the Canadian National Team's offer of a four-year, fully paid education at the University of Manitoba.

But the national program folded after a year and Dryden signed on for weekend duty with the Canadiens' farm team while studying law at McGill University in Montreal through the week.

Then came the fabled 1971 call-up, a giddy playoff ride past a superb Boston Bruins' team led by Bobby Orr and Phil Esposito, a six-game handling of the

Minnesota North Stars and a seven-game victory over the Chicago Black Hawks. It was one of the Canadiens' most unlikely titles and Dryden, the Conn Smythe Trophy winner, was the star.

Two years later, in the second season of a two-year, $90,000-a-year contract, Dryden stunned the hockey world by quitting the Canadiens. The club had refused to renegotiate his contract and Dryden took an articling job for $125 a week. His was the holdout that stuck. The Canadiens lost in the quarterfinals, and the following autumn Dryden was back in the fold—at $200,000 per year.

Dryden would win six Stanley Cups and five Vezina Trophies and provide the perfect counterweight to Montreal's great scoring ability. It usually took the Habs a period to become interested enough to elevate the tenor of a contest, and the early tenuous moments of a game or a period invariably belonged to Dryden.

Dryden's greatness was a marriage of the physical and the mental. He was a good athlete and moved his 6-foot-4 frame quickly, economically and efficiently. His height and quickness meant that he always had a chance to make the save.

Just as importantly, Dryden knew when the Canadiens needed a big save. If his

Denis Brodeur

gaudy .758 winning percentage is a testimony to the greatness of his teammates, it also speaks to his ability to fortify that greatness.

"Many times, I've reached for the phone between periods and said to (GM Sam Pollock), 'Sam, we're in trouble,' " former Canadiens' coach Scotty Bowman once recalled. "But then they'd get tired of shooting the puck at Dryden and we'd win the game. Many times."

Dryden needed information. Between shots he monitored the out-of-town scoring and delivered an update to his teammates at every intermission.

Away from the rink, he interviewed everyone, journalists, maitre d's and cab drivers, on everything from working conditions to kitchen overheads and profit per portion served. He rejected cliches in favor

of reasoned answers and deplored the athlete-as-gladiator metaphor so often favored by writers and broadcasters.

"A lot of athletes give you the end-of-the world story if they lose, but if you give up a goal or lose a game, it isn't the

KEN DRYDEN		1971-79
Born: Aug. 8, 1947 Hamilton, Ont.		
Teams: Montreal		
NHL	Regular	Playoffs
Seasons	7	8
Games	397	112
W-L-T	258-57-74	80-32
W Pct.	.758	.714
GAA	2.24	2.40
Shutouts	46	10
All-Star: 6 (First-5, Second-1)		
Trophies: 7 (Smythe-1, Calder-1, Vezina-5)		
Stanley Cup Championships 6		

end of the world," Dryden told interviewers. "It's trained into athletes to say something like that, it's for public consumption. Sports is just like selling encyclopedias. There shouldn't be this mythological aura surrounding it."

Bruins' bad boy Derek Sanderson was among those who sneered at Dryden's cerebral outlook and activities. "So what if he joined Nader's Raiders?" Sanderson said. "Maybe I'll join the Peace Corps."

But Dryden's ability and his obvious pleasure in the game made his distinctions palatable. "He's very popular," a teammate once said, "but if he had a string of bad games, we'd learn to hate him in a hurry."

Dryden retired in 1979 at 31, effectively ending a Canadiens' dynasty he helped author.

They Called Him 'The Big M'

One day, when Toronto Maple Leafs' star Frank Mahovlich could no longer cope with the indignities heaped upon him by coach Punch Imlach, he asked his doctor what to do.

"The doctor told me to sort of pull an imaginary curtain around myself whenever Punch was around," Mahovlich told a reporter in 1965. "I've been doing it and I feel a lot better."

A genial, gentle man, Mahovlich was probably the most charismatic and certainly the most gifted player the Leafs have enjoyed. If not for the curtain, or rather the forces that necessitated it, Mahovlich and not Bobby Hull might have been the dominant player of his generation.

'The Big M,' a homesick boy plucked from Northern Ontario to star for Toronto's St. Michael's College juniors, was a star before the city he played in knew how to treat one. An arresting skater, stickhandler and shooter, Mahovlich burst into the NHL as a Calder Trophy candidate and can't-miss superstar. He outduelled Hull for rookie-of-the-year honors and had 11 more goals than Hull (42-31) during their first two seasons.

In 1961, Mahovlich scored 43 goals in 56 games but his quest for 50 died when his scoring pace withered over the last 14

contests. The aborted drive for 50 weighed heavily on Mahovlich. He would never again score more than 36 as a Maple Leaf.

When he met Roger Maris, who was recovering from nightmarish demands after

breaking Babe Ruth's record for home runs in a season, Mahovlich is reported to have told him, "I'm one fellow who is able to appreciate the ordeal you went through last season."

While Hull would routinely break the 50 mark, Mahovlich, saddled with a defensively oriented team, had to be satisfied not with prodigious scoring totals, but periodic bursts of artistry. "Bobby Hull may score more goals," said Mahovlich's teammate Dave Keon, "but no one scores better goals than Frank."

To Leaf fans, Mahovlich's talents seemed so limitless, any game in which he was held scoreless must have been one he was taking off. He was booed, regularly and voraciously and Imlach never bothered to pronounce his name correctly.

The son of a hard-rock miner from Timmins, Mahovlich found that stardom brought a new life, but not necessarily a better one, than the one he left as a boy. "Hockey is different than the vision I had as a kid," he said. "Then, I thought if I ever got to the NHL it would be the answer to life. I found out it isn't. I enjoy hockey, it's a satisfying job when things are right, but some nights, it's frustrating."

His skills, so obviously mismanaged in Toronto, created universal demand. Chicago Black Hawks' owner Jim Norris, in

FRANK MAHOVLICH 1957-74		
Born: Jan. 10, 1938 Timmins, Ont.		
Teams: Toronto, Detroit, Montreal		
NHL	**Regular**	**Playoffs**
Seasons	17	16
Games	1,181	137
Goals	533	51
Assists	570	67
Points	1,103	118
Penalties	1,056	163
All-Star: 9 (First-3, Second-6)		
Trophies: 1 (Calder-1)		
Stanley Cup Championships 6		

a night of revelry, offered to buy
Mahovlich from the Maple Leafs for $1 million.

The Leafs accepted and then reneged in
the morning light. Finally, after Mahovlich
left the team and was treated for depression, Toronto traded its 30-year-old superstar to Detroit.

Mahovlich delivered two sterling seasons in Detroit, registering 49-goal and
38-goal seasons. Gordie Howe was the
focus in Detroit and he was sympathetic
to the harrows inflicted on Mahovlich in
Toronto.

"It was," Mahovlich would say, "like a
giant weight had been lifted off my shoulder."

The rebuilding Red Wings shipped him
to Montreal in 1971 for a package of players that included Mickey Redmond.
Mahovlich spent three banner seasons in
Montreal, earning two Stanley Cups to
accompany the four he earned in Toronto.
His 14 playoff goals in 1971 were an NHL
record. Mahovlich changed his style somewhat in Montreal, showing off his playmaking skills by leading the team in
assists three straight seasons.

A nine-time NHL all-star, Mahovlich
spent his athletic dotage in the World
Hockey Association, with Toronto and then
Birmingham, where he earned nearly a
million dollars before retiring at 40. But
for Frank Mahovlich, the curtain lifted with
the trade to Detroit.

"Eleven years I played with Frank
Mahovlich in Toronto and I didn't say 22
words to the guy," said Bobby Baun, a
teammate, first in Toronto then with the
Red Wings. "Nobody understood him so it
was easier to stay away from him. But
now Frank's a different person."

Captain Of Courage And Conviction

Milt Schmidt says one of the highlights of his life came four decades ago with a handshake and a lesson in the warrior's code. Schmidt and Eddie Shore were the best of the Boston Bruins for the club's first 40 years and Schmidt waged regular and incendiary battles with the Montreal Canadiens' Elmer Lach, Detroit Red Wings' Sid Abel and Toronto Maple Leafs' Ted Kennedy.

But even those wars paled when compared to the career-long feud that pitted Schmidt against 'Black Jack' Stewart, the Detroit Red Wings' brutal and intimidating defenseman. "It used to begin," remembered Schmidt's longtime linemate Woody Dumart, "about the time they blew the whistle to start the game."

The truce came years after the two had retired. "I was coaching the Bruins and I remember one day our dressing room door opened and it was Jack Stewart," Schmidt recalled. "We shook hands and talked a bit about the old times and Jack said to me, 'Weren't we a crazy couple of fools.' The moral of the story is that after the battles, you can have respect for each other."

Schmidt was a warrior shaped by the Depression. He was 11 when the stock market crashed and the NHL in which he would star reflected the desperation and toughness of the times.

Schmidt led the Bruins to two Stanley Cups and won a scoring championship in 1940 when he finished with 22 goals and 52 points.

His linemates Woody Dumart and Bobby Bauer finished second and third. With Schmidt at the club's core, the Bruins, fortified by the stellar goaltending of Frank Brimsek, were poised to become the league's next powerhouse.

But the 'Kraut Line' enlisted en masse in the Royal Canadian Air Force and was posted overseas in 1942–after first winning the Canadian senior championship Allan Cup with the Ottawa RCAF. Schmidt, a flying officer, returned to the NHL after spending 35 months in England and while those who reconstruct his career inevitably point to the loss of three years of prime playing time, Schmidt never does.

"We never looked at it with the point of view that we were losing something," Schmidt said. "The way we looked at it, we were just lucky to be coming back."

"We," for Schmidt, has always been the Krauts, with Bauer on the right wing and Dumart on the left. Bauer and Dumart, three and two years older than Schmidt, played on the same Kitchener Greenshirts junior team and the threesome saw their first action as a line in 1936-37 with Providence of the American League.

Schmidt was talented but small–he weighed just 147 pounds at 18–but he was promoted to the NHL the following year to kick off what would be an eight-year run of success for the 'Kraut Line.'

Each player had particular strengths. Bauer, a three-time Lady Byng winner, was an elegant player and gifted stickhandler.

Woody Dumart / Lynn Patrick / Milt Schmidt

Nat Turofsky/HHOF

MILT SCHMIDT	1937-55	
Born: March 5, 1918 Kitchener, Ont.		
Teams: Boston		
NHL	Regular	Playoffs
Seasons	16	13
Games	776	86
Goals	229	24
Assists	346	25
Points	575	49
Penalties	466	60
All-Star: 4 (First-3, Second-1)		
Trophies: 2 (Hart-1, Ross-1)		
Stanley Cup Championships	2	

Dumart was an excellent goal-scorer and a determined cornerman. But clearly, the line rotated around Schmidt.

Considered the top two-way NHL player of the late 1940s, Schmidt had top-drawer offensive skills and had his two best offensive seasons after the war, in 1946-47 (62 points) and 1950-51 (61 points). He was a strong skater and clever stickhandler with great finish. He considered it a point of pride that he was first in the corner at both ends of the rink.

Because of his style, Schmidt endured a long string of injuries. In addition to the usual litany of cuts, sprains and bruises, he suffered shoulder separations, torn chest cartilage and a broken jaw, but it was his knees that would trouble him most.

Schmidt tore cartilage in both knees leaving his left, in the words of one writer, "resembling a small smoked ham" for most of his career.

But it was his style, determined and angry, that powered the 'Kraut Line' and the Bruins. The will to win never ebbed.

"If we had lost a game, and Milt saw somebody smiling he'd get mad as hell," Dumart said . "He couldn't understand somebody enjoying themselves after a game that we lost. He was really a tough, tough guy that way."

Schmidt was a Bruin for a life, coaching or acting as general manager from 1955 to 1972. It was Schmidt who paved the way for two more Cups when he traded for Phil Esposito from the Chicago Black Hawks in 1967. Esposito, like Schmidt, would be a great captain.

Blueline Bullet: Speed Thrills

The NHL Guide and Record Book does not lie. Paul Coffey left the Edmonton Oilers 12 seasons ago. Combine the games he has played in the colors of the Pittsburgh Penguins, Los Angeles Kings, Detroit Red Wings, Hartford Whalers, Philadelphia Flyers and Chicago Black Hawks, and you realize he has skated more often in other people's colors than in the blue, orange and white.

And yet, the NHL's most prolific offensive defenseman still seems of the Oil. No matter where he has journeyed, he has spoken reverently of Edmonton and delivered the searing offensive talents first produced in the Alberta capital.

Coffey found hockey by accident. He played minor hockey for fun and had no idea his extraordinary skating and offensive skills would be in demand.

"I was playing for the Toronto Young Nats in my first year of midget," he said. "I was 15 years old, and I didn't have a clue about junior hockey or how to get there. I just played. I remember going to a game and someone on the team saying, 'There are Toronto Marlie scouts in the crowd tonight.' I still remember to this day saying 'Scouts? What do you mean?' I remember talking to my dad in the car on the way home and trying to find out what went on."

Coffey was drafted by the Ontario League's Sault Ste. Marie Greyhounds and

traded to the Kitchener Rangers, where he sharpened his offensive instincts out of necessity.

"We had a really bad team in Kitchener my last year there and I had to rush the puck a lot because it was always in our end," he once said.

The Oilers drafted him sixth overall in the 1980 NHL entry draft and it took half a season for coach Glen Sather's constant prodding to attack to finally take hold. Coffey scored seven goals and notched 27 points after the Christmas break of his rookie season and scored in all three games as the Oilers hammered the Montreal Canadiens in three straight games to eliminate the Canadiens and announce their ascendancy to the NHL elite.

In Edmonton, Coffey won three Stanley Cups, garnered two Norris Trophies, and, in 1986, he broke Bobby Orr's record for most goals in a season, scoring his 47th on an end-to-end rush.

Coffey's 138-point 1985-86 campaign is the second highest total ever for a defenseman, behind Orr's 139, and his 48 goals is the most ever for a rearguard.

Speed, the calling card of that Oiler team, was the most obvious of Coffey's gifts.

"Bobby Orr was the greatest skating defenseman ever, but Paul is right there," said longtime Oilers' coach John Muckler. "He glides faster than a lot of people skate."

PAUL COFFEY	1980-present	
Born: June 1, 1961 Weston, Ont.		
Teams: Edmonton, Pittsburgh, L.A., Detroit, Hartford, Philadelphia, Chicago		
NHL	**Regular**	**Playoffs**
Seasons	18	15
Games	1,268	189
Goals	383	59
Assists	1,090	136
Points	1,473	195
Penalties	1,704	262
All-Star: 8 (First-4, Second-4)		
Trophies: 3 (Norris-3)		
Stanley Cup Championships	4	

Bruce Bennett/BBS

Coffey won the NHL's fastest skating competition in 1991 and Orr, himself, said his father compared Coffey favorably to Bobby.

But lost in the blur of Coffey's remarkably smooth stride was the brilliance of his passing instincts. Unquestionably, no NHL defenseman has ever delivered the long distance pass as consistently and accurately as did Coffey.

Long criticized for his lacklustre defensive play, Coffey broke up a Soviet 2-on-1 to set up Mike Bossy's winning goal for Canada in the 1984 Canada Cup. And while he has never showcased the remarkable all-around game of Raymond Bourque, criticizing Coffey for poor defensive play is like trashing William Shakespeare for bad penmanship.

Coffey left the Oilers when they would not re-negotiate his contract as they did for Wayne Gretzky and Mark Messier.

He won a Stanley Cup—and recorded the fourth and fifth 100-point seasons of his career—riding shotgun for Mario Lemieux in Pittsburgh.

Already the quest has taken him to more cities than any other player in the top 25 of the NHL's all-time leading scorers and in Detroit, Coffey staged a renaissance, winning his third Norris Trophy in 1995 and his first since leaving Edmonton.

Individually, he may have already established playoff scoring marks (59 goals, 136 assists, 195 points) no defenseman will ever equal.

He holds defenseman records for single-season playoff goals (12), assists (25) and points (37).

The chance to take one more tour of duty with Gretzky and Messier nudged Coffey into the 1996 World Cup of Hockey and his quest for a fifth Cup drives him still.

"Winning the Stanley Cup when you're young is like going on vacation when you're 20," Coffey said. "Take the same vacation when you're in your thirties and you know how to do it much better."

Hockey Heaven Times Eleven

Denis Brodeur

Maurice Richard was very good at being great. Henri Richard was great at being very good.

That, in a nutshell, is the difference between the player THN judges to be the fifth greatest player of all-time and his brother, Henri (Pocket Rocket) Richard.

Rocket Richard was the most dramatic hockey player ever to grace the NHL, but aside from the essential question of goal-scoring, his brother was a better player.

"Henri is a better all-around player than I ever was." Maurice Richard said. "He stickhandles better, controls the puck more and skates faster. He's better in every way except in goal-scoring." Henri delivered more seasons, played more games and accrued more regular season and playoff points than the Rocket.

The second-best goal-scorer in the Richard family still managed to outscore Hall of Fame gunners such as Andy Bathgate and Nels Stewart, but if the real measure of the professional is victories, the little Richard stands on the top of the mountain.

Henri Richard was a first team all-star only one time, but more summers than not he went home to a parade. He won 11 Stanley Cups in 20 NHL seasons. The great

Rocket, by comparison, won eight and only two others, Jean Beliveau and Yvan Cournoyer, broke double figures with 10. Former Boston Celtics' star Bill Russell, also an 11-time champion, is the only North American athlete to have as many big league championships as Richard.

Just 5-foot-7 and 160 pounds, Richard was the best little man to step into the NHL. Dave Keon, the Toronto Maple Leafs Hall of Fame center, was among the legion of smallish players who learned not only how to survive but also thrive in the NHL by watching Henri Richard.

Henri was only six when Maurice broke in with the Canadiens. Because of the 15-year gap in age, "Maurice was more like an uncle to me." said Henri.

Henri eschewed comparisons with his brother. His sister dated a plumber and when someone asked, that's the profession to which Henri Richard said he aspired.

Inside, though, he knew better.

"Playing hockey was what I wanted to do since I was six years old," Richard said. "I wanted to play with Montreal. Without hockey, I don't know what I would have done."

While his talent and drive were unquestioned, Richard's size made the NHL a longshot.

He weighed only 120 pounds as a star with the Jr. Canadiens, but he filled out and eventually made the Canadiens just in time to fit into the supporting cast of the

club's five-Cup run from 1955-56 through 1959-1960.

A prolific goal-scorer in junior (Richard had 56 goals and 109 points in 1953-54) he never scored more than 30 goals or recorded more than 80 points in a season. Instead, he fashioned himself into a steady 20-goal-scorer as a pro, one whose skating, tenacity, positioning and playmaking made him an outstanding NHL player. Richard led the league in assists twice.

"I thought I wanted to be like Maurice, but I soon found out I couldn't be like him," Henri said. "I just couldn't put the puck in the net. So I had to change my style."

That style made him a perfect counterpoint to the Rocket, whom he centered for his first five seasons in the league.

"Henri kept me in the league a year or two longer than I normally would have

stayed," said the Rocket. "The way he skated, the way he worked, he made my job easy, much easier than I would have found it otherwise."

"You can take (Jean) Beliveau and all the others," said former Canadiens' defenseman Ken Reardon. "Give me Henri. That little bugger could skate for five minutes without getting tired."

HENRI RICHARD		1955-75
Born: Feb. 29, 1936 Montreal		
Teams: Montreal		
NHL	Regular	Playoffs
Seasons	20	18
Games	1,256	180
Goals	358	49
Assists	688	80
Points	1,046	129
Penalties	928	181
All-Star: 3 (First-1, Second-2)		
Trophies: 1 (Masterton-1)		
Stanley Cup Championships		11

When he arrived in the league, Henri Richard was unilingual and he was so intimidated by the hallowed Forum, he did not feel at home enough to shave there for 10 years. He matured, however, into a respected leader and captain. After quarrelling with then-coach Al MacNeil in the 1971 finals, Richard scored the tying and Stanley Cup-winning goal in Game 7 at Chicago Stadium.

Richard also scored the controversial Cup winner in 1966 when he knocked in the decisive goal with his arm while sliding on the ice. The losing Detroit Red Wings were incensed the goal counted.

"They say there's no room for small players in the game," said former teammate Pete Mahovlich. "I'll tell you something: if they have the same fire and drive that Henri Richard had, there's always room for players like that."

True MVP: Most Versatile Player

The bars were mostly dives but at 15, Bryan Trottier, lead singer and guitarist for The Trottier Family, didn't have much to compare them to anyway.

"We'd make music, not money," he said of the nights spent singing with his father, Buzz, and other family members in bars in Southern Alberta and Saskatchewan. "We'd try to sing too. Sad songs, all broken romances and busted dreams...like country songs are."

Along with four brothers and a sister, Trottier grew up on a cattle ranch near Val Marie, Sask., then a town of about 250 people. He learned to skate on the Frenchman River, the same river Buzz did.

Bryan started rodeo when he was nine and wasn't given time off from his chores to get into organized hockey until he was 10. Instead, he sharpened his skills on the river, often playing with his dog Rowdy. It was a quintessentially Canadian childhood and Bryan mourned when Rowdy died at 11 without a tooth in his head.

Trottier came to the attention of the New York Islanders largely by fluke. Former Islander Earl Ingarfield noticed Trottier during negotiations to buy the Western League's Swift Current Broncos and move them to Lethbridge. The Islanders didn't even know of the existence of an underage draft, a league invention designed to limit the damage of the World Hockey Association's policy of drafting players who were under 18 and not yet eligible for the NHL draft.

The Islanders took Ingarfield's recommendation to draft Trottier and the industrious center went 22nd in the 1974 amateur draft.

After a standout year in Lethbridge, 19-year-old Bryan Trottier stepped into the NHL with a flourish, scoring three goals and two assists in his first home game. Trottier took home the Calder Trophy as the league's top rookie and broke Marcel Dionne's record for points by a rookie. He still ranks seventh all-time in rookie points (95).

At 5-foot-10 and 200 pounds, Trottier wasn't huge but had a marvelously versatile game.

"He could pass the puck left or right, knock somebody off the puck and then make a wonderful play," said Islanders' general manager Bill Torrey. "He had the nice soft touch but he also could knock over a moose."

Trottier was a throwback, a player toughened by rural life. "Bryan could play with any man on any team in any era," Gordie Howe once said. "When there's a loose puck, he's always there to get it."

Trottier played 15 years with the Islanders and finished as the club's all-time leader in assists and points. He won a scoring title, a Hart Trophy and four Stanley Cups. His playoff feats included registering at least one point in a record 27 consecutive playoff games over three years, starting with a Conn Smythe Trophy-winning 1980 post-season. His 23 assists during the 1982 playoffs eclipsed Bobby Orr's record by four.

However, his departure from New York was ignominious. When Trottier's game began to slip, the Islanders exercised an optional buy-out clause that paid him a fraction of the full value of the contract and dropped him at 33.

He would emerge from retirement to win two Stanley Cups with the Pittsburgh Penguins. He along with Red Kelly, Dick Duff, Frank Mahovlich and Larry Murphy are the only players to win two or more Cups with two teams.

But in the meantime, financial ruin struck Trottier, who declared bankruptcy with debts of $9.7 million. Devastated, he developed clinical depression and, like many people afflicted with the disease, flirted with the idea of suicide. Medication and therapy have returned him to good health.

The tragedies of the songs he once sung had come and gone. In the end, Trottier's story is one of surviving those broken dreams and heartbreak...like the people in country songs do.

BRYAN TROTTIER	1975-94	
Born: July 18, 1956 Val Marie, Sask.		
Teams: Islanders, Pittsburgh		
NHL	Regular	Playoffs
Seasons	18	17
Games	1,279	221
Goals	524	71
Assists	901	113
Points	1,425	184
Penalties	912	277
All-Star: 4 (First-2, Second-2)		
Trophies: 4 (Hart-1, Ross-1, Smythe-1, Calder-1)		
Stanley Cup Championships	6	

Stubborn Streak And Cup Streak

Dickie Moore was the grit that made the polish gleam, the mortar obscured by the sheer grandeur of the Montreal Canadiens' colossus.

Never pressed to overcome a lack of talent, he struggled instead with the rigors inflicted on his body. As a boy he was hit by a car, nearly had his lip chewed off by a dog and broke both legs. His knee problems were considered so severe, they threatened to end his career in Montreal before it began. As a pro, he would play through a chronology of injuries: he broke his collar bone twice, tore cartilage in both knees and underwent several shoulder operations.

Moore played with a broken wrist for the final three months of the season to win the first of two consecutive scoring titles in 1957-58 but found life on top of the scoring parade provided as much distraction as satisfaction.

"Sometimes I feel I'd rather be down about the middle of the scoring list," he said. "Then people don't notice you too much. When I first broke in, I used to wonder what it would be like to lead the league. Now that I know, it sort of scares me."

Moore's 96 points in 1958-59 were the most recorded in NHL history and would stand as the top mark for seven years, but far more telling are his six Stanley Cups, including five in a row with the great Canadiens' teams of the late 1950s. Maurice Richard called him the best left winger he ever played with. Moore could play all three forward positions and when Richard, Bernie Geoffrion or even Jean Beliveau went down to injuries, Moore stepped in.

The resolve that would mark his career was evident from the start. Moore was one of eight brothers from the working class Montreal neighborhood of Park Extension. The Moores travelled as a pack, loudly supporting their own. Once, after losing much of the previous season to a knee injury, Moore staggered the Canadiens' brass by jumping into the stands during an exhibition game to defend his brother in a fight.

Not only was he fiercely protective of those around him, Moore was intractable when he made a decision. A star with the Montreal Jr. Canadiens, he could see he wouldn't immediately crack the big club in 1951, but still balked when the Habs offered the $7,500 minimum. He was making $20 a week working at the railroad but would not sign until he got a $2,000 bonus.

"Moore has always been a stubborn man," said longtime Montreal Gazette writer Red Fisher. "He was argumentative. Maybe that's what made him a great hockey player. He played all out and with heart in everything he did, on and off the ice."

Moore belatedly signed with the Canadiens at Christmas, 1951, and was immediately inserted on Rocket Richard's line. "He can't skate much and I don't know whether he can handle the puck," coach Dick Irvin said of Moore. "I do know he's a competitor."

Tough and unyielding, Moore was nonetheless an honorable competitor. He never accrued more than 68 minutes in penalties while averaging 26 goals through his nine full-time seasons with Montreal.

Moore was 32 and coming off a 24-goal season when Canadiens' general manager Frank Selke asked him to report to his office and discuss a possible trade. Moore refused and quit the Canadiens for his business ventures.

He would not return to the Canadiens, even though Selke tried to woo him back for the next year's playoff run. Instead, he worked elsewhere, first with the Toronto Maple Leafs for 38 games in 1964-65 and then as a 36-year-old as a member of the St. Louis Blues in 1967-68. With his knees well-rested Moore scored 14 playoff points for the Blues, the second-highest total of his career.

"He was a great team man, maybe the best I have ever known," said Henri Richard. "He was a very hard worker who would do anything to help the team. Dickie Moore would sacrifice anything to help a friend."

DICKIE MOORE	1951-68	
Born: Jan. 6, 1931 Montreal		
Teams: Montreal, Toronto, St. Louis		
NHL	**Regular**	**Playoffs**
Seasons	14	14
Games	719	135
Goals	261	46
Assists	347	64
Points	608	110
Penalties	652	122
All-Star: 3 (First-2, Second–1)		
Trophies: 2 (Ross-2)		
Stanley Cup Championships	6	

Harold Barkley Archives

Surviving, Thriving In 'Mug's Racket'

He was, by profession, instinct and inclination, a crowd pleaser. Fans loved Newsy Lalonde, one of the NHL's first great rambunctious stars. And he loved them right back.

"I can't go anywhere on a bus or in a club, unless there's somebody there who wants to talk to me." he once told an interviewer. "I tell you, it's the most wonderful thing. It's worth more than money."

Born in 1887, Lalonde worked as a newspaper reporter and printer at the Cornwall Freeholder as a youth and thus earned the nickname he would carry the rest of his life. The son of a Cornwall cobbler, he was 19 when he played his first professional season in Woodstock, Ont., and caught the eye of scouts connected to the network of senior teams that dotted Canada. The next year, Sault Ste. Marie (Ont.) of the International League offered him $35 a week and a one-way ticket to the Soo. Lalonde left with all the money he had ($16), but was nearly poisoned in his first game when he took a swig of a bottle on the bench that was supposed to be whisky, but turned out to be ammonia.

Although he would lead his league in scoring five times and twice led the NHL as a member of the Montreal Canadiens, hockey always remained Lalonde's second

favorite sport. He made more money playing lacrosse and was named Canada's best lacrosse player of the half-century.

In 1909 at the old, wooden natural-ice Jubilee rink on Ste. Catherine Street in Montreal, Lalonde was in the lineup when

the Canadian Athletic Club, the forerunner of the Montreal Canadiens, played its inaugural game.

Lalonde played lacrosse or hockey in Montreal, Toronto, Regina, Saskatoon, Vancouver and New York. He would win the scoring derby in four pro hockey leagues–the National Association, Western League, NHL and Pacific Coast League. His best NHL season came in 1919-20 when

he scored 36 goals and 42 points. But one year later, he won the scoring championship when he became the first player to lead the league in goals (33), assists (eight) and points (41).

Lalonde's six goals against the Toronto Maple Leafs on Jan. 10, 1920, a record for three weeks until Quebec Bulldog Joe Malone scored seven, is the second- most ever in an NHL game.

Lalonde's recklessness, as well as his puckhandling skills made him a star. Ted Reeve of the Toronto Telegram wrote: "...he was a marked man in more ways than one when he came out...middle height, deep chested, tremendously strong in the way of powerful Habitant stock, with the reflexes and gameness of a bull terrier."

"Lalonde was a survivor of a truly permissive age when hockey was genuinely a mug's racket," wrote one sportswriter. "(It was) mottled with roughnecks who preferred to drink an opponent's blood at body temperature, or near there."

His battles with Quebec defenseman Joe Hall were legendary. Hall nearly severed Newsy's windpipe in Quebec. The next game saw Hall carve Newsy for 18 stitches. As soon as he got back to the ice, Lalonde shattered Hall's collarbone. "But there was nothing personal," said Lalonde. "When

Hall later joined Canadiens, we became friends and roomies."

Lalonde would view his rivals with equal equanimity. After Toronto defenseman Sprague Cleghorn nearly killed Lalonde in a game, police charged Cleghorn with assault. Lalonde pleaded to have the rugged defenseman acquitted in court but managed only to have his sentence set at a $200 fine.

Lalonde spent five seasons with the Canadiens before Montreal sent the 35-year-old center to Saskatoon of the Western League for Aurel Joliat. Lalonde would continue in hockey, but play just one more game in the NHL and retire from the New York Americans at 39.

Lalonde would earn $140,000 as a professional athlete, and buy the building that housed his father's shoemaking business, but the stock market crash of 1929 swept away $100,000 in life savings. Friends, and there were plenty, arranged a benefit on his behalf that raised $1,000 and he found work at a liquor store.

Lalonde, who died Nov. 21, 1970 at 83 in a Montreal convalescent home from complications caused by a hip injury, was always willing to talk about his wild young ways.

"Honestly, I never did see myself as a Richard, a Howe or a Lindsay," he said in 1954. "My forte was playmaking and my stride was deceptively fast. Every time I see Toronto play I see myself again in Teeder Kennedy—but with a helluva lot more goals."

NEWSY LALONDE		1917-27
Born: Oct. 31, 1887 Cornwall, Ont.		
Teams: Montreal, Americans		
NHL	Regular	Playoffs
Seasons	6	2
Games	99	12
Goals	124	22
Assists	27	1
Points	151	23
Penalties	122	19
All-Star: 0		
Trophies: 0		
Stanley Cup Championships		0

Man Of Distinction On And Off Ice

By virtue of statistics and trophies, Syl Apps does not belong among the 50 greatest players of all-time.

While he would grasp the Stanley Cup three times, Apps never won a scoring championship and drew no closer to the Hart Trophy than runner-up.

And yet, his omission from the top 50 would be a grievous one. As the first radio superstar in the NHL, Apps remains a bigger-than-life figure in the minds of a generation.

Foster Hewitt's radio accounts trumpeted Apps' deeds in hearths across Canada. Thanks to the power of the new medium, most of Apps' admirers, and they were legion, never saw him play.

A devout Baptist who never swore, Apps didn't drink, eschewed smoking and never complained. His game was compulsively clean, powerful and riveting. Newspaper pictures showed him to be upright, tall and square-jawed.

Apps, college-educated and a former Olympic athlete, was, in fact, everything Toronto Maple Leafs' owner Conn Smythe believed a star and a captain should be.

In Apps, Smythe found a hero fit for public consumption and Apps would remain one throughout a life that included a career as a noted provincial politician and one-time Corrections Minister. Despite

a neurological disease that has robbed him of the ability to speak, Apps remains the same virtuous, industrious man he has always been.

"In the National Hockey League, where most players act as though they were candidates for a job in a slaughter-house," intoned Sport magazine during Apps' prime, "Sylvanus Apps is as out of place as an orchid on a hamburger."

"He was," said Ted (Teeder) Kennedy, Apps' successor as Maple Leafs' captain, "as fine a man as ever lived."

Charles Joseph Sylvanus Apps was born in 1915 in Paris, Ont., a small town 90 minutes from Toronto. The Apps were upper-middle class people. Ernest Apps operated a drugstore in town and his wife in the winter would flood a stretch of alley near the family home for skating.

Syl, the middle child, was good at everything. He excelled in track and field, golf and hockey, was chosen his high school valedictorian and attended McMaster University in nearby Hamilton.

A burgeoning interest in the pole vault earned him a spot on the Canadian Olympic team and a sixth-place finish at the 1936 Olympics.

Smythe heard reports of Apps' prowess as a hockey player, but when he saw him tear through the University of Toronto defense as a McMaster running back, he knew he had stumbled upon a prodigy.

Apps, however, was unsure he wanted to be a professional hockey player. "In my circle, professional athletes were not looked upon as the right sort," Apps said.

What he did know was that he needed a job so he could marry and start a family. The 21-year-old Apps stepped into the Maple Leafs' lineup in 1937 and won the Calder Trophy for rookie of the year. If he wasn't the best player in the league, he was certainly one of the most charismatic. A powerful skater, he was a magnificent

stickhandler with a deft passing touch. Detroit Red Wings' general manager Jack Adams called him the greatest center he had ever seen.

Apps, a five-time NHL all-star, led the league in assists in 1936-37 and 1937-38 and won the Lady Byng Trophy in 1941-42. He recorded just 56 penalty minutes during his 10-season career, including a penalty-free 1941-42 campaign.

Apps compiled a virtuous off-ice resume as well. In 1949 he was named Canadian Father of the Year. That brought a $1,000 check which he promptly turned over to charity.

He was also a member of the Ontario parliament for Kingston and the Islands from 1963 to 1980.

Apps played seven seasons with the Leafs, missed two while in the service, and then came back to post seasons of 24, 25 and 26 goals. He captained the Leafs for six seasons.

At 33 and burdened with injuries, Apps told Smythe he would retire after hitting the 200-goal mark. Smythe felt Apps had two or three more productive seasons left. He was, after all coming off career highs in goals and points, but a hat trick in the 1947-48 season finale in Detroit pushed Apps to 201 career goals.

Smythe offered Apps a blank check to come back. Apps actually relented and agreed to return, but when he discovered Teeder Kennedy had been named captain, he didn't want to cause a problem, so he remained retired.

SYL APPS		1936-48
Born: Jan. 18, 1915 Paris, Ont.		
Teams: Toronto		
NHL	**Regular**	**Playoffs**
Seasons	10	8
Games	423	69
Goals	201	25
Assists	231	29
Points	432	54
Penalties	56	8
All-Star: 5 (First-2, Second-3)		
Trophies: 2 (Calder-1, Byng-1)		
Stanley Cup Championships		3

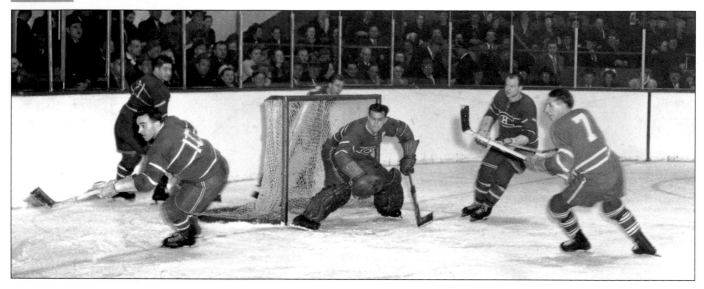

The Wonderful Dr. Strangeglove

Left or right, love it or hate it, Bill Durnan never could decide. Durnan, considered by many the greatest goalie of hockey's modern era upon his death in 1972, was spectacularly ambidextrous on the ice and terribly ambiguous off it.

Thanks to gloves that could be used to catch or stickhandle, Durnan parlayed a trick he learned as a school boy into a devastating weapon for NHL shooters. When the puck moved to a shooter on his left, Durnan quickly transferred his stick to his right hand. If the puck went to the other side of the rink, Durnan switched again. No matter what side the shooter approached, he faced Durnan's glove hand.

"You move your hand a lot faster than you move your body," Durnan said. "When you can use both hands, you've always got an open hand guarding the wide part of the net."

The trick, picked up from a coach in a Toronto church league, worked because Durnan was a wonderfully gifted athlete. He was considered one of the best young fastball pitchers in the country–leading his Montreal team to four consecutive provincial titles–and was so dominant in the nets as a boy, he went through one minor hockey season without allowing a goal.

Durnan's expected ascension to the Toronto Maple Leafs ended just prior to his 20th birthday when he severely injured a knee wrestling with a friend. The Leafs, convinced he could not come back, dropped him from their protected list. He would earn a palatable living playing senior hockey until the Montreal Canadiens signed him as a 28-year-old rookie in 1943. Durnan was a sensation and won the Vezina Trophy in his rookie season. His hands were so quick, it was said he only wore pads for effect.

"It was remarkable the way he was able to switch that stick from one hand to the other," said Canadiens' teammate Toe Blake. "I've never seen anybody else who could do that. At his best, nobody was as good. Nobody."

Over seven seasons, Durnan and the Canadiens won the Vezina trophy six times, losing out only in 1948 to the Maple Leafs' Turk Broda, the man who inherited the job for which Durnan had once seemed destined.

Twice Durnan's name was engraved on the Stanley Cup, six times he was named a first team all-star. It wasn't until 1965-66 that another goalie, Glenn Hall, would equal and later surpass his record of six first team all-star selections.

BILL DURNAN	1943-50	
Born: Jan. 22, 1915 Toronto		
Teams: Montreal		
NHL	Regular	Playoffs
Seasons	7	6
Games	383	45
W-L-T	208-112-62	27-18
W Pct	.626	.600
GAA	2.36	2.07
Shutouts	34	2
All-Star: 6 (First-6)		
Trophies: 6 (Vezina-6)		
Stanley Cup Championships	2	

Durnan was the last NHL goalie to post four consecutive shutouts. His shutout streak of 309 minutes and 21 seconds in 1948-49 is the fourth longest in NHL history.

Durnan was also the last goalie to serve as an NHL team captain. His many journeys to discuss issues with referees prompted the league to change its rules and prohibit goalies from being captain.

Steadfastly competitive, he nonetheless spent his career wondering whether injury or his mounting inability to take the pressure of his position would make every season, every game, his last.

"I figure hockey is a one-year career," he once told an interviewer. "I figure I may be fired next week, or I may decide to quit the week after. In that way, I gear myself for shock. If it doesn't come, so much the better. I carry on the best I can."

Durnan knew carrying one goalie, the standard practice of his day, put an unbearable strain on netminders. Still, he hated the idea of giving up his position.

"All I ever wanted to do was stay in the nets, no matter how I was playing," he said after his career was over. "In my day, I didn't even want the practice goalie in the same city. I guess (Canadiens' coach) Dick Irvin wrapped it up best when he said, 'When a star is injured or rested, another star is born.' Get it?"

Finally, after suffering a severe gash in his head from an opponent's skate during the 1950 playoffs, Durnan left the ice and didn't come back. Age and the rigors of

his position had finally outdistanced his desire to play.

"My nerves are shot and I know it," Durnan said. "It got so bad that I couldn't sleep the night before a game. I couldn't even keep my meals down. I felt that nothing was worth that kind of agony."

Durnan spent his post-NHL life in sales and promotions for brewing companies.

In 1972, he had been feeling poorly for months but stubbornly refused to see a doctor. Death came in the form of a stroke on Oct. 31, only two weeks after Broda, a frequent companion at Toronto area racetracks, died of a heart attack.

He was eulogized as "an easy-going, quietly humorous man who never seemed to realize how good he was at sports or how welcome he was to any assemblage."

True Believer In Own Powers

P atrick Roy became one of the NHL's greatest goalies by recognizing success as his birthright. Roy, after all, is a name fit for a King.

"You know," he told his friend, Pierre Turgeon, the day of his trade from the Montreal Canadiens to the Colorado Avalanche, "I'm going to win the Stanley Cup." Six months later, Roy made himself a prophet.

Born to a francophone father and an anglophone mother in the Quebec City suburb of Ste.-Foy, Roy was blessed with athletic bloodlines. His mother was a nationally ranked synchronized swimmer, his father a superb tennis player and amateur ballplayer.

But more than genetics separated Roy from the pack. From the outset, he displayed an unflagging belief in himself. Despite giving up an average of 5.32 goals per game with a bad Granby Bisons team from 1982-85, Roy escaped the Quebec Junior Hockey League with his confidence intact.

"I learned to deal with the frustrations of losing ," Roy would say later. "Now I appreciate more the enjoyment of winning."

Following his third junior season, Roy was sent to the American League's Sherbrooke Canadiens to witness the pro life as a spectator and third-string goaltender. But he impressed Sherbrooke coach Pierre Creamer, who went with a gut instinct and played the 19-year-old Roy in

the post-season despite only one full game of professional experience. Roy went 10-3 and led Sherbrooke to the Calder

PATRICK ROY	1985-present	
Born: Oct. 5, 1965 Quebec City, Que.		
Teams: Montreal, Colorado		
NHL	Regular	Playoffs
Seasons	13	12
Games	717	160
W-L-T	380-224-87	99-59
W Pct.	.591	.619
GAA	2.69	2.38
Shutouts	41	11
All-Star: 5 (First-3, Second-2)		
Trophies: 5 (Smythe-2, Vezina-3)		
Stanley Cup Championships		3

Cup. The legend had been born. When incumbent Steve Penney stumbled in the Montreal goal, the 21-year-old Roy earned the first-string job and after a respectable regular season, backstopped the Canadiens to their 1986 Cup victory with a memorable playoff goaltending performance. It earned him his first of two Conn Smythe awards.

"When I'm in the net, I feel I can stop all the shots," Roy said, with characteristic candor that post-season. "Some nights, I make some saves that I don't even see. It's great."

With Roy, the Canadiens were able to consistently contend despite the erratic talent level of the team in front of him. He lifted Montreal to the Stanley Cup final again in 1989 and delivered a scintillating playoff run in 1993, winning the Stanley Cup and lifting the Habs to 10 straight sudden-death overtime victories.

In the homestretch of that run came a defining Roy moment: he smothered a dangerous scoring chance in the final against Los Angeles, looked toward Los Angeles forward Tomas Sandstrom, smiled and winked.

"I knew Sandstrom was taking lots of shots, but not getting anything," Roy said. "And I knew he wasn't going to beat me."

It was a typical Roy gesture, cocksure and laced with bravado but also delivered for effect. Roy might seem flashy, but his is a game built not so much on reflex as a

magnificent grasp of technique. Behind the snippets of trash talk and showmanship, a craftsman has always toiled.

Patrick-mania peaked in 1993-94 when he returned to backstop the Canadiens only a few days after having his appendix removed. But even he could not overcome an often patchwork lineup and the Canadiens lost in the first round of the playoffs.

If being a member of Canadiens' hockey royalty suited Roy, his exalted status did not suit the Habs. In December of 1995, Roy, unhappy with coach Mario Tremblay, confronted team president Ronald Corey behind the Canadiens' bench during a blowout loss to the Red Wings. Four days later, Roy was shipped to Colorado.

He is credited with influencing an entire generation of goalies in Quebec who saw Roy as the Canadiens' most celebrated player and aspired to become puckstoppers rather than goal-scorers. His style of play, dropping to the ice more than convention dictated, has influenced goalies everywhere.

Roy brought his old presence to his new hockey home. The Avalanche stormed to the franchise's first-ever Stanley Cup victory and he padded his reputation as the era's preeminent money goaltender by fashioning a 2.10 goals against average.

Roy's total of 99 post-season wins is the highest ever and he also owns the career marks for playoff games and post-season minutes.

The swagger has always been backed up by the stats and he continues to build a formidable case for inclusion in the all-time NHL netminding elite. "He's right up there with the select few, guys like Gretzky and Messier," said former Avalanche coach Marc Crawford. "He's motivated to be the best goalie of all-time."

In fact, Roy's ambition is to play at least until he passes Terry Sawchuk's all-time leading win total–447. Roy entered 1998-99 just 67 victories away, about two seasons' work for him.

Here's Looking At You, Kid

Charlie Conacher was a Toronto Maple Leafs' hockey legend minted and forged in hard times.

Conacher was the driving force behind hockey's first superstar unit, the 'Kid Line.'

A dominant, aggressive player, he led or held a share of the league lead in goal-scoring five times and lifted a fledgling Toronto team and its followers out of the grey of the Depression.

"I was born in one of Toronto's high-class slums," said Conacher, one of 10 children. "We didn't have a pretzel, we didn't have enough money to buy toothpaste."

Conacher did have a rich athletic pedigree. His brother, Lionel, would become a famous football, hockey, baseball and lacrosse star and Canada's athlete of the first half-century.

Charlie was 15 and a poor skater when his brother broke into the NHL with the Pittsburgh Pirates in 1925-26.

By then, Charlie was already through with school and a regular star of a daily game among the jobless in Toronto's Jesse Ketchum park.

It was known as the Pogie Hockey League and, inspired by the rise of his brother to the NHL, Charlie was determined to shine. "I worked on my skating until I thought my legs would drop off,"

Conacher once told a friend. Conacher became a star with the junior and senior Marlboros and scored 20 goals in 38 games as a Maple Leafs' rookie in 1929-30.

Midway through that season, Conacher was paired with Joe Primeau, an elegant 23-year-old center, and 18-year-old left winger Harvey 'Busher' Jackson. The 'Kid Line' would pile up more than 850 points over seven seasons. Born only a few months after the stock market crash, its members came to symbolize the elements of success in a time of widespread failure. Primeau was dignified and gentlemanly. Jackson was clever and opportunistic. Conacher, determination piled six-foot-one inches high, was the owner of the hardest shot in the league. A five-time all-star, the 'Bomber' delivered four seasons of more than 30 goals.

"The Kid Line offered relief from the sorrow and the desperation a world-wide depression had created," wrote Toronto Star columnist Milt Dunnell. "If three young men could come off the ponds, the open-air rinks and the frozen creeks to command international attention, there was hope for the man whose modest ambition was to find a job."

He was the hometown boy who made good, the roustabout sportsman who drove a cream-colored sports coupe around Toronto. During a playful argument with roommate Baldy Cotton, Conacher

Nat Turofsky/HHOF

100

held him out a seventh-floor hotel window until Cotton, who was deathly afraid of heights, conceded the point.

Once, he tied and gagged King Clancy in his hotel room. Had general manager Frank Selke not heard Clancy's muffled shouts while passing his door, he would never have made the game that night.

Injuries would drastically hamper Conn Smythe's 'Big Blue Bomber'. By his mid-twenties Conacher would be hurt more often than not, mostly with wrist and knee problems.

He broke into goal-scoring double figures only once in his last five years in the league and was through at 31.

By then, he had forged the foundations of a successful business. The kid from the wrong side of the tracks had long since made it good when he died of throat cancer Dec. 30, 1967 at 57.

"Yes, the fondest memories I have of Charlie were the ones that found us scrounging apples off other people's trees or getting a freshly-baked loaf of bread from Canada Bread," wrote longtime friend Red Burnett of the Toronto Star.

"We'd dig out the doughy center, pack the cavity with butter and what a treat. There were crap and card games in the park, pick-up sides, battles with gangs from other parks, all of it valuable in learning the art of survival.

"That was my Conacher, leader and champion of the poor sweats who knew what it was to be hungry and without a dime."

CHARLIE CONACHER		1929-41
Born: Dec. 10, 1909 Toronto		
Teams: Toronto, Detroit, Americans		
NHL	Regular	Playoffs
Seasons	12	9
Games	459	49
Goals	225	17
Assists	173	18
Points	398	35
Penalties	523	49
All-Star: 5 (First-3, Second-2)		
Trophies: 2 (Ross-2)		
Stanley Cup Championships		1

Singular Talent Sets Him Apart

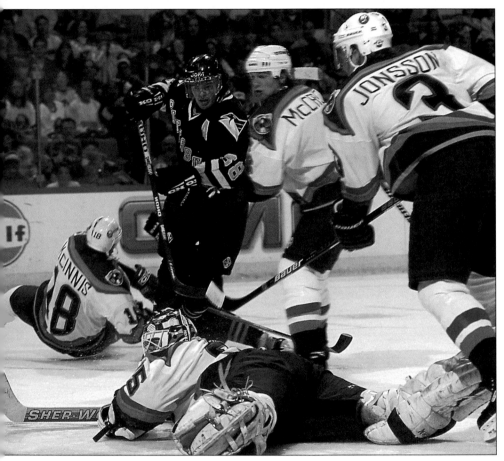

Buried deep inside the body of the man, the joy of the boy remains intact; these are the crowning days of the manchild the hockey world knows as Jaromir Jagr.

Mario Lemieux is ensconced in a plush retirement. Jagr, nicknamed 'Mario Jr.' because it's an anagram for his first name, has officially become the nucleus of the Pittsburgh Penguins, a star in apex.

He arrived in the NHL in 1990, flashing flowing locks, a foreign number (his 68 commemorates the year of the Soviet invasion of his native Czechoslovakia) and staggering talent.

From his first day in the league, Jagr was one of its most arresting players, a sculpted 6-foot-2, 216-pound hockey-playing pterodactyl who could weave past or over defensemen at will.

Not even the magnificent Lemieux delivered the goal-scoring esthetics Jagr turned in virtually every night.

After taking the measure of the league in his first four seasons, Jagr claimed the scoring title in 1994-95 and followed that with a 62-goal, 149-point encore in 1995-96. He established NHL marks for assists (87) and points by a right winger that memorable season.

While his game is stylish and Euro-flashy, his values are of the Original Six. Unlike Lemieux, Jagr will not dive to earn a penalty. He delivers goal-scoring volume with value-added degrees of difficulty. He plays hurt and is impossible to intimidate.

But he is 26 and soon, if he doesn't already, will have more money than he could ever spend.

One day the desire to perform will ebb, some of the gratification he finds on the ice will come to him in the form of a wife or child or another element of life.

The man-child will be a man, as much provider as performer and, like it became for Lemieux, there will be few, if any, mountains worth climbing.

Jagr has already won two Stanley Cups–the second of which he played a huge role–which pre-empts the familiar story line of a career spent in search of a championship.

He has thrived in the post-season and delivered when it counted, most prominently burying the New York Rangers and Boston Bruins in the playoffs in 1992 when Lemieux was felled by an Adam Graves slash.

He has no need to search for mentors. The late Bob Johnson, the Penguins' coach when Jagr arrived in 1990, remains a father figure whose memory will never diminish. "He will always be the number one coach to me," Jagr has said.

He has spent time in the company of the world's greatest player and learned. "I always watch him," Jagr said of Lemieux. "If I don't know something I just watch him. I can learn so much from him in practice and then I try those things in a game."

So are the legions of fans who have watched him. In an era of dump-and-chase, when the game's artistry has been replaced by vandals spray-painting the game with clutch-and-grab tactics, Jagr unfurls highlight-reel goals nightly. He was the only player last season to crack the century mark in points with 102, the lowest full-season total since Stan Mikita's 87 points in 1966-67.

In an increasingly corporate, buttoned-down NHL, his game flows as dramatically and naturally as his trademark locks.

"The comparable player is Frank Mahovlich," Scotty Bowman once said. "When Frank had full speed ahead and he had the defenseman backing off at the line, he could go inside or outside. He had that great reach. Both players could control the puck so well."

When healthy, Jagr is nothing if not consistent, delivering goals game in and game out, not in unpredictable bunches. All this has come through an unvarnished love of playing, of reaching a little further, but it likely won't last forever. The residue of money permeates the NHL.

Jagr revels in the luxury his artistry has wrought, but somehow the art remains in volume and in excellence, untainted. "To him," said his longtime linemate Ron Francis, "it's still pure."

As long as it remains that way, Jagr will remain among the league's most bankable and charismatic stars. But be warned, someday the manchild will cut his hair and grow up like everyone else.

JAROMIR JAGR	1990-present	
Born: Feb. 15, 1972 Kladno, Czech.		
Teams: Pittsburgh		
NHL	**Regular**	**Playoffs**
Seasons	8	8
Games	581	104
Goals	301	50
Assists	434	57
Points	735	107
Penalties	435	81
All-Star: 4 (First-3, Second-1)		
Trophies: 2 (Ross-2)		
Stanley Cup Championships		2

Steve Babineau/SA

Little Big Man Super Scorer

His was a Hall-of-Fame, if not glory-filled career shaped by two choices. One was made for him, the other Marcel Dionne made himself.

Dionne was the second player chosen in the 1971 amateur draft, one spot behind the Montreal Canadiens' Guy Lafleur, and the penalty for finishing as runner-up would be steep.

Dionne's home would be on the other side of the hockey universe from Montreal with a once-proud team rendered moribund by administrative dry rot: the Detroit Red Wings.

Initially, Dionne, the son of a Drummondville Que., steel mill foreman, seemed a good fit for working class Detroit. Dionne, not Lafleur, would set the new points standard for rookies the following season, but his four seasons in Detroit would be largely miserable.

When his contract expired, Dionne became the first high-profile free agent to sign with another team. The Los Angeles Kings were willing to come up with $1.5 million over five years and Dionne jumped into a hockey wasteland.

But the Kings spent the first several years of Dionne's tenure foolishly unloading high draft choices in lopsided deals. The difference between playing in Los Angeles and Detroit turned out to be the weather, not the standings—although there had been cause for sunny optimism. The Kings recorded their all-time best mark in 1974-75, the season before Dionne's arrival.

"Back then, we had guys like Butch Goring, Rogie Vachon and me and I thought the Kings would build around that," Dionne said. "It didn't take long before I realized I had entered the exact same situation I had left in Detroit."

Although he was a choppy skater, and he stood only 5-foot-8, Dionne was a remarkable talent. He could take or give a pass flawlessly on his forehand and backhand and he was solid on his skates.

The centerpiece of the 'Triple Crown Line' with Dave Taylor and Charlie Simmer, Dionne recorded six 50-goal seasons in seven seasons, reached 100 points eight times and won his sole scoring title in 1979-80. He collected the Art Ross Trophy that season because he scored more goals than Wayne Gretzky (53-51), who also finished with 137 points.

As the best player on a floundering franchise, Dionne would endure a career-long inquisition that his were singular and therefore selfish talents. The Kings posted only four winning seasons in the 12 years in which Dionne toiled there and won just three of 12 playoff series.

"Some critics have said that all I've ever cared about was scoring my points," Dionne once said. "Some people have called me moody because I didn't kiss their butt and some people have said I was the biggest problem with the Kings. But I don't like to lose, no matter how I play personally."

Dionne provoked ample discussion. For every critic there was a supporter.

"He's become an all-around star," Scotty Bowman said of Dionne in his prime. "He has to rank right up there with the best small men who ever played the game, such as Henri Richard and Dave Keon and Stan Mikita. He can play for me, for any one, any time, any place."

Dionne was 35 when the Kings traded him to the New York Rangers in 1987. Although the Rangers were better than the Kings, he had gone from a team which hadn't won a Cup in 19 years to one that hadn't won in 46.

Dionne would retire at 37 as the third-highest point-scorer in NHL history and he would be critical of the league's accent on goonism until his final days as a player. But while Lafleur would enjoy five championships, the man chosen one spot behind would become one of the most talented players never to sip from the Stanley Cup. "I was born to be in the pack, to be second best," Dionne said. "But I know in my own mind what I have done."

MARCEL DIONNE		1971-89
Born: Aug. 3, 1951 Drummondville, Que.		
Teams: Detroit, Los Angeles, Rangers		
NHL	Regular	Playoffs
Seasons	18	9
Games	1,348	49
Goals	731	21
Assists	1,040	24
Points	1,771	45
Penalties	600	17
All-Star: 3 (First-2, Second-1)		
Trophies: 1 (Ross-1)		
Stanley Cup Championships		0

Bruce Bennett/BBS

Setting NHL's Goal Standard

They called him 'Phantom' Joe Malone and a phantom he remains.

There is no mental image of him, no archival footage, only a few black and white prints and the irrefutable footprint of his greatness in the NHL record book.

Highest goals-per-game average, one season: Joe Malone, Montreal Canadiens, 1917-1918, 44 goals in 20 games. 2.20 goals per game. Most goals one game: seven, Joe Malone, Quebec Bulldogs, Jan. 31, 1920. Bulldogs 10, Toronto St. Pats' 6.

These are the last and most lasting traces of Joe Malone, records rendered untouchable not just by the greatness of the player, but also by the player's place in history.

Malone, who died in Quebec City, May 15, 1969, knew as much. "I'm getting so many calls about my scoring records," an exasperated Malone told The Hockey News a few months before his death.

"I'm naturally proud of them, but they belong in the past. It's not fair to compare the players from my era to the Mahovlichs and Richards."

When Malone began playing hockey, the game still employed a rover and forward passing was prohibited for players on offense.

Even when he turned pro, substitution was an afterthought and star players played every minute of every game.

"We didn't go up and down the rink like they do now," Malone said. "Today's game is much faster. We'd hustle when opportunities presented themselves, but the rest of the time, we'd loaf. At least I did. It was the only way you could go the entire 60 minutes."

Malone and Newsy Lalonde were the NHL's best offensive players when the National Hockey Association, a forerunner to the NHL, folded in 1917. Malone was picked up by the Canadiens, who moved him to Lalonde's left and installed Didier Pitre, another eventual Hall of Famer, on the right side.

Malone, then 26, celebrated the move with five goals in the Canadiens' season opener and a hat trick in his second contest. He was a dominating stickhandler and a superior skater, but his greatest asset was his hockey instinct. "I didn't have the hardest shot in the world," he said, "but I was where the puck was going most of the time."

Malone would play only 20 of the 22 games the Canadiens scheduled in that NHL's first season. "I missed one game because the arena of the Montreal Wanderers burnt down," he said once. "I missed another for reasons I never could remember, either I was hurt or drunk. I can't remember which."

Three years later, Malone, then with the

Quebec Bulldogs, skated through minus 20-degree temperatures to record the NHL's first and only seven-goal game against Toronto St. Patrick's in a half-full Quebec Coliseum. Malone had scored eight goals once and seven three times, all in NHA games.

A toolmaker by trade, Joe Malone never made more than $2,000 a year playing hockey.

He won four NHA-NHL scoring titles, and played out the string in a second engagement with the Canadiens in 1923-24 at 33.

"I took a look at a kid in our training camp in Grimsby, Ont., and I knew right then I was headed for the easy chair," Malone told The Hockey News, "He was Howie Morenz and in practice, he moved past me so fast, I thought I was standing still."

But Joe Malone had done his part. He finished with 146 goals and 21 assists, good for 167 points. That total, accrued over 125 games, was the best in the league's short history.

In a different time, Malone's feats may have earned him a more lasting place.

"Joe might have been the most prolific scorer of all-time if they had played more games in those days," said Frank Selke, the former Canadiens executive who saw Malone as a young pro.

The game would go much faster still, but the first toddler steps and a place in the record book that bears it out, will always belong to Joe Malone.

JOE MALONE		1917-24
Born: Feb. 28, 1890 Sillery, Que.		
Teams: Montreal, Quebec, Hamilton		
NHL	**Regular**	**Playoffs**
Seasons	7	3
Games	125	9
Goals	146	5
Assists	21	0
Points	167	5
Penalties	35	0
All-Star: 0		
Trophies: 2 (Ross-2)		
Stanley Cup Championships		1

Warrior's Credo: Play To Win

Hockey is a game built upon two poles. Every night, glorious and joyful skill abuts brutality and intimidation.

On the sparsely populated median between the two you will find Chris Chelios. Chelios and Ray Bourque have long jockeyed as the dominant all-round defensemen of their era, but if Bourque made beating the Boston Bruins difficult, Chelios made surviving a date with the Chicago Blackhawks an ordeal.

A veteran of 15 NHL campaigns, Chelios has already accumulated more than 2,100 penalty minutes, a total sentence 500 minutes longer than that racked up by Gordie Howe over almost twice as many years in the NHL. Chelios' superb instincts, strong skating and top-drawer offensive gifts meant he could have been a Norris Trophy candidate without repeatedly bloodying his nose. He became a three-time Norris winner by continually bloodying the opposition's.

"He's just a lousy person," longtime foe Brian Propp once said. "He never goes after any tough guys. He just goes after guys who don't fight when no one else who will (fight) is on the ice."

"Obviously he's got good skills," then-Bruin Randy Burridge said of Chelios, "but he'll backstab you any time he gets the chance."

No one will dispute Chelios' will to

win. "A lot of people fight for the puck," ESPN analyst Bill Clement once observed. "Chris plays like he's fighting for his life."

"You have to know him" said veteran NHLer Luc Robitaille. "Telling Chris Chelios he can't play hockey is like cut-

ting off his arm. Nobody wants to play more than him." That drive sometimes gets the better of Chelios.

When he saw his chance to play blocked by the owners' lockout of 1994, he did what he always does. He lashed out.

"If I was Gary Bettman I'd be worried about my family," Chelios said during the dog days of the lockout. "I'd be worried about my well-being now. Some crazed fans or even a player, who knows, they might take matters into their own hands and figure they get him out of the way and things might get settled."

Chelios quickly and profusely apologized for his words, but his friends understood.

"Chris wears his heart on his sleeve," said his agent Tom Reich. The dichotomy between good and bad bathes Chelios. The same intimidator who wields his stick like a scythe is well-known for his charitable activities in Chicago. His teammates, both past and present, speak of a loyal and generous man.

"I've walked with him down Ste. Catherine Street and he has stopped to give a bum five dollars or taken him into a diner to buy him lunch," said former Montreal Canadiens' teammate Tom Kurvers. "He has a huge heart."

Chelios, a Chicago native, used big-city drive to carve out a career. As a teen, he was twice cut from junior teams

in Canada. After one failed stint he had to borrow money from strangers to get to San Diego from a Detroit bus station. But Chelios, a two-time Western Collegiate all-star with the Wisconsin Badgers, grew and added 40 pounds in his late teens, landed a spot in the U.S. Olympic program and eventually won a Norris Trophy and a Stanley Cup with the Canadiens.

Traded to Chicago in a one-sided deal for Denis Savard in 1990, Chelios continued to blossom with the Hawks and entrenched his standing as the most menacing skilled defenseman of his time. He has collected more than 60 points seven times and earned more than 100 penalty minutes 11 times.

A six-time all-star, Chelios is a gifted instinctual player. "Chris Chelios is the best defenseman in the league," Mighty Ducks of Anaheim star Paul Kariya once said. "He gives no gap (between himself and the oncoming forward). When you're going forward, most defensemen go

back, but it seems like he's going forward and back at the same time. There's always pressure on the puck."

During the inaugural World Cup tournament, Team USA wanted Chelios so badly he was allowed to join the team on his own schedule. He was at his best playing for his country, foiling Team Canada attacks when it counted most and the U.S. skated off with the Cup and bragging rights over Canada.

Good and bad remain the Alpha and the Omega for Chris Chelios and, while tempered by age, he said he will remain the same player until his final stride.

"As long as my teammates and coaches are happy with me, that's all that matters," Chelios said. "I'm not going to change."

CHRIS CHELIOS	1984-present	
Born: Jan. 25, 1962 Chicago		
Teams: Montreal, Chicago		
NHL	Regular	Playoffs
Seasons	15	14
Games	1,001	163
Goals	156	28
Assists	606	88
Points	762	116
Penalties	2,189	319
All-Star: 6 (First-4, Second-2)		
Trophies: 3 (Norris-3)		
Stanley Cup Championships	1	

Hallmarks Were Power, Precision

First the name, then the man. Born in Newmarket, north of Toronto, Dit Clapper was christened Aubrey Victor. His parents were determined to call him Vic, "but I couldn't say Vic," Clapper once recalled. "I'd lisp my name and it came out Dit."

Dit Clapper was the NHL's most admirable star during the time between the final days of Howie Morenz to the starburst that was Maurice Richard. Above all, he was a powerful man, 6-foot-2, 200 pounds, slow to anger, but hellish to deal with when stirred. One of the few ways to provoke him was to mess his hair, which he combed neatly, the part just a little off center.

When Clapper broke into the NHL with the Boston Bruins in 1927, the Detroit Red Wings, Chicago Black Hawks and New York Rangers were in their second seasons. In his third season, big Dit Clapper scored 41 goals in 44 games. His game was powerful and precise. "He was so very good in so many ways, but he stood out for one thing," said Bobby Bauer, a Bruins star on the 'Kraut Line.' "He made so few mistakes."

As the league's first 20-year player, Clapper seemed as constant as time itself and was capable of winning kindness, even toward opponents. When a young, injury-prone Maurice Richard showed a habit of bursting through center ice with his head down, Clapper wrapped his huge arms around the Rocket and told him, "Keep your head up in this league, kid."

A quarter-century after Clapper retired, sportswriter Dick Beddoes noted this conversation between sportswriters describing a prominent Boston player: "He's no Clapper," said the writer, "but he's a hell of a guy."

Rousing Clapper and living to tell the tale became a badge of honor. In one of his rare fights, Clapper hit bantamweight Rabbit McVeigh of the New York Americans three times on the chin. After the fight, McVeigh skated to manager Red Dutton and chortled "Gee, can I take it?"

Clapper was so deeply respected inside the game that when he punched referee and eventual league president Clarence Campbell during a fracas, he was suspended for only a game. Campbell told the media that he, not Clapper, was responsible for the incident because he called the Boston star a name.

After 11 years up front—during which Clapper earned two berths on the second all-star team as a right winger—he moved to defense to succeed Eddie Shore and added nine years along the blueline. No players, save Red Kelly and Mark Howe, would navigate the position change as smoothly as Clapper, who would earn three first team and one second team all-star selections after the switch. He is the only player to be named an all-star at defense and forward.

Clapper was a player-coach for the Bruins for his final two NHL seasons before moving behind the bench in civilian clothes. He was inducted into the Hall of Fame the day after he retired. But coaching didn't agree with him. At the Bruins' 1949 break-up banquet, he stunned his audience by announcing he was quitting. "Being a coach is a lousy job," he said. "I couldn't abuse these players. They're my friends."

He was 42 when he moved to Peterborough, Ont., and began operating a sporting goods store. But his popularity in Boston would remain undiminished by time. In 1983, when Bruins' general manager Harry Sinden suggested taking Clapper's number 5 out of retirement and assigning it to Guy Lapointe, he touched off a firestorm of criticism, even though Clapper had been dead for five years. Clapper would suffer his first stroke at 65 and be confined to a wheelchair for the final five years of his life. He died Jan. 21, 1978.

During his lengthy reign, Clapper stood for strength and resilience. When a young Gordie Howe was asked his goal, he said he wanted to last 20 years, "just like Clapper."

DIT CLAPPER		1927-47
Born: Feb. 9, 1907 Newmarket, Ont.		
Teams: Boston		
NHL	Regular	Playoffs
Seasons	20	16
Games	833	82
Goals	228	13
Assists	246	17
Points	474	30
Penalties	462	50
All-Star: 6 (First-3, Second-3)		
Trophies: 0		
Stanley Cup Championships		3

Banging The Drum For Boom Boom

In the blush of strong play or another Montreal Canadiens' victory, Bernie Geoffrion would commandeer any podium, be it a bench, a trainer's table or a nightclub stage, and unveil a strong, polished singing voice. He was a one-of-a-kind personality and after his playing days, Geoffrion would become a folk hero as much for his accent and humor, first as coach of the Atlanta Flames and then as pitchman for Lite beer.

But when he did not score, there was only a leaden silence in Bernie Geoffrion. In those moments, the only thing his wife could do with him was push him into an easy chair and play the recordings of his favorite singer, the famous Mario Lanza.

Behind Geoffrion's bigger-than-life persona, lay a depth of feeling built to the very same scale. "When goals don't come, there is no song," he once told a reporter. "That is a mistake, I know, but how can I sing when I am not happy?"

Geoffrion's story is about mountainous achievement, both personal and professional, mined with sadness and disappointment.

The fine singing voice that earned him an appearance on a Canadian variety show was ruined by a wayward shot against Boston that damaged his throat and put him in hospital for 22 days.

He was a glorious star in a firmament already crowded with them, a pretender when he fell short of outstripping Maurice Richard and Jean Beliveau and a usurper when he did.

That Geoffrion was a great player is beyond dispute. The nicknames 'Boom Boom' and 'Boomer' were homages to the sound his tremendous shot made when it found the Forum boards. He is credited with pioneering the slapshot and, decades later, there is no doubt the sound of Boom Boom's shot was heard around the hockey world.

"When Maurice Richard hangs up his skates, that youngster will take over as the greatest player in the NHL," Canadiens' coach Dick Irvin said after watching Geoffrion break into the league. "He can score goals with the best in the league and he has got a shot that rates above Charlie Conacher's."

Geoffrion was the rookie of the year in 1951-52 and would become the first player since Richard to score 50 goals when he reached the half-century mark in 1960-61. It took a Herculean effort; Geoffrion scored

BERNIE GEOFFRION		1950-68
Born: Feb. 16, 1931 Montreal		
Teams: Montreal, Rangers		
NHL	**Regular**	**Playoffs**
Seasons	16	16
Games	883	132
Goals	393	58
Assists	429	60
Points	822	118
Penalties	689	88
All-Star: 3 (First-1, Second-2)		
Trophies: 4 (Hart-1, Ross-2, Calder-1)		
Stanley Cup Championships		6

Hockey Hall of Fame

23 goals in his last 26 games to reach the standard. Geoffrion played only 64 games of a 70-game schedule.

Geoffrion was an intense competitor, who would suffer gruesome injuries and invariably return ahead of schedule. In 1958, he collapsed during a Canadiens' practice and needed emergency stomach surgery to survive. Naturally, he was back in time for the playoffs. In 1961, Geoffrion insisted Doug Harvey cut a cast off his leg so he could play in the playoff semifinals against the Chicago Black Hawks.

By the mid-1960s, only Howe and Richard had more career goals than Geoffrion. He won the Hart Trophy in his 50-goal year, earned two scoring championships and six Stanley Cups.

In 1955, Geoffrion won his first points title by passing Richard, who had been suspended for striking an official. Canadiens' fans, incensed over Richard's suspension by NHL president Clarence Campbell, booed their young star and showered threats on him. In what should have been his greatest professional moment, Geoffrion was accorded police protection. The scoring title still didn't earn him first team all-star status. That, too, went to Richard. "Usually it is not too much to expect to be on the first team when you have scored more points than anyone else," Geoffrion said.

When Richard retired, first Doug Harvey, then Jean Beliveau was elected team captain, even though he was not one of three assistants from the previous year. Geoffrion, who had worn the A, was devastated by the decision to go with Beliveau.

"If I did not have the desire, if I wasn't fit to lead, would I have come back so often from injuries?" asked Geoffrion. "There were many times when everybody told me to quit. My doctor told me to stop playing, but I came back."

He would come back one more time, emerging from retirement to play two seasons with the New York Rangers (1966-67 and 1967-68) before quitting as a player for good.

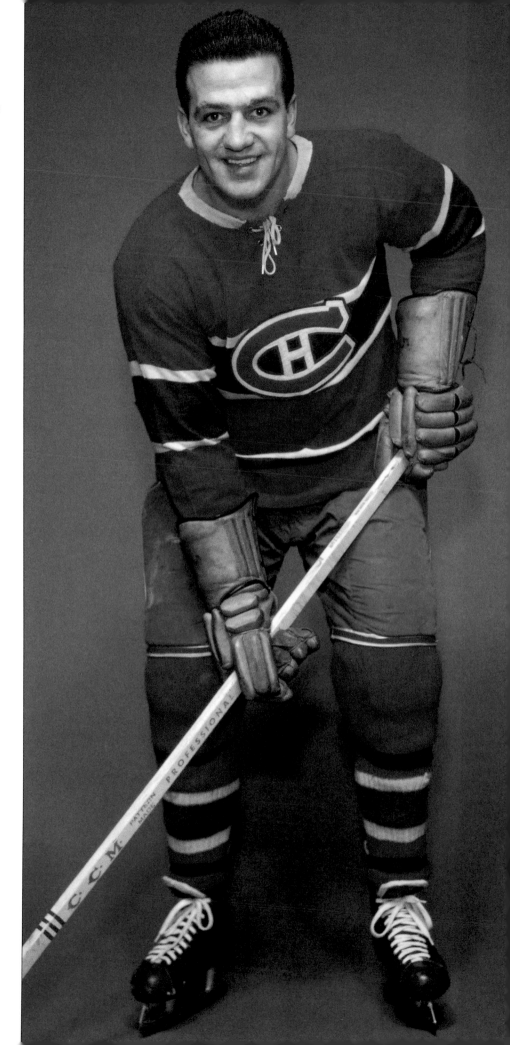

Strength Down The Middle

Death came in a moment that defined Tim Horton's life. He was killed en route to his real home from his adopted one on a night he once again defied the aging process.

The 44-year-old Buffalo Sabres' defenseman was driving to his Fort Erie, Ont. home from Maple Leaf Gardens when he

Listed at 5-foot-10, Horton was closer to 5-foot-8, yet he was the NHL's reigning strongman. But stories of his strength invariably mention his compassion. When the Boston Bruins' cocky rookie Derek Sanderson tried to fight Horton, the Toronto defender wrapped his arms around the upstart—in what was called the

'Horton Hug'—and convinced him never to issue the challenge again. "I had to try him once, but I heard a cracking sound and I figured it was my ribs cracking one by one," Sanderson said.

Horton exceeded 100 penalty minutes only once during his 22 full seasons in the NHL. "I like to play the body not the

went off the road Feb. 20, 1974 near St. Catharines. Despite missing the third period of the previous night's game because of an injury, Horton was named the third star.

He died a hockey player and a gentleman, one of the game's best defensemen and most peaceable personalities. "Horton's one weakness," said longtime Toronto Maple Leafs' coach Punch Imlach, "is that he hasn't got a mean bone in his body. If he had, they would have had to make a rule against him."

TIM HORTON		1952-74
Born: Jan. 12, 1930 Cochrane, Ont.		
Teams: Toronto, Rangers, Pittsburgh, Buffalo		
NHL	**Regular**	**Playoffs**
Seasons	22	17
Games	1,446	126
Goals	115	11
Assists	403	39
Points	518	50
Penalties	1,611	183
All-Star: 6 (First-3, Second-3)		
Trophies: 0		
Stanley Cup Championships		4

puck, but I don't really look for fights," he once explained.

He was tremendously efficient defensively. "You see the way he turns those forwards against the boards," said then Philadelphia Flyers' general manager Keith Allen. "He just pins them there. They're in a trap and they know it. Nobody coming down his side wants anything to do with him."

A solid offensive player with a devastating slapshot and a willingness to head to open ice, Horton was the most dominant

and complete Maple Leafs' defenseman ever. He hit double figures in goals three times during his career in the NHL.

"Game in and game out," said Norm Ullman, a teammate as well as an opponent, "Tim Horton has been the best defenseman in hockey over the past 15 years."

Twice, Horton was named runner-up for the Norris Trophy and he was named to the NHL all-star team six times, three times as a first team all-star. The 16 points he compiled in the 1961-62 Stanley Cup playoffs was a league record for defensemen.

Horton had been a Maple Leaf or in the system for 23 years when Toronto traded him to the New York Rangers in 1969-70. He would retire three times, but eventually the lure of the game and loyalty to a former teammate brought him back. After a season-and-a-half in New York, Horton signed with a Pittsburgh Penguins' team coached by former teammate Red Kelly.

Then Imlach came calling. Horton played one season and most of the next with the Sabres and remained one of the team's best players, despite his longstanding nearsightedness and advancing years. At the time of his death, he was the NHL's second-oldest player and telling friends he was finally ready to devote himself full-time to the Canadian-based coffee and donut chain that still bears his name.

"Maybe it's just a bad habit I've acquired," said Horton, when asked why he kept coming back. "I like to play hockey. And besides, I've got a lot of time ahead to sit behind a desk."

Straw That Stirred The Drink

It was a pre-game sight that provided infinite comfort to New York Rangers' coach Lester Patrick.

In the hubbub of the dressing room, he would spy his captain, Bill Cook, rubbing his palms against his hockey pants, rocking gently on his stool.

"He'd be a bundle of nerves, just aching to get at it and break the tension," Patrick said. "The placid player can be depended on for a safe, steady game, but for the kind of inspired hockey needed to win championships, I need the Bill Cooks. When it comes right down to the crunch, the other players will follow the Bill Cooks."

Today, he would be called a premier power forward, but before there was such a term there were two words to describe a gifted goal-scorer who delivered as much grit as he did polish. From his first days as a senior hockey player in Sault Ste. Marie, Ont., they called him 'Bad Bill' because of his rough play and, until the arrival of Maurice Richard, Cook reigned as the dominant right winger in the NHL. With his brother Bun, at left wing and Frank Boucher at center, Cook was the linchpin of the Rangers' vaunted 'A Line,' aka the 'Bread Line.'

broadcaster Foster Hewitt was asked if he had ever seen a comparable caliber of passing.

"There aren't many people around to remember, I guess, but the way the Russians play reminds me of the old New York Rangers, especially the line of Frank Boucher, and Bill and Bun Cook," Hewitt said. "If anything, they were a little better. It always seemed to me that they had the puck on a string."

The driving force behind the Rangers' Stanley Cup wins in 1928 and 1933, Bill Cook ruled the Broadway Blueshirts in a way even Patrick never could. The Rangers won the Stanley Cup in their second season, and although he was 30 when he arrived in New York, Cook would captain the team for 10 seasons.

"Lester really didn't bother us too much in life at any time," Cook once said. "Most of the substance that came out of getting any quality out of the team came from about three or four of us. We would try to bring out a little animal instinct of winning it, and it seemed to work."

Cook waded through the NHL version of warfare; he was one of the league's top fighters and had a legendary brawl with Nelson Crutchfield of the Montreal

"We had three lines on the old Rangers," remembers journeyman forward Murray Murdoch. "The third line was just happy to be there. The second line did as they were told and the first line did as they pleased."

In 1972, when the Soviet National Team was showcasing its astonishing skill level in the Summit Series, venerable Canadian

Canadiens in 1935. But Cook had seen the real thing. An artilleryman in World War I, he saw heavy action in some of the bloodiest battle zones in France before being commissioned to soft detail, training cavalry recruits in England. Cook chafed in Britain for two years and finally volunteered for active service, assisting in what would ultimately be a losing battle for the Royal Russian Army against the Bolsheviks. Cook would don a sheet and snowshoes and scout out Bolshevik positions for the infantry, double back and lend a hand with the shelling.

Discharged with military honors, he tried his hand as a pro in 1922 with the Saskatoon Sheiks of the old Western League. When the league disbanded at the end of 1925-26, Bill and Bun Cook were sold to the Rangers.

The Western League was at least the equal of the NHL and as if to prove that very point, Cook won the scoring title in his first year in New York. He led the league in scoring again in 1932-33 when he scored a league high 28 goals and added 22 assists. Cook would lead the NHL in goals three times.

When his playing career ended, Cook turned to coaching, first with Cleveland in the American League and later for the Rangers in the early 1950s, but he would earn only 34 wins in 117 NHL games.

In 1984, shortly before his death at 90, Bill Cook remained content. "We had," he said, "the most wonderful times of any hockey club."

BILL COOK		1926-37
Born: Oct. 9, 1895 Brantford, Ont.		
Teams: Rangers		
NHL	Regular	Playoffs
Seasons	11	9
Games	474	46
Goals	229	13
Assists	138	11
Points	367	24
Penalties	386	72
All-Star: 4 (First-3, Second-1)		
Trophies: 2 (Ross-2)		
Stanley Cup Championships		2

Substance More Than Style

Stonefaced, Johnny Bucyk watched them go, friends and teammates, one by one, sent packing back to real life. The Boston Bruins' all-time leader in games outplayed most of them and outlasted them all.

"It breaks your heart when a club lets your buddies go," Bucyk once told a writer. "But you can't be soft about it. It's a hard game and a hard life and you do the best you can."

Bucyk did the best he could for as long as he could and he was a champion on both counts. Twenty-one Boston seasons, 545 goals, both club records. Another mark, 1,436 games as a Bruin will fall under Ray Bourque's relentless assault.

Bucyk grew up poor in Edmonton. His father, Sam, was out of work for four years during the Depression and he died when John was 11. Pearl Bucyk worked picking potatoes for $1 a day and wrapped meat in a factory for 36 cents an hour to support the family.

"I used to wash the clothes in a big tub and then I would throw the water out into the backyard," she told an interviewer, "In the winter, it would freeze over and make a rink, a blue rink from the blue in the water. All the kids would be on the rink

and they would ask me to throw more rinse water out: 'Please Mrs. Bucyk, please throw some more water out.' "

John was big and athletic, but because of his family's poverty (he didn't get his own pair of skates until he was 13), he was a painfully slow skater. His minor hockey coach ordered him to skate between periods and arranged for figure skating lessons, done with a private coach through the summer so the other kids wouldn't find out. Still, when he began playing junior hockey for the Edmonton Oil Kings, he couldn't even cross over his right skate.

Blessed with good size, Bucyk willed himself into being an NHL player. "It's an old saying, but if you want something

badly enough, you'll get it," said Ken McCauley, one of Bucyk's minor hockey coaches. "Johnny Bucyk wanted it a little more than the next guy."

Bucyk made the NHL, but languished as a third-line left winger for two seasons after breaking in with the Detroit Red Wings in 1955. Still, his consistent improvement as a pro was impossible to ignore and when Wings' general manager Jack Adams decided to re-acquire Terry Sawchuk from Boston in 1957, Bucyk was the price he paid.

Boston meant a reunion with junior teammates Bronco Horvath and Vic Stasiuk. The 'Uke Line,' named for the Ukrainian background of all three, starred for six seasons in Boston, but even their stellar play could not lift the Bruins. Boston made the playoffs twice in Bucyk's first 10 years in Boston and 'Chief,' nicknamed for his dark looks, tasted defeat often and with unfailing reluctance.

The arrival of Bobby Orr and, soon after Phil Esposito, would change that. In 1967, at 32, Bucyk found himself on a winning club and posted his first 30-goal season. "Management had to weed out and trade off the guys who couldn't stop thinking like losers," said Derek Sanderson. "They had to have guys who think of winning and nothing else. The Chief always had that, never will lose it."

Bucyk won his first Cup two days before his 35th birthday and enjoyed his first 50-goal season a year later to become the oldest player ever to do so. Bucyk recorded seven 30-goal seasons after age 32.

While he went from one of the league's hardest hitters to being a two-time Lady Byng winner, the offensive element of his game never changed. Bucyk, 6-foot-1 and 215 pounds, operated within spitting distance of the crease. "Johnny Bucyk," wrote Toronto *Star* columnist Milt Dunnell "is as obvious as a goal post."

"I've thought of myself as a spear-carrier, not a star, really," Bucyk once said. "I'm not a glamour guy and I've just gone along getting what I could out of every game. It has added up."

So did the price he had to pay. Late in his career, Bucyk could not sleep on either side because of lingering damage from separated shoulders. A back injury made sleeping face up impossible, so Bucyk grabbed gulps of sleep from his stomach.

When his career ended at 43, Bucyk stood as the fourth-leading NHL goal-scorer and point-producer of all-time. The kid from Edmonton had proven again the race to the Hall of Fame goes not always to the fastest, but to the steadiest in body and heart.

JOHNNY BUCYK		1955-78
Born: May 12, 1935 Edmonton		
Teams: Detroit, Boston		
NHL	Regular	Playoffs
Seasons	23	14
Games	1,540	124
Goals	556	41
Assists	813	62
Points	1,369	103
Penalties	497	42
All-Star: 2 (First-1, Second-1)		
Trophies: 2 (Byng-2)		
Stanley Cup Championships		2

Zero Hero
Efficiency Expert

After hockey, little George Hainsworth remade himself into a municipal politician in Kitchener, Ont. He flourished as a fixer, the kind of careful, deliberate councillor who thrives in public service whenever the populace has the good sense to elect him.

He was that kind of man. Only 5-foot-5, Hainsworth stood out as the premier technician of his time. Because he was so small, Hainsworth learned to use every inch available to guard the net.

"He was," said Elmer Ferguson, the Montreal *Herald* hockey scribe, "almost mechanical in his perfection. He was completely devoid of expression in the course of a game. He did his duties with the absolute minimum of movement and utter apparent lack of effort. You could describe Little George's methods as being phlegmatic and frigid."

Despite breaking into the NHL as a 31-year-old rookie, Hainsworth would win three Vezina Trophies—including the first ever presented—and log 11 NHL campaigns, split between the Montreal Canadiens and Toronto Maple Leafs.

In his third season, Hainsworth surrendered just 43 goals in 44 games with the Canadiens and posted 22 shutouts. He blanked opponents 49 times in his first 132 NHL games and the Canadiens led the league in goals against all three seasons.

But like many methodical men, Hainsworth yearned to be a showstopper, the kind of flashy netminder that made

every save seem exciting. "I wish I could play like (flashy Black Hawks' goalie Charlie) Gardiner, the way he can put on a show," Hainsworth once told a writer. "But I can't play that way. The only way I can play is the way I can play."

Hainsworth was born in Toronto's Kew Beach in 1895, but his family moved to

Kitchener, where he distinguished himself as a gifted baseball and hockey player. Championships followed him throughout his amateur career and, after several seasons of professional play in Saskatoon, he pursued the lure of bigger money to Montreal in 1926 to succeed Georges Vezina, the great netminder who had been killed the previous season by pneumonia.

Hainsworth backstopped the Canadiens to Stanley Cups in 1930 and 1931, but after seven banner seasons, the Canadiens dispatched him to Toronto in 1933 for Lorne Chabot. Hainsworth spent three more seasons with the Leafs and split his final year between the Habs and Leafs before retiring. He shared the ice with the greatest stars of the pre-war era: Howie Morenz and Aurel Joliat in Montreal; Charlie Conacher, Joe Primeau and King Clancy in Toronto.

Gifted in everything but showmanship, Hainsworth's 94 career shutouts stood as the standard until Terry Sawchuk posted 103. His record of 22 shutouts in a season is likely unattainable. The last goalie to come within hailing distance of the mark was Tony Esposito, who racked up 15 shutouts in 1969-70.

Hainsworth retired with a 1.91 goals-against average. In 52 playoff games, he limited opponents to 1.93 goals per game and posted eight shutouts. He had a 5-0-1 mark and 0.75 goals-against average when the Canadiens won the 1930 Cup.

Despite his spectacularly solid play, he

never finished as a first or second team all-star. The practice of choosing all-stars began midway through Hainsworth's career.

The Black Hawks' Gardiner, Boston star Tiny Thompson and New York American Roy Worters were dominant in 1931 when the selection of all-star teams began.

Hainsworth lost just one game to injury over 11 seasons when he retired at 41. An electrician in the off-season, he went to work full time for an electronics firm before winning election as an alder-

GEORGE HAINSWORTH 1926-37		
Born: June 26, 1895 Toronto		
Teams: Montreal, Toronto		
NHL	Regular	Playoffs
Seasons	11	10
Games	465	52
W-L-T	246-145-74	21-26-5
W Pct.	.609	.471
GAA	1.91	1.93
Shutouts	94	8
All-Star: 0		
Trophies: 3 (Vezina-3)		
Stanley Cup Championships	2	

man in Kitchener. His most lasting achievement was his contribution to the construction of the main hockey arena in Kitchener, first known as the Kitchener Memorial Auditorium and now as the Dom Cardillo Arena, after a former mayor of the city.

On Oct. 9, 1950, Hainsworth was on his way home from visiting his son when the car he was driving collided with a small truck. The impact broke Hainsworth's ribs. At 57, hockey's Mechanical Man died of a pierced heart.

Explosive Force Shredded Foes

Timing was the one and only element of greatness to elude Gilbert Perreault. Had he been born a year earlier, Perreault would automatically have been the territorial property of the Montreal Canadiens, a teammate and eventual successor to his idol, Jean Beliveau, with all the attendant grooming and expectations.

But Gilbert Perreault, the youngest of six children and son of a railway engineer, was born in Victoriaville, Que., Nov. 13, 1950. Instead of assuming what had been the birthright of the Quebecois star, Perreault would become The Franchise, the Buffalo star around which undistinguished players and uncomprehending coaches would rotate.

Perreault's game was a startling combination of vision, powerful skating and shooting, and most of all, wondrous stickhandling. He won the Calder Trophy going away and set a rookie points record en route. "If anybody breaks these records," Phil Esposito said after his 76-goal, 152-point season in 1971, "it will be Gilbert Perreault."

As a child, Perreault preferred street hockey to playing on ice and didn't skate until he was eight. He learned to stickhandle watching Beliveau on television. But he kept the puck closer to his body than Beliveau, sacrificing reach for control. Despite his late start, he quickly developed a wide, powerful skating stride.

At 16, Perreault moved to Montreal and starred for two years with the Jr. Canadiens. His obvious skills made him the coveted prize of the NHL's two most recent expansion teams, the Sabres and Vancouver Canucks. Two spins of a wheel of fortune by NHL president Clarence Campbell and Perreault was Buffalo-bound.

In a poll of Buffalo fans, he would be remembered as the greatest athlete that city would accommodate. Perreault outdistanced O.J. Simpson, then the greatest rusher in National Football League history, as the best athlete to perform in Buffalo. But aside from some superb years between Rene Robert and

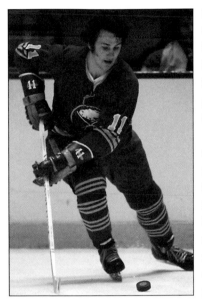

Rick Martin as the centerpiece of the 'French Connection' and the club's 1975 run to the Stanley Cup final, Perreault's tenure with the team would be diminished marginally by his inability to elevate the franchise to the ultimate prize. (The Sabres, though, did finish first or second eight times during his career.)

He was a superb stickhandler in the salad days of the dump and chase, an ephemeral player in an era dominated, first by the brute force and opportunism of the Philadelphia Flyers and the team-wide virtuosity of a powerhouse edition of the Canadiens. Perreault never challenged the 50-goal plateau and reached the 100-point barrier only twice, but he scored 30 or more goals 10 times and holds all major Buffalo team offensive records.

The Sabres' inability to break into the playoff elite would become an indictment of their star. Perreault was shy and soft-spoken. His personality and lack of team success were married into the idea that his lack of passion was holding him and the team back. "I was the team's big scorer and that's the guy who gets blamed when the team doesn't win," Perreault once said. "But it takes everyone on a team to win. People who think I didn't want to win very much just didn't know me."

Whether he did care enough was the subject of debate.

"Bert was a player who maybe didn't always want to be the greatest," conceded longtime teammate Craig Ramsay. "He was a very intense man," countered linemate Mike Foligno. "He had a lot of pride and always wanted to do well."

By the time Scotty Bowman had left Buffalo and the Edmonton Oilers returned offensive fireworks to the fore, Perreault was playing out his final days. Perreault had been born too early as well as too late, the era that followed would have suited him as well as the one that preceded him.

"If Perreault was 18 or 19 now," Flyers' general manager Bobby Clarke said in 1986, at the height of the NHL's run-and-gun era, "he'd blow this league apart."

GILBERT PERREAULT	1970-87	
Born: Nov. 13, 1950 Victoriaville, Que.		
Teams: Buffalo		
NHL	Regular	Playoffs
Seasons	17	11
Games	1,191	90
Goals	512	33
Assists	814	70
Points	1,326	103
Penalties	500	44
All-Star: 2 (Second-2)		
Trophies: 2 (Calder-1, Byng-1)		
Stanley Cup Championships	0	

Bruce Bennett/BBS

Slick (And Sick) Pivot Dominated

Max Bentley always said he felt worse than he looked. Trouble was, he looked like death warmed over.

He was just 5-foot-8 and a grey pallor enveloped his sickly 140 pounds. "This is the first time I've seen a walking ghost," Chicago Black Hawks' general manager Bill Tobin once remarked after seeing Bentley in particularly gaunt form.

In 1940, a year before Bentley landed in Chicago, the Montreal Canadiens, sure they had unearthed a star from the Saskatchewan soil, invited him to their training camp. The Canadiens' doctor soon uncovered what he believed to be evidence of a bum heart.

"This young man has a serious heart condition," the attending physician told the newspapers. "My advice is that he should go home and never again play hockey. If he doesn't take things easy, he will not last a year."

Bentley went back to Delisle, Sask., but after a few months figured that any fate was better than not playing. When he didn't die, he earned a tryout with the Hawks, largely on the recommendation of his brother Doug, a Chicago stalwart of the day. In his third season with the Hawks, Max Bentley broke through for 26 goals and 70 points. He not only looked like a ghost, he was every bit as difficult to collar.

With his brother on the left side and sniping Bill Mosienko on the right, Bentley

held the reins of the 'Pony Line.' A superb stickhandler, he would navigate the puck from his own end into enemy territory before delivering a perfect pass to a streaking teammate.

"My idea was to try to set up somebody," Bentley once said. "I'd beat two or three guys and then make a pass."

Bentley was pure finesse, right down to the slicked back hair he sported. He was called the 'Dipsy Doodling Dandy' and 'Dandy from Delisle.'

"Max was one of the very few players who could make a fantastic play while still going at full speed," said Boston Bruins' star Milt Schmidt. "We'd say before a game, 'Let's get a hold of Bentley and we'll win.' But we never could catch him."

When Wayne Gretzky broke into the league, oldtimers compared him most often to Max Bentley. Bentley said he considered that a great compliment, but "the difference is that Gretzky carries it from the blueline in, while I often took it in starting from behind my own net."

Gretzky and Bentley share a piece of NHL history. Each scored four goals in a single period, an NHL record. Red Berenson and Harvey Jackson also did it.

The youngest of 13 children, Max constantly complained of aches and pains–some real, some imagined–that ran the gamut from a dry throat to burning eyes to an upset stomach. At one time or another he convinced himself he had ulcers, kidney trouble, diabetes and cancer of the hip. The Bentley boys regularly complained to each other.

"If Doug had the flu, Max had the flu and a bad knee," said longtime NHL executive Emile Francis. "It never seemed to stop. I remember one day when Max listed his ailments and Doug listed his, which were just a little more severe than his brother's. Finally, Max said with a little smile, 'Geez Doug, just once let me be the sickest.' "

Nat Turofsky/HHOF

Bentley won a Lady Byng and two scoring championships with the Hawks, but Chicago was convinced they needed more depth and shipped the 27-year-old Bentley to the Toronto Maple Leafs for five serviceable bodies in November of 1947. Only the trade of Phil Esposito to Boston 30 years later would eclipse the Bentley deal as the worst in Black Hawks' history. The Hawks finished in the cellar eight of the next 10 seasons.

In Toronto, Bentley would thrive as the flashy counterpoint to the Leafs' rugged captain Ted Kennedy. As Bentley aged, his standing as the team's leading hypochondriac grew beyond challenge, but the worse he seemed to feel, the better he would play. "Max is dying," Maple Leafs'

MAX BENTLEY		1940-54
Born: March 1, 1920 Delisle, Sask.		
Teams: Chicago, Toronto, Rangers		
NHL	Regular	Playoffs
Seasons	12	8
Games	646	51
Goals	245	18
Assists	299	27
Points	544	45
Penalties	179	14
All-Star: 2 (First-1, Second-1)		
Trophies: 4 (Hart-1, Ross-2, Byng-1)		
Stanley Cup Championships		3

coach Hap Day once wisecracked before a game, "so we can't expect more than two goals from him."

While he would win his only three Stanley Cups in Toronto, Bentley remains in the eyes of most, forever a Black Hawk. He finished with one season as a Ranger in 1953-54, so he and Doug could play one more season together. Max played three seasons in the Western League before retiring to the farm in Delisle for good in 1959. He died of cancer at 64.

The bad heart was imagined. But for Max Bentley, the greatness was real and tangible.

125

From Sensation To Statesman

There was, in the young Brad Park, a recklessness that defined his life on the ice and off.

His wife-to-be, Gerry, noticed the first time she visited him at the Toronto home of his parents.

The family was gathered around the pool for a swim, but Brad was out of sight. "Where's Brad," asked Gerry. "Up on the roof," Brad's mother Betty replied casually. "He always jumps in from there."

In his rookie season, Park had the temerity to level Gordie Howe with a clean hip check. A few minutes later, Howe slashed the young Ranger in the throat. Park, unintimidated, croaked out a string of curses and vowed revenge.

From brash kid to geriatric chessmaster, in New York, Boston and for his final two seasons, Detroit, Brad Park would exemplify the life cycle of the professional hockey player.

He entered the league a jug-eared daredevil and then settled into a sterling prime with the New York Rangers. His years of dotage late in his career with the Bruins and Red Wings were exercises in which wisdom and experience continually held age and injury at bay. Drafted No. 1 overall by the Rangers in 1966, Park broke into

the league as a 20-year-old, surrounded by elders. He made impressions, mostly in the chests of NHLers of various status, and quickly emerged as the best defenseman (not named Bobby Orr) of his era.

The comparison was always an odious

one. Neither Park, nor any other defenseman had Orr's skating ability, but Park's game was rugged and efficient.

A better comparison could be made between Park and a Chicago Black Hawks' Hall of Fame defender.

"Park reminds me of Pierre Pilote," Chicago coach Bill Reay said in 1971. "Both were relatively compact men who could accelerate better than most forwards."

Park enjoyed a splendid prime. He scored 24 goals in 1971-72 and became the first defenseman in 30 years to register two hat tricks in the same season.

He was also every bit the modern player. Park challenged the Rangers with a holdout in his second year. His book, *Play the Man*, was uncommonly candid, he broke longstanding precedent and badmouthed Boston fans and players. The rink was a hole, Park wrote, many of the players were thugs and the fans were animals.

Maturity, Park would learn, means ruefully living with the consequences of youth. By the time he was 28, his knees were in tatters. He would endure five major knee surgeries and four arthroscopic procedures. The Rangers, sensing that the injuries would soon cut Park's value, and mindful of the need for a box-office draw, packaged Jean

126

Ratelle along with Park in a deal that brought Phil Esposito and Carol Vadnais to Manhattan.

Park quickly made peace with Boston fans with several years of sterling play and found a perfect hockey home in Beantown. The Bruins, a tight-checking team that played half its games in the small Boston Garden, provided a perfect venue for Park's withering range.

"My wheels aren't as good, but my brain is better," Park once said. "When I was younger and quicker I was capable of controlling a whole game over the whole rink. Now I've got to be content to control our zone. I move up only when the opportunity is outstanding, and not always then. Basically, I'm prepared to do less and do it well rather than try doing what I used to do and do it badly."

Park would hit double figures in goals five times with the Bruins and squeeze out two more seasons with the Red Wings. He would finish a five-time first team all-star, two-time second team all-star and six-time runner-up in Norris Trophy balloting. And while Park would never win a Stanley Cup, he made the playoffs every season of his career–matching Ray Bourque for the third-longest such streak (17)–and tied with Orr for third-most goals by a defenseman in a single playoff year (nine).

The contemporaries he would outlast included even the great Orr. From prodigy to prime-time player and elder statesman, Park did it all.

BRAD PARK		1968-85
Born: July 6, 1948 Toronto		
Teams: Rangers, Boston, Detroit		
NHL	Regular	Playoffs
Seasons	17	17
Games	1,113	161
Goals	213	35
Assists	683	90
Points	896	125
Penalties	1,429	217
All-Star: 7 (First-5, Second-2)		
Trophies: 1 (Masterton-1)		
Stanley Cup Championships		0

Responsible And Responsive

To the luckless, the knack of being at the right place is about coincidence and good fortune. The lucky know better: winners manipulate circumstance, they don't wait for it.

He may not have controlled his professional destination, but no NHL player worked more shrewdly to prepare for and maximize his situation as one of the greatest European players to star in the NHL, Jari Kurri.

Kurri became an Edmonton Oiler on a misunderstanding. A common belief among NHL teams in 1980–that Finland had all its young prospects tied to the national team–dampened interest in Finnish players among NHL scouts. But Edmonton scout Barry Fraser knew Kurri hadn't signed a contract in his homeland and landed the 17-year-old Finnish star with the Oilers' fourth-round choice.

Nature had blessed Kurri with spectacular hand-eye coordination and a powerful skating stride, and even before he arrived, Kurri understood he could score at the NHL level. But he also knew he would have to do more than score to play with Gretzky, who had arrived in the NHL the year before.

"I knew I'd be with Wayne and that defensive work would be very important," Kurri said. "I had a role to play. I was an up-and-down, two-way winger, so it had to be a matter of complete concentration." About Christmas, 1980, Kurri succeeded journeyman Blair MacDonald on Gretzky's right side in a game against Quebec.

Kurri intuitively understood Gretzky's game. Kurri regularly veered into the high slot on his off-wing and his whipsaw shot allowed him to exploit the milli-second of extra time that came enclosed in most Gretzky passes. "Jari is very calm when he gets in around the net with the puck," Gretzky once said. "He makes the move he wants to make when he wants to make it. We see the game the same way."

In that rookie season, Kurri scored 25 of

his 32 goals after landing with Gretzky. He would score more than 50 goals four times in the eight years he and Gretzky shared Oilers' blue.

Kurri set a record for goals by a right winger in 1984-85 with 71 and added a record-tying 19 in 18 games as the Oilers breezed to their second consecutive Stanley Cup. Kurri led the NHL in playoff goals four of the five times Edmonton won the Cup; he is third all-time in post-season goals and points and fourth in assists.

During the Oilers' Stanley Cup run, coach Glen Sather was asked to describe the perfect left winger for Gretzky. "The ideal guy would have a good shot and a quick release. He'd have the speed to get into the holes. He'd be big. He'd give Gretzky good passes. He'd do what Kurri does on the right side."

But when the Oilers traded Gretzky to Los Angeles in 1988, Kurri had 102- and 93-point seasons and proved himself a stand-alone star–as if that were necessary for someone who had scored a minimum of 30 goals 10 straight seasons. Kurri also collected 10 goals in the Oilers' 1990 post-Gretzky Stanley Cup victory.

Kurri became a hockey vagabond: a Gretzky reunion in Los Angeles was followed by stints with the New York Rangers, Mighty Ducks of Anaheim and finally, the Colorado Avalanche. The complete game that earned Jari Kurri a spot with hockey's premier talent kept him employed in his athletic old age until his retirement after the 1997-98 season, but stories of Kurri will invariably include the name Wayne Gretzky.

If Kurri was the luckiest player on the planet, surely Wayne Gretzky was number two. How would Gretzky's stardom had been impeded had he not been gifted with a defensively advanced star who could cradle his wonderful passes and scoot over to cover No. 99's check on the same shift?

"Wayne helped me a lot," Kurri said, "but I think I helped him too."

JARI KURRI	1980-1998	
Born: May 18, 1960 Helsinki		
Teams: Edmonton, Los Angeles, Rangers, Anaheim, Colorado		
NHL	**Regular**	**Playoffs**
Seasons	17	14
Games	1,251	200
Goals	601	106
Assists	797	127
Points	1,398	233
Penalties	545	123
All-Star: 5 (First-2, Second-3)		
Trophies: 1 (Byng-1)		
Stanley Cup Championships		5

Dan Hamilton

Top 50 Update

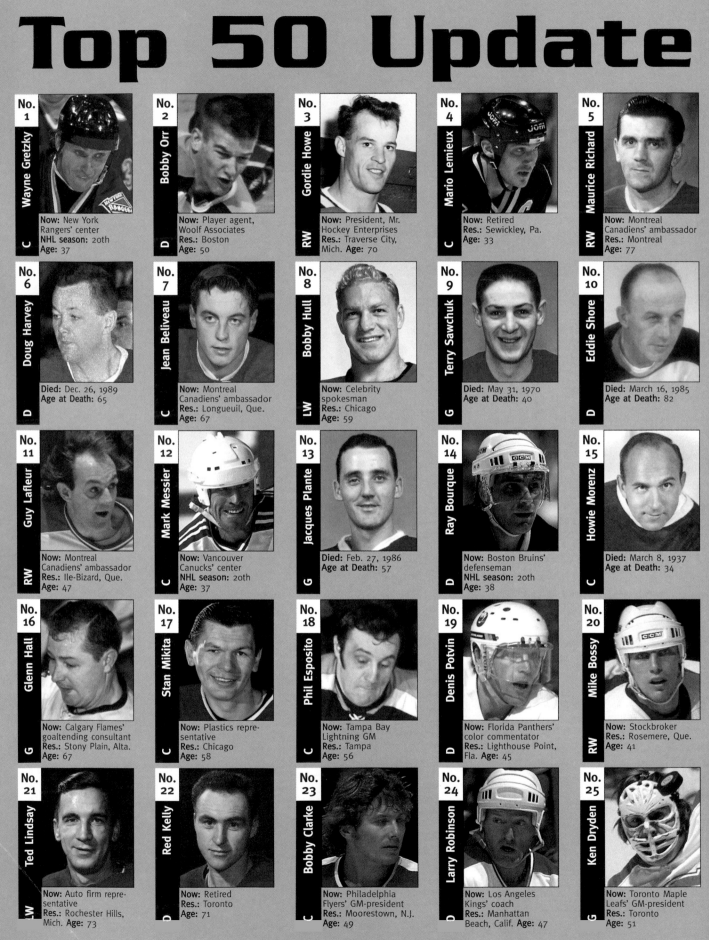

No. 1 — Wayne Gretzky (C)
Now: New York Rangers' center
NHL season: 20th
Age: 37

No. 2 — Bobby Orr (D)
Now: Player agent, Woolf Associates
Res.: Boston
Age: 50

No. 3 — Gordie Howe (RW)
Now: President, Mr. Hockey Enterprises
Res.: Traverse City, Mich. Age: 70

No. 4 — Mario Lemieux (C)
Now: Retired
Res.: Sewickley, Pa.
Age: 33

No. 5 — Maurice Richard (RW)
Now: Montreal Canadiens' ambassador
Res.: Montreal
Age: 77

No. 6 — Doug Harvey (D)
Died: Dec. 26, 1989
Age at Death: 65

No. 7 — Jean Beliveau (C)
Now: Montreal Canadiens' ambassador
Res.: Longueuil, Que.
Age: 67

No. 8 — Bobby Hull (LW)
Now: Celebrity spokesman
Res.: Chicago
Age: 59

No. 9 — Terry Sawchuk (G)
Died: May 31, 1970
Age at Death: 40

No. 10 — Eddie Shore (D)
Died: March 16, 1985
Age at Death: 82

No. 11 — Guy Lafleur (RW)
Now: Montreal Canadiens' ambassador
Res.: Ile-Bizard, Que.
Age: 47

No. 12 — Mark Messier (C)
Now: Vancouver Canucks' center
NHL season: 20th
Age: 37

No. 13 — Jacques Plante (G)
Died: Feb. 27, 1986
Age at Death: 57

No. 14 — Ray Bourque (D)
Now: Boston Bruins' defenseman
NHL season: 20th
Age: 38

No. 15 — Howie Morenz (C)
Died: March 8, 1937
Age at Death: 34

No. 16 — Glenn Hall (G)
Now: Calgary Flames' goaltending consultant
Res.: Stony Plain, Alta.
Age: 67

No. 17 — Stan Mikita (C)
Now: Plastics representative
Res.: Chicago
Age: 58

No. 18 — Phil Esposito (C)
Now: Tampa Bay Lightning GM
Res.: Tampa
Age: 56

No. 19 — Denis Potvin (D)
Now: Florida Panthers' color commentator
Res.: Lighthouse Point, Fla. Age: 45

No. 20 — Mike Bossy (RW)
Now: Stockbroker
Res.: Rosemere, Que.
Age: 41

No. 21 — Ted Lindsay (LW)
Now: Auto firm representative
Res.: Rochester Hills, Mich. Age: 73

No. 22 — Red Kelly (D)
Now: Retired
Res.: Toronto
Age: 71

No. 23 — Bobby Clarke (C)
Now: Philadelphia Flyers' GM-president
Res.: Moorestown, N.J.
Age: 49

No. 24 — Larry Robinson (D)
Now: Los Angeles Kings' coach
Res.: Manhattan Beach, Calif. Age: 47

No. 25 — Ken Dryden (G)
Now: Toronto Maple Leafs' GM-president
Res.: Toronto
Age: 51

Top 50 Update

No. 26 Frank Mahovlich — LW
Now: Canadian senator
Res.: Unionville, Ont.
Age: 60

No. 27 Milt Schmidt — C
Now: Retired
Res.: Dover, Mass.
Age: 80

No. 28 Paul Coffey — D
Now: Chicago Black Hawks' defenseman
NHL season: 19th
Age: 37

No. 29 Henri Richard — C
Now: Montreal Canadiens' ambassador
Res.: Laval, Que.
Age: 62

No. 30 Bryan Trottier — C
Now: Colorado Avalanche assistant coach
Res.: Portland, Me.
Age: 42

No. 31 Dickie Moore — LW
Now: Owner, industrial equipment rentals
Res.: Montreal
Age: 67

No. 32 Newsy Lalonde — C
Died: Nov. 21, 1970
Age at Death: 84

No. 33 Syl Apps — C
Now: Retired
Res.: Kingston, Ont.
Age: 83

No. 34 Bill Durnan — G
Died: Oct. 31, 1972
Age at Death: 57

No. 35 Patrick Roy — G
Now: Colorado Avalanche goaltender
NHL season: 14th
Age: 33

No. 36 Charlie Conacher — RW
Died: Dec. 30, 1967
Age at Death: 58

No. 37 Jaromir Jagr — RW
Now: Pittsburgh Penguins' right winger
NHL season: 9th
Age: 26

No. 38 Marcel Dionne — C
Now: Memorabilia company owner
Res.: Clarence, N.Y.
Age: 47

No. 39 Joe Malone — C
Died: May 15, 1969
Age at Death: 79

No. 40 Chris Chelios — D
Now: Chicago Black Hawks' defenseman
NHL season: 16th
Age: 36

No. 41 Dit Clapper — D
Died: Jan. 21, 1978
Age at Death: 70

No. 42 Bernie Geoffrion — RW
Now: Retired
Res.: Marietta, Ga.
Age: 67

No. 43 Tim Horton — D
Died: Feb. 21, 1974
Age at Death: 44

No. 44 Bill Cook — RW
Died: April 6, 1986
Age at Death: 90

No. 45 Johnny Bucyk — LW
Now: Boston Bruins' director alumni services
Res.: Boxford, Mass.
Age: 63

No. 46 George Hainsworth — G
Died: Oct. 9, 1950
Age at Death: 55

No. 47 Gilbert Perreault — C
Now: Buffalo Sabres' community relations
Res.: Victoriaville, Que.
Age: 48

No. 48 Max Bentley — C
Died: Jan. 19, 1984
Age at Death: 63

No. 49 Brad Park — D
Now: Sports equipment salesman
Res.: Lynnfield, Mass.
Age: 50

No. 50 Jari Kurri — RW
Now: Retired
Res.: Helsinki, Finland
Age: 38

131

THE NEXT
50

No. 95
Dominik Hasek

By
Michael
Ulmer

They lined up more than 3,500 strong to make The Hockey News Top 100. Nine players jumped the queue to make hockey history by comprising the only three lines to earn high honors intact. All three members of the 'Production Line,' 'Punch Line' and 'Kid Line' rank among the very best to play the game.

Of the thousands of other combinations that have appeared in the NHL, none can make that claim.

Leading the way is the Detroit Red Wings' threesome of right winger Gordie Howe, center Sid Abel and left winger Ted Lindsay. They rank No. 1 all-time on the basis of individual rankings. Howe is

unit went on to a lengthy coaching career (Abel and Blake). The 'Kid Line' was together from late in 1929 through the mid-1930s.

To be sure there have been other great lines, but none made it intact to the Top 100.

The Edmonton Oilers' Wayne Gretzky, No. 1-ranked player of all-time, and Jari Kurri, No. 50, didn't have a regular left winger. The New York Islanders' Mike Bossy, No. 20, and Bryan Trottier, No. 30, both made the Top 50, but longtime linemate Clark Gillies wasn't a strong candidate. Max and Doug Bentley, Nos. 48 and 73, respectively, join the Richards as the only siblings among the Top 10, but Chicago

Gordie Howe

Sid Abel

Ted Lindsay

No. 3, Lindsay No. 21 and Abel No. 85. Collectively, that ranks the 'Production Line' marginally ahead of Montreal Canadiens' right winger Rocket Richard, No. 5, left winger Toe Blake, No. 66, and center Elmer Lach, No. 68. The Toronto Maple Leafs' unit of right winger Charlie Conacher, No. 36, left winger Harvey (Busher) Jackson, No. 55, and center Joe Primeau, No. 92, also made the list as a line.

It's often said lines are greater than the sum of their parts. It's difficult to imagine that could be said of these legendary lines.

The 'Production Line' was together six years during the late-1940s and early-1950s while the 'Punch Line' dominated for five years during the 1940s. There are striking similarities between the two. All six players won scoring titles (although not all while linemates), both lines finished 1-2-3 in NHL scoring once, and one member of each

Black Hawk 'Pony Line' teammate Bill Mosienko didn't crack the elite group. Only Milt Schmidt, No. 27, made it from the Boston Bruins' 'Kraut Line'; neither Woody Dumart nor Bobby Bauer did.

Leading the way in the second half of the Top 100 is two-time Hart Trophy winner Nels Stewart, the Montreal Maroons' superstar center who was the all-time leader in goals and assists at the time of his retirement in 1940. With Bill Cowley (No. 53), Frank Boucher (No. 61), Cy Denneny (No. 62) and Elmer Lach (No. 68) all earning berths in the Top 100, only one player who has been an all-time NHL offensive leader isn't ranked among the all-time greats.

Center Syd Howe played for five NHL teams, most notably with the Red Wings, and retired with 528 points in 1946—but for all his points there is no greater glory.

No. 60
Turk Broda

They called him 'Old Poison' and during the mid-1920s and 1930s, Nels Stewart was that and more. Stewart, Babe Siebert and Hooley Smith combined for one of the most famous lines in hockey's early days, the Montreal Maroons' 'S Line.'

Stewart scored 134 goals and added 56 assists and was the line's premier marksman in the five years the three played for the Maroons. A hulking 200-pounder in an era dominated by smaller, more nimble talents, he looked slow, but was quick

enough to score 324 goals in stints with the Maroons, Boston Bruins and New York Americans.

Stewart scored an astonishing 34 goals in just 36 games, won the Hart Trophy, scoring title and the Stanley Cup in his rookie season (1925-26). He added another Hart in 1929-30.

Stewart was the all-time leading NHL goal-scorer, from 1936-37 through 1952-53, until he was passed by Rocket Richard. Stewart was also the most penalized player in league history with 953 minutes when he retired in 1940.

No. 51	Nels Stewart	
	Center	1925-40

Born: Dec. 29, 1902 Montreal, Que.
Died: Aug. 21, 1952 (Age 56)
Teams: Maroons, Boston, Americans

NHL	Regular	Playoffs
Seasons	15	12
Games	650	54
Goals	324	15
Assists	191	13
Points	515	28
Penalties	953	61

All-Star: 0
Trophies: 3 (Hart-2, Ross-1)

Stanley Cup Championships 1

No. 52	King Clancy	
	Defenseman	1921-37

Born: Feb. 25, 1903 Ottawa, Ont.
Died: Nov. 10, 1986 (Age 83)
Teams: Ottawa, Toronto

NHL	Regular	Playoffs
Seasons	16	13
Games	593	61
Goals	137	9
Assists	143	8
Points	280	17
Penalties	904	92

All-Star: 4 (First-2, Second-2)
Trophies: None

Stanley Cup Championships 3

He was born to be a King. Francis Clancy's father, an outstanding football star, was the original King Clancy. The younger Clancy was a star defenseman for nine seasons with the Ottawa Senators and produced 13-, 14- and 17-goal seasons.

When Conn Smythe began looking around the league in 1930 for someone to put his Toronto Maple Leafs over the top, he settled on Clancy and, using proceeds won at the track, landed the Ottawa defenseman for $35,000 and two players. Clancy

led the Maple Leafs in 1931-32 to their first Cup victory.

A two-time first all-star, Clancy gave Smythe seven more seasons, tried his hand at coaching the Montreal Maroons and then, after only half a season, traded a fedora for a whistle. Clancy refereed for 11 years until 1949.

He returned to the Maple Leafs in 1953 and served as head coach for three seasons. He became assistant GM to Punch Imlach and, for the last 20 years of his life, acted as a goodwill ambassador.

<table>
<tr><td>No. 53</td><td>Bill Cowley
Center 1934-47</td></tr>
</table>

| **Born:** June 12, 1912 Bristol, Que. |
| **Died:** Dec. 31, 1993 (Age 81) |
| **Teams:** St. Louis, Boston |

NHL	Regular	Playoffs
Seasons	13	11
Games	549	64
Goals	195	12
Assists	353	34
Points	548	46
Penalties	143	22

All-Star: 5 (First-4, Second-1)
Trophies: 3 (Hart-2, Ross-1)

Stanley Cup Championships 2

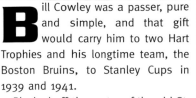

Bill Cowley was a passer, pure and simple, and that gift would carry him to two Hart Trophies and his longtime team, the Boston Bruins, to Stanley Cups in 1939 and 1941.

Plucked off the roster of the old St. Louis Eagles a year after the Ottawa Senators moved south, Cowley won the 1941 scoring title with 17 goals and 45 assists in 46 games. It was said that he made better wings than Boeing.

He led the league in assists three times and was on his way to a record-breaking season in 1943-44 with 71 points in 36 games before a broken leg ended his season in January. Cowley surpassed Joe Primeau's old record for assists in a season with 45 in 1940-41 and centered Boston's 'Three Gun Line' of Cowley, Roy Conacher and Eddie Wiseman.

A dependable playoff scorer, Cowley contributed 12 goals and 34 assists in 64 playoff games, including a 14-point performance in 1939.

He played 12 seasons for the Bruins before retiring in 1947.

The successor to Mario Lemieux as the game's outstanding big man, Lindros arrived in the NHL amidst controversy. Heralded as a can't-miss NHL prospect since his early teens, Lindros defied convention and insisted the Ontario Hockey League change its rules so he could be traded to the Oshawa Generals, a team of his choosing.

At 18, he refused to sign with the NHL team that drafted him, the Quebec Nordiques, and created a bidding war that landed him in

Philadelphia in a massive nine-player deal. The impact of that deal resonates today, as Lindros has assumed the mantle of the game's most dominant personality. No NHL player has ever combined Lindros' size, skill and skating ability with such willingness to play physically.

Lindros led the league in points in 1994-95 and won the Hart Trophy. He has scored 40 or more goals three times and his ascension to the forefront of the league was formalized with his Team Canada captaincy at the 1998 Olympics.

<table>
<tr><td>No. 54</td><td>Eric Lindros
Center 1992-Present</td></tr>
</table>

| **Born:** Feb. 28, 1973 London, Ont. |
| **Teams:** Philadelphia |

NHL	Regular	Playoffs
Seasons	6	4
Games	360	48
Goals	223	23
Assists	284	33
Points	507	56
Penalties	743	118

All-Star: 2 (First-1, Second-1)
Trophies: 1 (Hart-1)

Stanley Cup Championships 0

<table>
<tr><td>No. 55</td><td>Harvey Jackson
Left Winger 1929-44</td></tr>
</table>

| **Born:** Jan. 19, 1911 Toronto |
| **Died:** June 25, 1966 (Age 55) |
| **Teams:** Toronto, Americans, Boston |

NHL	Regular	Playoffs
Seasons	15	12
Games	633	71
Goals	241	18
Assists	234	12
Points	475	30
Penalties	437	53

All-Star: 5 (First-4, Second-1)
Trophies: 1 (Ross-1)

Stanley Cup Championships 1

The nickname 'Busher,' short for bush-leaguer, was a reproach the cocksure Harvey Jackson received as a rookie Toronto Maple Leaf. Darkly handsome and gifted with a tremendous shot and great lateral movement, Jackson manned the left side on the magnificent 'Kid Line' with Joe Primeau and Charlie Conacher. They tore through NHL defenses during the 1930s.

Jackson delivered four straight 20-goal seasons during the line's heyday and led the league in scoring during the Leafs' 1931-32 Stanley Cup

championship season with 53 points. Montreal Canadiens general manager Frank Selke called Jackson "the classiest player of all-time."

When the 'Kid Line' was broken up by Primeau's retirement in 1936, Jackson shifted to a line with his brother, Art, and Pep Kelly and the following year with Gordie Drillon and Syl Apps. Jackson scored 48 goals in his final three seasons with Toronto before being traded to the New York Americans. He played three years in Boston before retiring in 1944.

Peter Stastny was 23 in 1980 when he slipped away from his Czechoslovakian Bratislava club during the European Cup hockey championship in Austria to Quebec City and the Nordiques.

A superb passer and playmaker, Stastny was a rugged player who could not be intimidated and was the centerpiece of a dashing Nordiques team. The Stastnys–Peter at center with brothers Marian and Anton–were reunited in Quebec City a year after Peter fled the coun-

try but it was Peter who emerged as the dominant star.

Stastny reached the 100-point plateau in each of his first six seasons and only Wayne Gretzky scored more points than Stastny in the 1980s. Stastny played for nine-and-a-half seasons in Quebec before he was traded to New Jersey in March, 1990.

Stastny remains the all-time leading scorer for the Nordiques-Colorado Avalanche franchise and the only player in team history to break the 1,000-point plateau.

<table>
<tr><td>No. 56</td><td>Peter Stastny
Center 1980-95</td></tr>
</table>

| **Born:** Sept. 18. 1956 Bratislava, Czech. |
| **Teams:** Quebec, New Jersey, St. Louis |

NHL	Regular	Playoffs
Seasons	15	12
Games	977	93
Goals	450	33
Assists	789	72
Points	1,239	105
Penalties	824	123

All-Star: 5 (First-4, Second-1)
Trophies: 1 (Ross-1)

Stanley Cup Championships 0

Teeder Kennedy learned the work ethic that defined him at the feet of his mother, Margaret. Gordon Kennedy was killed in a hunting accident in November, 1925, just a month before the birth of his son. Needing extra money to feed and shelter her four children, Margaret Kennedy moonlighted in an arena snack bar and kept her son nearby. Ted Kennedy became a rink rat.

"We played for hours," Kennedy once recalled. "In order to get on free, we would clean the ice. Then, later we could have a shinny game for an hour."

Despite a clunky skating style, Kennedy became a fierce and determined player who led the Maple Leafs to five Stanley Cups over his 14-year career.

A gifted face-off artist and charismatic performer, Kennedy was awarded the Hart Trophy in 1955 despite scoring only 10 goals, his lowest total as a regular. The award was a homage to a brilliant career and his standing as a most tenacious and powerful captain.

It almost ended for Andy Bathgate before it began. The Winnipeg native injured his left knee after absorbing a bodycheck in his first shift with the Guelph Juniors in 1951.

A steel plate was fixed into the knee and while he would eventually reach stardom as an NHLer, the knee troubled Bathgate throughout his career.

A two-time first all-star in an era that included right wingers Gordie Howe and Maurice Richard, Bathgate was an efficient skater, a terrific shoot-

er and a sublime puckhandler who led the league in assists two times.

He won the Hart Trophy in 1959 for a 40-goal, 88-point season and tied Bobby Hull for the scoring title in 1962. Bathgate won his only Stanley Cup in 1964 with the Leafs.

Despite 17 seasons as a goaltending nemesis, Bathgate's greatest contribution to the game benefited goaltenders. It was his shot that tore into the face of Jacques Plante, Nov. 1, 1959, that prompted Plante, against the wishes of coach Toe Blake, to return to the ice wearing a face mask.

Pierre Pilote got a late start in hockey–he didn't play his first organized game until he was 16. Still, he quickly emerged as a superb all-around defenseman. A solid rusher, Pilote's passing touch may have rivaled Doug Harvey's.

Pilote was an effective defensive player who was clever with his stick and determined when dealing with traffic in front of his own net.

He proved to be a steady force for the Black Hawks. He didn't miss a game in his first five

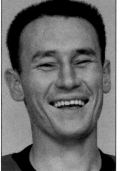

years and was captain for Chicago's Stanley Cup victory in 1961.

Pilote was voted to eight consecutive first or second all-star teams and was chosen a first all-star for five consecutive years from 1962-63 through 1966-67. He won his first Norris Trophy in 1963, ending Doug Harvey's reign as the NHL's top defenseman. Pilote would win again in 1964 and 1965, then finish twice more as runner-up, bridging the gap between the Harvey era and Bobby Orr's first of eight consecutive Norris Trophies.

Above all, Turk Broda was a presence. "He hasn't a nerve in his body," said Detroit Red Wings' coach-GM Jack Adams. "He could tend goal in a tornado and never blink an eye."

In 1936, Toronto Maple Leafs' owner Conn Smythe bought Broda from the International League's Detroit Olympics for the record price of $8,000. Just 22, Broda replaced George Hainsworth in the Leafs' net and spent 14 seasons there, interrupted by two years he served in the Canadian armed forces.

Broda rang up 62 regular season shutouts and a 2.53 goals-against average and won two Vezina Trophies.

But it was in the post-season that he most earned his keep. A five-time Cup winner, Broda won 60 of 101 playoff games and compiled 13 shutouts and a 2.15 average.

He fought weight problems through his career–the very public struggle was dubbed the 'Battle of the Bulge'–but his athletic style made him a huge favorite with Leaf fans.

<table>
<tr><td>No.
61</td><td>Frank Boucher
Center   1921-44</td></tr>
</table>

Born: Oct. 7, 1901 Ottawa
Died: Dec. 12, 1977 (Age 76)
Teams: Ottawa, Rangers

NHL	Regular	Playoffs
Seasons	14	11
Games	557	56
Goals	161	16
Assists	262	18
Points	423	34
Penalties	119	12

All-Star: 4 (First 3, Second-1)
Trophies: 7 (Byng-7)

Stanley Cup Championships 2

rancois Xavier Boucher was a New York Rangers' star of uncommon grace and style. A member of an Ottawa hockey-playing family that included three other big-leaguers, Boucher instead joined the North West Mounted Police at 17. But he reconsidered and jumped at the chance to play pro with the 1921-22 Ottawa Senators.

Boucher was unable to scratch out playing time on the talent-laden Senators and played four years with Vancouver in the Pacific Coast League before moving to New York in 1926.

He became a sensation on Broadway, centering Bill and Bun Cook. The graceful line was one of the most dominant units in the NHL during the late-20s to mid-30s.

Boucher retired in 1944 with 423 points after 13 seasons with the Rangers and was named to three first all-star teams.

He won the Lady Byng Trophy seven times in eight seasons (he was runner-up once) and set a standard for clean, effective play so prodigious, he was given the trophy to keep after his last win in 1935.

The most potent tributes to Cy Denneny are these: In 11 NHL seasons (1917-1929) with the Ottawa Senators, he had four seasons in which he averaged better than a goal a game and broke the 20-goal barrier seven times.

A four-time Cup winner with the Senators, Denneny never finished lower than fourth in league scoring in his first 10 years.

Among players with 200 or more NHL goals, Denneny's career goals-per-game ratio of .755 (246 goals in 326 games) is third behind Mario

Lemieux (.823) and Mike Bossy (.762). His best season came in 1917-18 when he scored 36 goals in only 22 games.

One of the earliest proponents of a curved stick, Denneny would stand on his blade until he got the curve he wanted.

He became a player-coach for Boston in 1928-29 and led the Bruins to the Stanley Cup. He also coached the Senators in 1932-33, their last season before an absence from the NHL that spanned seven decades and ended with a return in 1992.

<table>
<tr><td>No.
62</td><td>Cy Denneny
Left Winger   1917-29</td></tr>
</table>

Born: Dec. 23, 1891 Farran's Point, Ont.
Died: Sept. 10, 1970 (Age 78)
Teams: Ottawa, Boston

NHL	Regular	Playoffs
Seasons	12	10
Games	326	41
Goals	246	18
Assists	69	3
Points	315	21
Penalties	210	31

All-Star: 0
Trophies: 1 (Ross-1)

Stanley Cup Championships 5

<table>
<tr><td>No.
63</td><td>Bernie Parent
Goalie   1965-79</td></tr>
</table>

Born: April 3, 1945 Montreal
Teams: Boston, Philadelphia, Toronto

NHL	Regular	Playoffs
Seasons	13	9
Games	608	71
W-L-T	270-197-121	38-33
W. Pct.	.562	.535
GAA	2.55	2.43
Shutouts	54	6

All-Star: 2 (First-2)
Trophies: 4 (Vezina-2, Smythe-2)

Stanley Cup Championships 2

In his first organized hockey game, Bernie Parent, just 11, allowed 20 goals. It got considerably better. Parent was the brick wall on which the Philadelphia Flyers built two Stanley Cup wins.

Parent played 57 games for Boston before the Flyers landed him in the 1967 expansion draft. Philadelphia shipped him to Toronto in 1971 but the World Hockey Association's Philadelphia Blazers signed Parent for what would be a one-year stint in 1972-73.

The Flyers realized their mistake and re-

acquired Parent's rights as he went on to win the Conn Smythe Trophy in their 1974 and 1975 Cup years.

A superb, positional goalie, Parent won the Vezina Trophy in 1975 and shared the award with Tony Esposito in 1974. He also had back-to-back 12-shutout seasons and was a first all-star both years. That total wasn't matched for almost 25 years until Dominik Hasek's 13 in 1997-98.

A marvelous money goaltender, Parent fashioned a 2.43 goals-against average in 71 playoff games.

He was, and always will be 'The Golden Brett,' a remarkably candid and talented superstar linked in temperament and talent to his father, Bobby Hull, hockey's 'Golden Jet.'

The Blues acquired Hull from the Calgary Flames in 1988. In one of hockey's most lopsided trades, Hull and Steve Bozek went to the Blues in return for journeyman goalie Rick Wamsley and defenseman Rob Ramage.

In St. Louis, Hull emerged as a bona-fide sniper and posted three consecutive seasons of

70 or more goals, 72, 86 and 70, from 1989-90 through 1991-1992. He led the league in goals all three years and totaled 228. Only Wayne Gretzky, with 250 goals from 1981-82 through 1983-84 has had a more prolific three seasons.

Hull is a cunning player with a knack for avoiding checkers and materializing in prime scoring location where he can unfurl devastating slap or wrist shots. A Hart Trophy winner in 1991, Hull has averaged better than a point a game in the post-season.

<table>
<tr><td>No.
64</td><td>Brett Hull
Right Winger   1986-Present</td></tr>
</table>

Born: Aug. 9, 1964 Belleville, Ont.
Teams: Calgary, St. Louis, Dallas

NHL	Regular	Playoffs
Seasons	11	13
Games	801	108
Goals	554	69
Assists	433	51
Points	987	120
Penalties	298	51

All-Star: 3 (First-3)
Trophies: 2 (Hart-1, Byng-1)

Stanley Cup Championships 0

They called him the 'Mighty Atom' and the 'Little Giant,' this sprite of a player (5-foot-6 and 136 pounds) who played left wing for Howie Morenz.

Aurel Joliat was a star fullback with the Ottawa Rough Riders and the Regina Wascana Boat Club before a broken leg prompted him to devote his talents to hockey.

During his second season, Joliat was teamed with Morenz and he became Morenz's confidante and curator of his legend. It was Joliat who visited Morenz in his hospital

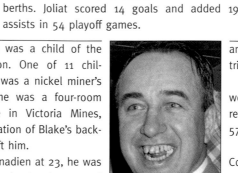

room after a leg injury ended the latter's career. Joliat said Morenz indicated he would rather die than quit playing for the Montreal Canadiens. When Morenz suddenly died, Joliat attributed it to a broken heart.

But Joliat was a magnificent talent in his own right, a great two-way player whose 270 goals would tie Morenz on the all-time list. He won three Stanley Cups (1924, 1930 and 1931), the Hart Trophy (1934) and four all-star berths. Joliat scored 14 goals and added 19 assists in 54 playoff games.

No. 65	Aurel Joliat	
	Left Winger	1922-38

Born: Aug. 29, 1901 Ottawa
Died: June 2, 1986 (Age 84)
Teams: Montreal

NHL	Regular	Playoffs
Seasons	16	13
Games	654	54
Goals	270	14
Assists	190	19
Points	460	33
Penalties	757	89

All-Star: 4 (First-1, Second-3)
Trophies: 1 (Hart-1)

Stanley Cup Championships 3

No. 66	Toe Blake	
	Left Winger	1935-48

Born: Aug. 21, 1912 Victoria Mines, Ont.
Died: May 17, 1993 (Age 80)
Teams: Maroons, Montreal

NHL	Regular	Playoffs
Seasons	14	10
Games	578	58
Goals	235	25
Assists	292	37
Points	527	62
Penalties	272	23

All-Star: 5 (First-3, Second-2)
Trophies: 3 (Hart-1, Ross-1, Byng-1)

Stanley Cup Championships 3

Toe Blake was a child of the Depression. One of 11 children, he was a nickel miner's son whose home was a four-room company house in Victoria Mines, Ont. The desperation of Blake's background never left him.

A Montreal Canadien at 23, he was the team's toughest player and among its most skilled. Paired with Maurice Richard and Elmer Lach to create the 'Punch Line,' Blake was a clutch player with two Stanley Cup winning goals (1944 and 1946). Blake acted as a firewall between Richard

and the legions of lesser players who tried to take him on.

A three-time first all-star, Blake won the scoring title in 1938-39 and recorded 235 goals and 527 points in 578 games.

Blake was closing in on Bill Cowley's record for most career points (548) when a badly broken leg ended his career in January, 1948.

He returned in 1955 to coach the Canadiens and guided Montreal to a coaching record eight Stanley Cups before retiring in 1968.

Boston fans were outraged when Frank Brimsek replaced Tiny Thompson in the Bruins nets early in the 1938-39 season. But Brimsek won 12 of his first 15 games, six by shutout, and earned the Calder and Vezina Trophies. Only three other goalies, Tony Esposito, Tom Barrasso and Ed Belfour have won the Calder and the Vezina in the same season.

'Mr. Zero' had a 1.56 goals-against average and recorded 10 shutouts in his rookie season. He led the Bruins to the Stanley Cup thanks to a

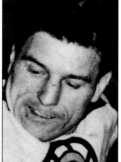

sparkling 1.25 GAA in the playoffs. He added another Cup in 1941 and won his second Vezina in 1942. He was selected to all-star teams eight times.

Brimsek devoted two years of his prime to the war effort, serving with the U.S. Coast Guard aboard a patrol boat in the South Pacific and never recaptured his form after returning. "I was a little shaky when I got back," he once said. "My legs and my nerves were shot." He played nine years with the Bruins before a final season with the Chicago Black Hawks.

No. 67	Frank Brimsek	
	Goalie	1938-50

Born: Sept. 26, 1913 Eveleth, Minn.
Teams: Boston, Chicago

NHL	Regular	Playoffs
Seasons	10	9
Games	514	68
W-L-T	252-182-80	32-36
W. Pct.	.568	.471
GAA	2.70	2.56
Shutouts	40	2

All-Star: 8 (First-2, Second-6)
Trophies: 3 (Vezina-2, Calder-1)

Stanley Cup Championships 2

No. 68	Elmer Lach	
	Center	1940-54

Born: Jan. 22, 1918 Nokomis, Sask.
Teams: Montreal

NHL	Regular	Playoffs
Seasons	14	11
Games	664	76
Goals	215	19
Assists	408	45
Points	623	64
Penalties	478	36

All-Star: 5 (First-3, Second-2)
Trophies: 3 (Ross-2, Hart-1)

Stanley Cup Championships 3

Elmer Lach was the playmaking arm and defensive conscience of the Montreal Canadiens' great 'Punch Line.' A glorious passer, Lach broke Bill Cowley's standard for career assists and total points in the same 1952 season and stood as the all-time points leader until Maurice Richard passed him in 1953-54. Gordie Howe would better Lach's career assist mark four seasons later.

The 'Punch Line' produced more than 700 points in four-and-a-half years together. While Lach's stickhandling and passing skills were

excellent, Canadiens' coach Dick Irvin said Lach was more valuable for his rugged defense than his offense. He never let his opponents off lightly.

"When it comes to giving sly butt-ends and using his elbows, that Elmer Lach is in a class by himself," Chicago Black Hawks' tough guy Johnny Mariucci remarked.

Despite a frightful collection of injuries including a fractured skull, and a broken jaw, cheek and leg, Lach won the Hart Trophy in 1944-45, took home a scoring title in 1947-48 and won three Stanley Cups.

No. 69	**Dave Keon**	
	Center	1960-82

Born: March 22, 1940 Noranda, Que.
Teams: Toronto, Hartford

NHL	Regular	Playoffs
Seasons	18	13
Games	1,296	92
Goals	396	32
Assists	590	36
Points	986	68
Penalties	117	6

All-Star: 2 (Second-2)
Trophies: 4 (Byng-2, Calder-1, Smythe-1)

Stanley Cup Championships 4

Only 5-foot-9, Dave Keon was one of the best two-way centers to grace the NHL. Keon spent virtually every night of his NHL career checking the opposition's top center, yet still scored 396 goals and 986 points over 18 NHL seasons.

A peerless face-off man and penalty-killer, Keon was one of the league's most gifted technicians. He played a grinding game yet accrued only 117 minutes in 1,296 regular season games–an average of one minor penalty every 22 games.

He won four Stanley Cups in 15 seasons with the Leafs, two Lady Byng Trophies and, in 1967, the Conn Smythe Trophy.

He shifted to the World Hockey Association in 1975 and delivered four 20-goal seasons. He returned to the NHL in 1979 and played three seasons with the Hartford Whalers. Keon scored 32 goals in 92 playoff games and compiled only six penalty minutes. A taciturn man who was never comfortable with the glare of publicity, he retired after 22 professional seasons in 1982 at 42.

Grant Fuhr was the platform on which the Edmonton Oilers piled their pyrotechnics. While the Oilers' firewagon style never led to great statistics for Fuhr, it did garner him four Stanley Cup rings.

A runner-up for the Vezina Trophy in his rookie year as a 19-year-old, Fuhr was spectacular in style, extraordinarily durable and consistently unflappable.

"Have you ever seen a rookie goalie with as much poise as this kid," one-time Toronto Maple Leaf Billy Harris was asked. "Sure I have, Johnny Bower," Harris answered, "but he was 31 years old."

Fuhr was the backbone of the Oilers' dynasty during the 1980s but salary demands prompted his trade to Toronto in 1991.

Brief stops in Buffalo and Los Angeles almost put an end to his career but Fuhr bounced back after signing with the St. Louis Blues as a free agent in 1995. He set an NHL record with 79 games in 1995-96, including 76 consecutive starts.

No. 70	**Grant Fuhr**	
	Goalie	1981-Present

Born: Sept. 28, 1962 Spruce Grove, Alta.
Teams: Edmonton, Toronto, Buffalo, Los Angeles, St. Louis

NHL	Regular	Playoffs
Seasons	17	13
Games	806	137
W-L-T	382-271-104	86-44
W. Pct.	.573	.661
GAA	3.41	2.98
Shutouts	23	5

All-Star: 2 (First-1, Second-1)
Trophies: 1 (Vezina-1)

Stanley Cup Championships 4

No. 71	**Brian Leetch**	
	Defenseman	1988-Present

Born: March 3, 1968 Corpus Christi, Tex.
Teams: Rangers

NHL	Regular	Playoffs
Seasons	10	7
Games	725	82
Goals	164	28
Assists	536	61
Points	700	89
Penalties	357	30

All-Star: 5 (First-2, Second-3)
Trophies: 4 (Norris-2, Calder-1, Smythe-1)

Stanley Cup Championships 1

New York Rangers' superstar Brian Leetch has succeeded Paul Coffey as the game's pre-eminent rushing defenseman. Leetch made an immediate impact upon entering the league, scoring 23 goals and 71 points to win the Calder Trophy in 1989.

A brilliant skater and an intuitive passer, Leetch collected a career-high 102 points in 1992 to win the Norris Trophy.

He was awarded the Conn Smythe Trophy in the Rangers' 1994 Stanley Cup win with 11 goals

and 34 points in 23 games, making him the first American player to capture the award. Only Coffey, who had 37 points in 1985, has scored more points by a defenseman in one postseason.

Leetch captained the victorious U.S. team at the inaugural World Cup of Hockey in 1996 and holds or shares 34 Ranger records, including the club's playoff records for points (89) and assists (61) and goals by a defenseman (28). Leetch has recorded four 20-goal seasons and collected a second Norris in 1997.

Earl Seibert played 15 seasons in the NHL and stood out as one of the game's premier defensemen of his era. A solid 6-foot-2 and 210 pounds, Seibert pieced together a 10-year all-star string in stints with the New York Rangers (four-and-a-half seasons), Chicago Black Hawks (nine years) and for the final 43 games of his NHL career, the Detroit Red Wings.

An excellent rushing defenseman, Seibert scored 89 goals and recorded 276 points. He was also considered one of the best shot-block-

ers of his era, never afraid to use his body to prevent a goal.

It was Seibert who checked Howie Morenz into the Forum boards in 1937. Morenz caught a rut, broke his leg and died in hospital, and while he was innocent of any wrongdoing, Seibert was booed in Montreal for years.

A gentle player, he was extraordinarily powerful and therefore respected. "It's lucky he was a gentle boy," Eddie Shore once said, "because if he ever got mad, he'd have killed us all."

No. 72	**Earl Seibert**	
	Defenseman	1931-46

Born: Dec. 7, 1911 Kitchener, Ont.
Died: May 21, 1990 (Age 78)
Teams: Rangers, Chicago, Detroit

NHL	Regular	Playoffs
Seasons	15	11
Games	645	66
Goals	89	11
Assists	187	8
Points	276	19
Penalties	746	76

All-Star: 10 (First-4, Second-6)
Trophies: 0

Stanley Cup Championships 2

oug Bentley starred for 12 years with the Chicago Black Hawks as a shifty, two-way player who held down the left side of the famed 'Pony Line' that also featured his brother, Max, at center and right winger Bill Mosienko.

Only 5-foot-8 and 145 pounds, Bentley also played on a team with four of his six brothers in Drumheller, Alta., before making the move to the NHL as a 23-year-old rookie.

He didn't score more than a dozen goals in his first three seasons, but after being reunited with

his longtime center, Max, Doug captured the 1942-43 scoring title with 73 points, including 33 goals, and doubled his career points total.

Bentley bettered that production the following year with 77 points but lost the scoring title to the Bruins' Herbie Cain, who had 82 points.

A three-time first all-star, Bentley was a durable player at ease with all elements of the game and was named the Hawks' best player of the half-century in 1950. After a brief comeback with the New York Rangers, Bentley retired in 1954.

No. 73	Doug Bentley	
	Left Winger	1939-54

Born: Sept. 13, 1916 Delisle, Sask.
Died: November 24, 1972 (Age 56)
Teams: Chicago, Rangers

NHL	Regular	Playoffs
Seasons	13	5
Games	566	23
Goals	219	9
Assists	324	8
Points	543	17
Penalties	217	8

All-Star: 4 (First-3, Second-1)
Trophies: 1 (Ross-1)

Stanley Cup Championships 0

No. 74	Borje Salming	
	Defenseman	1973-90

Born: April 17, 1951 Kiruna, Sweden
Teams: Toronto, Detroit

NHL	Regular	Playoffs
Seasons	17	12
Games	1,148	81
Goals	150	12
Assists	637	37
Points	787	49
Penalties	1,344	91

All-Star: 6 (First-1, Second-5)
Trophies: 0

Stanley Cup Championships 0

e will be best remembered as the pioneer. Borje Salming was the first European player to shine in the NHL. Salming had to fight through goonism and racist jabs to attain standing among the elite NHL defensemen of his era.

Salming, an elegant passer and skater with a hard shot, was a six-time all-star in an era that spanned the careers of Bobby Orr, Denis Potvin, Brad Park and Montreal's 'Big Three' of Serge Savard, Guy Lapointe and Larry Robinson. Twice he was runner-up for the Norris Trophy

and he topped the 70-point mark four times.

Salming played 16 years for the Toronto Maple Leafs, represented Sweden at three Canada Cups and retired with 787 points. His 768 points in a Leaf jersey were good for third on the team's all-time list and 310 points better than the second-highest scoring blueliner, Tim Horton (458).

The gaunt Salming, who dominated both ends of the ice, capped his remarkable NHL career with one season as a Detroit Red Wing.

---

hey called him the 'Chicoutimi Cucumber' and it seemed nothing fazed Georges Vezina. Despite rules that prohibited goalies from dropping to their knees to stop the puck through most of his career, Vezina allowed just over three goals a game.

The Montreal Canadiens found Vezina in 1910 on a barnstorming swing, when he shut them out in an exhibition game. Vezina led Montreal to championships in the National Hockey Association and NHL, including two Stanley Cups.

Vezina played 328 consecutive games and 39 more in the playoffs before having to quit after the opening game of the 1925-26 season.

Despite an obvious illness, he started against Pittsburgh and fought throbbing chest pains. He began coughing up blood in the first intermission. Vezina left the rink and never returned.

He died four months later of tuberculosis at 38. His career would be immortalized a year later with creation of the Vezina Trophy, goaltending's highest honor.

No. 75	Georges Vezina	
	Goalie	1917-26

Born: Jan. 7, 1888 Chicoutimi, Que.
Died: March 26, 1926 (Age 38)
Teams: Montreal

NHL	Regular	Playoffs
Seasons	9	5
Games	191	26
W-L-T	104-81-5	17-8
W. Pct.	.561	.680
GAA	3.28	2.78
Shutouts	13	4

All-Star: 0
Trophies: 0

Stanley Cup Championships 2

No. 76	Charlie Gardiner	
	Goalie	1927-34

Born: Dec. 31, 1904 Edinburgh, Scotland
Died: June 12, 1934 (Age 29)
Teams: Chicago

NHL	Regular	Playoffs
Seasons	7	4
Games	316	21
W-L-T	112-152-52	12-6-3
W. Pct.	.437	.643
GAA	2.02	1.43
Shutouts	42	5

All-Star: 4 (First-3, Second-1)
Trophies: 2 (Vezina-2)

Stanley Cup Championships 1

eath found Chuck Gardiner when he was just 29, ending the career of one of the premier goalies of the 1920s and 1930s.

Born in Edinburgh, Scotland, but raised in Winnipeg, Gardiner starred with the Chicago Black Hawks for seven seasons. He posted a career 2.02 goals-against average and nailed down 42 shutouts.

A charismatic and fearless goalie, Gardiner's directions and exhortations filled whatever net he was minding and became a huge crowd favorite. Gardiner twice won the

Vezina Trophy and was a three-time first all-star. Howie Morenz called Gardiner the toughest goalie he ever faced.

Gardiner's final season turned out to be his best. He posted his lowest regular-season goals-against average (1.73) and allowed just 1.20 goals per game in the playoffs as the Hawks swept to the 1934 Stanley Cup despite having the worst offense in the league.

During the summer, Gardiner died after collapsing from a brain tumor in Winnipeg.

No. 77	Clint Benedict	
	Goalie	1917-30

Born: Sept. 26, 1894 Ottawa, Ont.		
Died: Nov. 12, 1976 (Age 82)		
Teams: Ottawa, Maroons		

NHL	Regular	Playoffs
Seasons	13	9
Games	362	48
W-L-T	191-142-28	25-18-4
W. Pct.	.568	.574
GAA	2.31	1.80
Shutouts	58	15

All-Star: 0
Trophies: 0

Stanley Cup Championships 4

Remembered as the father of the face mask, Ottawa Senators goalie Clint Benedict commissioned a leather mask from a Boston firm when Howie Morenz broke his nose with a shot during a game in 1929. The injury took six weeks to heal sufficiently to allow his return.

Benedict only kept the mask for a few days because the rigid nosepiece obscured his vision on low shots. Later that season, he suffered another broken nose and retired. The face mask would not return to an

NHL game until Jacques Plante insisted on wearing it 30 years later in 1959.

Benedict began playing senior hockey at 15 and enjoyed seven NHL seasons with the Senators and six with the Montreal Maroons, winning four Stanley Cups.

He compiled the league's best goals-against average for five straight years from 1918-1919 through 1922-23. Benedict went 25-18-4 in the playoffs and fashioned a 1.80 goals-against average in 48 games.

An elegant player who has hit the 50-goal mark five times, Steve Yzerman helped lead the Detroit Red Wings out of their post-Gordie Howe doldrums.

Yzerman scored 39 goals and recorded 87 points in his 1983-84 rookie year, as the Wings made the playoffs after a five-year absence, but he lost the Calder Trophy to Buffalo Sabres' goalie Tom Barrasso.

While Yzerman has emerged as one of the greatest Red Wings ever, he has played in the shadows of Mario Lemieux and Wayne Gretzky.

Yzerman has never been a first or second all-star, and never finished higher than third in the scoring race.

Still, Yzerman has thrived in the late-1980s and 1990s. He is one of only four players to top the 150-point barrier.

Yzerman provided sterling defense in the Wings' 1997 Stanley Cup victory, helping Detroit to its first Cup since 1955. He came back the next year to lead the Wings to another championship and won the Conn Smythe Trophy, the first major individual award of his career.

No. 78	Steve Yzerman	
	Center	1983-Present

Born: May 9, 1965 Cranbrook, B.C.		
Teams: Detroit		

NHL	Regular	Playoffs
Seasons	15	13
Games	1,098	135
Goals	563	52
Assists	846	83
Points	1,409	135
Penalties	740	68

All-Star: 0
Trophies: 1 (Smythe-1)

Stanley Cup Championships 2

No. 79	Tony Esposito	
	Goalie	1968-84

Born: April 23, 1943 Sault Ste. Marie, Ont.		
Teams: Montreal, Chicago		

NHL	Regular	Playoffs
Seasons	16	14
Games	886	99
W-L-T	423-306-152	45-53
W. Pct.	.566	.459
GAA	2.92	3.07
Shutouts	76	6

All-Star: 5 (First-3, Second-2)
Trophies: 4 (Vezina-3, Calder-1)

Stanley Cup Championships 1

They called him 'Tony O,' in honor of the record that he set 29 seasons ago, as a mop-haired rookie with the Chicago Black Hawks.

Esposito, claimed by Chicago off Montreal's roster for a $30,000 fee in the 1969 Intra-League draft, fashioned one of the most amazing rookie seasons in NHL history, posting 15 shutouts, two more than the modern-era record. Esposito won the Calder and Vezina Trophies that first season.

Over 15 seasons with the Black Hawks, he

reigned as one of the league's most unorthodox and best goalies, employing the butterfly style to great effect. Esposito earned first all-star status in 1970, 1972 and 1980, won a Vezina Trophy outright and shared two more.

A member of the 1972 Summit Series team and a workhorse who averaged 60 games a season, Esposito captured every title with the Black Hawks but the one that mattered most. Chicago advanced to the Stanley Cup finals in 1971 and 1973, but lost both times.

Battling Billy Smith was the glue that held together the New York Islanders' run of four Stanley Cups from 1979-80 through 1982-83. A zealous competitor who used his stick like a scythe to defend his crease, Smith was claimed from the Los Angeles Kings in the 1972 expansion draft.

Smith gained more fame, initially at least, for scoring goals than stopping them. On Nov. 28, 1979, he was the last Islander to touch the puck when, on a delayed penalty, Colorado Rockies' defenseman Rob

Ramage sent a pass by a teammate the length of the ice and into an empty net.

Smith split the goaltending duties with Glenn (Chico) Resch through the 1970s, but took a stranglehold of the playoff chores in 1980 once the Islander dynasty began.

Smith won his only Vezina Trophy in 1982, and claimed the Conn Smythe Trophy in 1983. He retired in 1989 with an NHL-record 88 playoff wins—Patrick Roy now holds the record (99)—making him one of the greatest post-season goalies ever.

No. 80	Billy Smith	
	Goalie	1971-89

Born: Dec. 12, 1950 Perth, Ont.		
Teams: Los Angeles, Islanders		

NHL	Regular	Playoffs
Seasons	18	13
Games	680	132
W-L-T	305-233-105	88-36
W. Pct.	.556	.710
GAA	3.17	2.73
Shutouts	22	5

All-Star: 1 (First-1)
Trophies: 2 (Vezina-1, Smythe-1)

Stanley Cup Championships 4

Serge Savard, a member of the Montreal Canadiens' vaunted 'Big Three' defense corps, was a prodigious winner.

In his 15 seasons manning the Canadiens' blueline, Savard won the Stanley Cup seven times, including four in a row from 1975-76 through 1978-79 and won the Conn Smythe Trophy in just his second season (1969). Savard was the only Canadian player in the 1972 Summit Series who did not play in a losing game.

After retiring from the Canadiens in 1981, he

was picked up by the Winnipeg Jets, who invested a $2,500 waiver wire fee. Savard helped the Jets improve by 48 points to earn a spot in the playoffs.

Despite incurring broken legs in his fourth and fifth seasons, limiting him to 60 games, Savard thrived as a gifted, resourceful defenseman for 17 seasons.

An outspoken critic of violence in hockey, Savard moved smoothly into the business world, but returned to manage the Canadiens for more than 12 seasons.

No. 81	Serge Savard	
	Defenseman	1966-83

Born: Jan. 22, 1946 Montreal, Que.
Teams: Montreal, Winnipeg

NHL	Regular	Playoffs
Seasons	17	14
Games	1,040	130
Goals	106	19
Assists	333	49
Points	439	68
Penalties	592	88

All-Star: 1 (Second-1)
Trophies: 2 (Smythe-1, Masterton-1)

Stanley Cup Championships 7

No. 82	Alex Delvecchio	
	Center	1951-74

Born: Dec. 4, 1931 Fort William, Ont.
Teams: Detroit

NHL	Regular	Playoffs
Seasons	24	14
Games	1,549	121
Goals	456	35
Assists	825	69
Points	1,281	104
Penalties	383	29

All-Star: 2 (Second-2)
Trophies: 3 (Byng-3)

Stanley Cup Championships 3

They called him 'Fats,' not because of his weight, but because Alex Delvecchio's cherub face seemed at all times to bear a smile.

In fact, over the course of 24 seasons with the Detroit Red Wings, Delvecchio was anything but soft. He defined durability, becoming the third NHLer to play 20 years, following in the skateprints of Dit Clapper and Gordie Howe.

Delvecchio embodied clean, stylish play and captured three Lady Byng Trophies. He never

accrued more than 37 penalty minutes in a season.

Delvecchio retired in 1974, second only to Howe, his longtime sidekick, for games and seasons, assists and points. Delvecchio never minded being stuck in Howe's shadow.

"Gordie Howe was the greatest, there's no doubt about it," he said. "When you got to play with him, you gave him the puck and you knew things were going to happen for your hockey team." Delvecchio missed only 43 games in his career, 22 with the same ankle injury.

Abadly broken leg when he was only 31 cut short Babe Dye's career and deprived the NHL of a gifted goal-scorer.

Dye arrived in the league in 1919 as a superb athlete even though he was only 5-foot-8 and 150 pounds. A football star and a good enough baseball prospect to warrant a $25,000 offer from the Philadelphia Phillies, Dye spent seven of his 11 NHL seasons with the Toronto St. Pats.

Thanks to astounding stickhandling and a hard, powerful shot, Dye scored 174 goals in his

first 169 games. He put together two 11-game goal-scoring streaks and twice scored five goals in a contest. He led the league in goals three times.

He had 11 goals and 13 points in 15 playoff games and won his only Stanley Cup with Toronto in 1921-22.

In 1927, Dye broke his leg in training camp and after two aborted comeback attempts, quit in 1931. Dye became an NHL referee for five years and then settled in Chicago, where he worked as a foreman for a paving company.

No. 83	Babe Dye	
	Right Winger	1919-31

Born: May 13, 1898 Hamilton, Ont.
Died: Jan. 2, 1962 (Age 63) **Teams:** Toronto, Hamilton, Chicago, Americans

NHL	Regular	Playoffs
Seasons	11	5
Games	269	15
Goals	202	11
Assists	41	2
Points	243	13
Penalties	200	18

All-Star: 0
Trophies: 2 (Ross-2)

Stanley Cup Championships 1

No. 84	Lorne Chabot	
	Goalie	1926-37

Born: Oct. 5, 1900 Montreal **Died:** Oct. 10, 1946 (Age 46) **Teams:** Rangers, Toronto, Chicago, Montreal, Maroons, Americans

NHL	Regular	Playoffs
Seasons	11	9
Games	411	37
W-L-T	206-140-65	13-17-6
W. Pct.	.580	.444
GAA	2.04	1.54
Shutouts	73	5

All-Star: 1 (First-1)
Trophies: 1 (Vezina-1)

Stanley Cup Championships 2

Hockey history loves Lorne Chabot. For one thing, Chabot invented the blocker by accident. In 1925, Chabot was playing goal for a senior team from Port Arthur, Ont., when he fashioned hockey's first blocker to protect a broken stick hand.

Chabot reached the NHL in 1926 as a 26-year-old rookie when Conn Smythe was hired to assemble talent for the fledgling New York Rangers. Chabot played well for two seasons but an eye injury prompted the Rangers to give up on him and

trade him to Smythe, who was now running the Maple Leafs. His departure from New York was most noteworthy for a bizarre publicity stunt in which Ranger press agents listed his name as Chabotsky during his rookie season to lure more Jewish fans.

It was Chabot whose eye injury led to Ranger coach-GM Lester Patrick's legendary appearance in the net for the 1928 playoffs. And it was Chabot who let in the goal in the sixth overtime period that ended the longest game in NHL history during the 1936 playoffs.

No. 85 — Sid Abel
Center 1939-54

Born: Feb. 22, 1918 Melville, Sask.		
Teams: Detroit, Chicago		

NHL	Regular	Playoffs
Seasons	14	13
Games	612	97
Goals	189	28
Assists	283	30
Points	472	58
Penalties	376	79

All-Star: 4 (First-2, Second-2)
Trophies: 1 (Hart-1)

Stanley Cup Championships 3

Sid Abel was the linchpin and veteran anchor on the Detroit Red Wings' overpowering 'Production Line.' Abel was 29 when the line was first assembled during the 1947-48 season. Gordie Howe, by comparison, was just 19 and Ted Lindsay, 22.

Thanks in large part to Abel's canny puck distribution, the line combined for 215 points, including 92 goals in 1949-50. The unit finished 1-2-3; Lindsay won the scoring title with 78 points, ahead of Abel (69) and Howe (68). Only the Boston Bruins' 'Kraut Line' and the Montreal Canadiens' 'Punch Line' had turned that trick.

After five glorious seasons, the 'Production Line' was broken up in the summer of 1952 when Abel, 34, asked to be traded to Chicago where he could be player-coach.

Twice a first team all-star and a three-time Cup winner, Abel won a Hart Trophy in 1949 and was captain of Detroit for six seasons. He returned to coach the Red Wings during the 1957-58 season and remained behind the bench for 10-1/2 years.

Bob Gainey was a steward of the game, a game-shaper who could change the flow and the direction without registering a point.

Gainey recorded four 20-goal seasons, but it was his ability to neutralize the opposition's top scorers that made him such an identifiable contributor to the Montreal Canadiens' four-year Stanley Cup run of the late-1970s. He won the Conn Smythe Trophy in 1979.

"I can't think of anybody who means more to

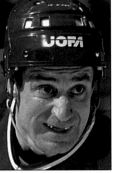

our team than Gainey," Serge Savard said. "A few guys, like (Larry) Robinson, (Guy) Lafleur and (Guy) Lapointe mean as much, but they're not more important than Gainey." The Selke Trophy for defensive excellence by a forward was conceived with Gainey in mind in 1977-78 and he won the award its first four years.

Gainey captained the Habs for seven seasons, second only to Jean Beliveau. He led the Canadiens to his fifth Stanley Cup (his only one as captain) in 1986.

No. 86 — Bob Gainey
Left Winger 1973-89

Born: Dec. 13, 1953 Peterborough, Ont.		
Teams: Montreal		

NHL	Regular	Playoffs
Seasons	16	16
Games	1,160	182
Goals	239	25
Assists	262	48
Points	501	73
Penalties	585	151

All-Star: 0
Trophies: 5 (Selke-4, Smythe-1)

Stanley Cup Championships 5

No. 87 — Johnny Bower
Goalie 1953-70

Born: Nov. 8, 1924 Prince Albert, Sask.		
Teams: Rangers, Toronto		

NHL	Regular	Playoffs
Seasons	15	10
Games	552	74
W-L-T	251-196-90	35-34
W. Pct.	.551	.507
GAA	2.52	2.52
Shutouts	37	5

All-Star: 1 (First-1)
Trophies: 2 (Vezina-2)

Stanley Cup Championships 4

Johnny Bower, the Toronto Maple Leafs goaltending great, was older even when he was young. Bower enlisted in the Canadian army at 17 for four years, two of which were spent overseas, and was discharged in time for a final year of junior with the Prince Albert Black Hawks.

Aside from a full season and bits of two more with the New York Rangers, Bower was a superb career minor-leaguer with a dozen minor league seasons to his credit. The Maple Leafs landed the genial Bower

in 1958 as a 34-year-old sophomore and he would be a key contributor to four Stanley Cups.

Bower became a first-time first all-star in 1961 at 37. He also captured a Vezina Trophy that year and shared another with teammate Terry Sawchuk in 1965.

He enjoyed a dozen seasons with the Maple Leafs and became known as the father of the goaltender poke check. He fashioned a career 2.52 goals-against average and won 251 games before his retirement in 1970 at age 45.

They called Sprague Cleghorn 'Peg' and of the rambunctious talents that dotted the NHL and its predecessors, he was perhaps the most unruly.

Cleghorn played for the Ottawa Senators, Toronto St. Pats, Montreal Canadiens and Boston Bruins during his 10 NHL years and spent 7 seasons in the National Hockey Association. Cleghorn was a rushing defenseman who once scored five goals for the National Hockey Association's Montreal Wanderers.

Cleghorn scored 163 pro goals, 84 in the NHL,

and his chippy, abrasive style made him one of the most notorious and colorful players in the NHL's earliest days.

He once disabled three Ottawa players in the same game and the next time had to be smuggled into the Ottawa rink via a furnace room door. Once in uniform, he skated to center ice and, turning slowly in all directions, defied both the crowd and the Senators to come and get him.

"All told," Cleghorn once said, "I figure I was in 50 stretcher-case fights."

No. 88 — Sprague Cleghorn
Defenseman 1918-28

Born: March 11, 1890 Montreal, Que.		
Died: July 11, 1956 (Age 66)		
Teams: Ottawa, Toronto, Montreal, Boston		

NHL	Regular	Playoffs
Seasons	10	8
Games	262	39
Goals	84	7
Assists	39	8
Points	123	15
Penalties	489	48

All-Star: 0
Trophies: 0

Stanley Cup Championships 3

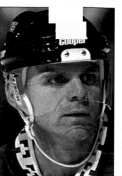

Mike Gartner has always been an NHL hybrid, part thoroughbred and part ploughhorse. He is a brilliant skater, twice named the NHL's fastest skater, and remarkably durable.

Gartner was gifted with a terrific shot and an unfailing instinct on attack. Gartner has been a gunner since his 36-goal rookie season in 1979-80 with the Washington Capitals. He increased his output to 48 in his sophomore year.

Gartner would hit the 40-goal mark seven more times in his career, which included a decade in Washington, parts of two years in Minnesota, four full seasons with the New York Rangers and tenures in Toronto and Phoenix. Once knocked for his teams' poor post-season records, Gartner has 43 playoff goals including eight in 13 games for the Rangers in 1992.

His standing as the fifth-highest goal-scorer in history is as much a testimony to his resilience as to his quicksilver skills. Only Wayne Gretzky, Gordie Howe, Marcel Dionne and Phil Esposito have found the net more.

No. 89	Mike Gartner	
	Right Winger	1979-Present

Born: Oct. 29, 1959 Ottawa, Ont.
Teams: Washington, Minnesota, Rangers, Toronto, Phoenix

NHL	Regular	Playoffs
Seasons	19	15
Games	1,432	122
Goals	708	43
Assists	627	50
Points	1,335	93
Penalties	1,159	125

All-Star: 0
Trophies: 0

Stanley Cup Championships 0

No. 90	Norm Ullman	
	Center	1955-75

Born: Dec. 26, 1935 Provost, Alta.
Teams: Detroit, Toronto

NHL	Regular	Playoffs
Seasons	20	14
Games	1,410	106
Goals	490	30
Assists	739	53
Points	1,229	83
Penalties	712	67

All-Star: 2 (First-1, Second-1)
Trophies: 0

Stanley Cup Championships 0

One of the great offensive centers in NHL history, Norm Ullman delivered 20 impeccable NHL seasons–13 for the Detroit Red Wings and seven with the Toronto Maple Leafs.

Ullman arrived in the NHL at 19 in the dying days of the Detroit Red Wings' dynasty and soon embarked on a 12-year run of 20-or-more-goal seasons. The Leafs landed Ullman, Paul Henderson and two others for four players, including Frank Mahovlich. But as he did in Detroit, Ullman found a team on the downswing and a year removed from Stanley Cup glory. Ullman scored 490 goals, assisted on 739 and stands 23rd on the all-time scoring list.

Ullman will also be remembered for his sterling forechecking game. During the 1965 playoffs against the Chicago Black Hawks, Ullman scored two goals for Detroit five seconds apart. It remains the fastest two goals by one player in playoff history. He finished his career with two productive seasons for the World Hockey Association's Edmonton Oilers before retiring in 1977 at 41.

History knows Dave (Sweeney) Schriner as a hard-shooting NHL left winger and the first Russian-born player to play in the NHL. Schriner was born in Saratov, Russia, but was raised in Calgary.

Schriner was a standout for the New York Americans and Toronto Maple Leafs during the 1930s and '40s. A rookie of the year thanks to an 18-goal debut with the 1934-35 New York Americans, Schriner was a star on Broadway for five years before he was traded to the Maple Leafs in a deal that saw former 'Kid Line' star 'Busher' Jackson and four others head to Manhattan.

Schriner, an offensive player who disdained backchecking, was a two-time scoring champion and won two Stanley Cups with Toronto.

In 1942, Schriner scored five goals as the Leafs rallied from a 3-0 deficit in games to defeat the Detroit Red Wings and win the Cup. The nickname 'Sweeney' was given to him as boy because a respected ballplayer named Bill Sweeney used to take him to the rink.

No. 91	Sweeney Schriner	
	Left Winger	1934-46

Born: Nov. 30, 1911 Saratov, Russia
Died: July 4, 1990 (Age 78)
Teams: Americans, Toronto

NHL	Regular	Playoffs
Seasons	11	8
Games	484	59
Goals	201	18
Assists	204	11
Points	405	29
Penalties	148	54

All-Star: 3 (First-2, Second-1)
Trophies: 3 (Ross-2, Calder-1)

Stanley Cup Championships 2

No. 92	Joe Primeau	
	Center	1928-36

Born: Jan. 24, 1906 Lindsay, Ont.
Died: May 14, 1989 (Age 83)
Teams: Toronto

NHL	Regular	Playoffs
Seasons	9	6
Games	310	38
Goals	66	5
Assists	177	18
Points	243	23
Penalties	105	12

All-Star: 1 (Second-1)
Trophies: 1 (Byng-1)

Stanley Cup Championships 1

They called him 'Gentleman Joe,' a smooth-passing center who held the reins of the Toronto Maple Leafs' fabulous 'Kid Line.'

Primeau's 37 assists, achieved in 1932, stood as the league standard for eight years. An NHL regular for only seven full seasons, Primeau was originally recruited by Conn Smythe for the New York Rangers, but when Smythe agreed to leave the Rangers, he took Primeau's rights with him.

Known for his clean play, Primeau won the Lady Byng Trophy and the Stanley Cup in 1931-32.

After the 1935-36 season, the man with two of the smoothest hands in the NHL retired at 30 and founded a successful concrete factory.

He would later distinguish himself as a superb coach and the only bench boss ever to win hockey's coaching hat trick–the Memorial Cup, emblematic of junior hockey supremacy, the Allan Cup, the top prize for senior hockey and, in 1951, the Stanley Cup with the Maple Leafs.

No. 93	Darryl Sittler	
	Center	1970-85

Born: Sept. 18, 1950 Kitchener, Ont.
Teams: Toronto, Philadelphia, Detroit

NHL	Regular	Playoffs
Seasons	15	14
Games	1,096	76
Goals	484	29
Assists	637	45
Points	1,121	74
Penalties	948	137

All-Star: 1 (Second-1)
Trophies: 0

Stanley Cup Championships 0

Darryl Sittler grew up in St. Jacob's, Ont., Mennonite country, and the rural work ethic never left him as an NHL star.

A determined player who melded good shooting and skating skills into a premium package, Sittler led the Toronto Maple Leafs in scoring or tied for the team lead from 1972-73 through 1979-80 and set 10 club records.

Sittler scored the series-winning goal in the 1976 Canada Cup and delivered two of the most spectacular nights in Leafs' history during the

1975-76 season–a 10-point effort against the Boston Bruins and a five-goal playoff game against the Philadelphia Flyers.

But even with a strong supporting cast that included Hall-of-Famers Lanny McDonald and Borje Salming, Sittler wasn't able to lift the Leafs past the mismanagement of owner Harold Ballard into the Stanley Cup finals.

Wanting more money, Sittler demanded and was granted a trade and spent nearly three seasons in Philadelphia and another with the Detroit Red Wings before retiring in 1985.

When finally given a premier chance, Joe Sakic demonstrated to the world what kind of a dominant talent he had become.

Sakic was the driving force in the Colorado Avalanche's 1996 Stanley Cup championship with a record six game-winning playoff goals and 18 goals overall, just one fewer than the post-season record. Sakic's 34 points were the best of those playoffs and he was awarded the Conn Smythe Trophy.

Although he has led the Quebec Nordiques-

Colorado franchise in scoring six times, the franchise's lack of post-season success gave critics a chance to knock Sakic's leadership, however different a story the numbers tell. For example: Sakic has scored 35 goals and 75 points over 57 playoff games.

A deceptive skater with a terrific shot, Sakic has played in seven all-star games and broke the 100-point barrier four times, including a career-high 120 points in 1995-96. Sakic has finished among the league's top 10 scorers four times.

No. 94	Joe Sakic	
	Center	1988-Present

Born: July 7, 1969 Burnaby, B.C.
Teams: Quebec-Colorado

NHL	Regular	Playoffs
Seasons	10	5
Games	719	57
Goals	334	35
Assists	549	40
Points	883	75
Penalties	311	36

All-Star: 0
Trophies: 1 (Smythe-1)

Stanley Cup Championships 1

No. 95	Dominik Hasek	
	Goalie	1990-Present

Born: Jan. 29, 1965 Pardubice, Czech.
Teams: Chicago, Buffalo

NHL	Regular	Playoffs
Seasons	7	7
Games	350	37
W-L-T	165-121-48	16-16
W. Pct.	.566	.500
GAA	2.34	2.22
Shutouts	33	3

All-Star: 4 (First-4)
Trophies: 6 (Vezina-4, Hart-2)

Stanley Cup Championships 0

From his first days as a Buffalo Sabre, Dominik Hasek was 'The Dominator,' the most baffling, intimidating goaltender of his time.

Hasek was a five-time Czechoslovakian goalie of the year and a three-time player of the year but was a washout in only 25 games with the Chicago Black Hawks. The Hawks dumped Hasek in the summer of 1992 to Buffalo in a deal that brought them journeyman forward Christian Ruuttu and a draft choice (Eric Daze). Hasek quickly beat out incum-

bent goalie Grant Fuhr and put together five consecutive sterling regular season performances.

Hasek was a first all-star in 1994, 1995, 1997 and 1998 and has captured four Vezina Trophies. In 1997 Hasek became the first goalie since Jacques Plante 25 years ago to win the Hart Trophy.

In 1997-98, Hasek recorded 13 shutouts, the most by an NHL goalie since Tony Esposito (15) in 1969-70. Hasek was the key contributor to the Czech Republic's gold medal victory at the 1998 Winter Olympics.

Babe Pratt was a winner. In a 26-year hockey career that spanned eight leagues, from junior to the pros, Babe Pratt was a champion 15 times.

Pratt would hop freight trains in Winnipeg to play for the famous Kenora (Ont.) Thistles. He nailed down a defense job on the New York Rangers' 1940 Stanley Cup winner and, teamed with defenseman Ott Heller, the two were on the ice for only 17 goals against over a 48-game schedule.

A Hart Trophy winner with the Toronto Maple

Leafs in 1944, Pratt set a new standard for defensemen with 57 points in 50 games, a record that stood for 16 years. In his first three seasons with the Leafs, Pratt scored 12, 17 and 18 goals and scored the Stanley Cup winner as the Leafs beat Detroit in the seventh game of the 1945 finals. His NHL career ended in 1947 after a brief stint with the Boston Bruins.

An affable, well-loved man, Pratt became the Vancouver Canucks' goodwill ambassador in 1970. He died of a heart attack in 1988 at the Pacific Coliseum during a Canucks game.

No. 96	Babe Pratt	
	Defenseman	1935-47

Born: Jan. 7, 1916 Stony Mountain, Man.
Died: Dec. 16, 1988 (Age 72)
Teams: Rangers, Toronto, Boston

NHL	Regular	Playoffs
Seasons	12	9
Games	517	63
Goals	83	12
Assists	209	17
Points	292	29
Penalties	463	90

All-Star: 2 (First-1, Second-1)
Trophies: 1 (Hart-1)

Stanley Cup Championships 2

They called him Black Jack and no one quite knew whether it was because of his shock of black hair or the countenance he brought to the ice.

The incarnation of the rock-ribbed defenseman who patrolled the blue-line during the 1940s, John Stewart was a feared defender for the Detroit Red Wings whose decade-long reign included legendary bouts with the Toronto Maple Leafs' Ted Kennedy and Boston Bruins' Milt Schmidt.

Stewart never scored more than five goals or 19 points in one of his 12 NHL seasons and captured only one Stanley Cup (1950).

While his career pre-dated the Norris Trophy, he nonetheless endures as the standard for rough, unyielding defensive play. It is said he was given his nickname by a rival forward who woke up in an emergency ward and asked, "Who hit me with the blackjack?"

"This is the best defenseman in the game," Detroit coach-GM Jack Adams once said. "He has everything."

No. 97 Jack Stewart
Defenseman 1938-52

Born: May 6, 1917 Pilot Mound, Man.
Died: May 25, 1983 (Age 66)
Teams: Detroit, Chicago

NHL	Regular	Playoffs
Seasons	12	9
Games	565	80
Goals	31	5
Assists	84	14
Points	115	19
Penalties	765	143

All-Star: 5 (First-3, Second-2)
Trophies: 0

Stanley Cup Championships 2

No. 98 Yvan Cournoyer
Right Winger 1963-79

Born: Nov. 22, 1943 Drummondville, Que.
Teams: Montreal

NHL	Regular	Playoffs
Seasons	16	12
Games	968	147
Goals	428	64
Assists	435	63
Points	863	127
Penalties	255	47

All-Star: 4 (Second-4)
Trophies: 1 (Smythe-1)

Stanley Cup Championships 10

One of the Montreal Canadiens' most exciting players, the player they called the 'Roadrunner' was always about blazing speed.

Bobby Orr and Bobby Hull were among the select few whose skating could compare with Yvan Cournoyer's startling quickness and acceleration. He scored 25 or more goals for 12 consecutive years, and reached 40 or more goals four times.

Cournoyer took home the Conn Smythe Trophy in 1973 when he scored a playoff-record 15

goals. He would remain a productive post-season performer throughout his career and scored 64 goals in 147 playoff games. Cournoyer played on 10 Stanley Cup winners, including four in a row, before a back injury forced him out of the game at 36.

Jean Beliveau (10 cups) and Henri Richard (11) are the only players with a comparable Stanley Cup championship total.

Cournoyer initiated the play that climaxed with Paul Henderson's game-winning goal in the 1972 Summit Series.

Toughened as a boy by war, Bill Gadsby was one of the NHL's most diligent, respected and durable defenseman.

At 12, Gadsby and his mother were aboard the Athenia and returning from England on the day World War II broke out. The Athenia was torpedoed and they spent five hours in the Atlantic Ocean before being rescued.

As the 25-year-old captain of the Chicago Black Hawks in 1952, Gadsby contracted polio, but after spending 10 days in the isolation ward of an Ottawa hospital, fought off the disease.

He would play 20 NHL seasons, with the Black Hawks, New York Rangers and Detroit Red Wings. A solid offensive player who hit double figures in goals three times, Gadsby was a three-time first all-star, a four-time second all-star and, at one time, held the NHL record for assists by a defenseman (46 in 1958-59).

Despite his excellence, he was never a member of a Stanley Cup winner and never won any of the major individual trophies.

No. 99 Bill Gadsby
Defenseman 1946-66

Born: Aug. 8, 1927 Calgary
Teams: Chicago, Rangers, Detroit

NHL	Regular	Playoffs
Seasons	20	8
Games	1,248	67
Goals	130	4
Assists	438	23
Points	568	27
Penalties	1,539	92

All-Star: 7 (First-3, Second-4)
Trophies: 0

Stanley Cup Championships 0

No. 100 Frank Nighbor
Center 1917-30

Born: Jan. 26, 1893 Pembroke, Ont.
Died: April 13, 1966 (Age 73)
Teams: Ottawa, Toronto

NHL	Regular	Playoffs
Seasons	13	9
Games	348	36
Goals	136	11
Assists	60	11
Points	196	22
Penalties	244	25

All-Star: 0
Trophies: 3 (Byng-2, Hart-1)

Stanley Cup Championships 4

They called Frank Nighbor the 'Flying Dutchman' and the 'Pembroke Peach,' and from the mid-1910s to late-1920s, Nighbor set a lofty standard for goal-scorers.

A right-shooting center who sometimes played left wing, the Pembroke native starred for 15 years with the Ottawa Senators. His first two seasons with the Senators were in the National Hockey Association before the club joined the NHL in 1917.

Nighbor twice scored five goals in a game against Quebec in 1917. A five-time Stanley Cup

winner, he finished among the top NHL 10 scorers four times and was the first winner of the Hart Trophy in 1924 and the inaugural Lady Byng in 1925, which was presented to Nighbor by Lady Byng, the wife of Canada's Governor General and a fervent hockey fan.

Nighbor won another Lady Byng in 1926. A solid defensive player, Nighbor thrived while playing 60 minutes a night and was considered the first skilled practitioner of the poke check.

He retired in 1929-30 after half a season with the Toronto Maple Leafs.

Dates With Destiny

BY ERIC DUHATSCHEK

One night in October, 1998, coach Pierre Page was barking out line combinations from behind the Anaheim Mighty Ducks' bench. This was early in his tenure with the team, right in the middle of Paul Kariya's contract dispute, when Page, caught up in the rhythm of the game, called: "Next up...Sacco... Pronger...Sundin." *Sundin*? Page coached Mats Sundin for three years with the Quebec Nordiques, but the player he wanted on the ice—and the one that jumped out anyway—was right winger Teemu Selanne. Now, apart from all his on-ice skills, Selanne possesses a mischievous sense of humor, so the next day he approached Page with a twinkle in his eye and introduced himself. "Hi," he said, "I'm Teemu Selanne. Nice to meet you."

Selanne, a Finn, and Sundin, a Swede, share more than their association with Page. They are both in the primes of careers pointing straight to the Hockey Hall of Fame. Among active players over 25, they are the most likely candidates for the next edition of the Top 100 players of all-time.

Selanne, at 28, is a year older than Sundin and, according to Page, "everything you'd want in a hockey player. He's skilled, he's bigger than you think, he's stronger than you think and he's quicker than you think. He went through

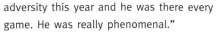

Nifty Nine

The Hockey News conducted voting for the top players in NHL history prior to the 1997 playoffs. Some candidates were caught in limbo. Those players fell into two categories—either not yet old enough to receive due consideration or not yet accomplished enough. Four older players stand out as potential future Top 100 players when the full length and breadth of their careers are considered. Teemu Selanne and Mats Sundin are 'A' candidates while Ron Francis and Pavel Bure rate 'B' status. Five players, then under age 25, stand out: Paul Kariya, Martin Brodeur, Bryan Berard, Peter Forsberg and Keith Tkachuk.

Teemu Selanne

adversity this year and he was there every game. He was really phenomenal."

The adversity stemmed from the fact that the Mighty Ducks struggled as a team largely because Kariya played only 22 games. In that respect, the 1997-98 season represented a coming out for Selanne, a curious development considering how he stood the NHL on its collective ear in his rookie season (1992-93) with a record 76 goals—23 more than the previous mark (53) set by Mike Bossy. It is a record that could stand forever. Selanne has been among the most consistent scorers in the league for the past six years and yet, there was always the underlying sense that he needed someone else to make him good.

They said it was Phil Housley's passing skills—plus the chance to play with Alexei Zhamnov and Keith Tkachuk—that enhanced his productivity with the Winnipeg Jets. They said he needed Kariya the previous season to get him to No. 2 scorer in NHL scoring. But with Kariya missing 60 games, Selanne scored 52 goals in 1997-98—or 28.1 per cent of the Ducks' goals in games that he played, the second-highest such mark in league history. (Brett Hull's 28.8 mark with the St. Louis Blues in 1990-91 is the best.) To Page, that is how last year went into the books, with Selanne, "showing what he could do without Kariya—by playing with all kinds of differ-

Mats Sundin

ent people, on different lines and he had a great attitude all the time."

The essence of Selanne's game is speed and he comes by his passion for it honestly. When he isn't playing hockey, Selanne races cars under a pseudonym—Teddy Flash. Selanne invented the nickname because he feared his original NHL employer, the Jets, would object.

Over time, the NHL has seen its share of fast skaters. What sets Selanne apart is that he can make plays at full speed. He can take a pass in stride, fend off the defenseman and juke himself into shooting position, all the while bearing down on the goalie. "You have to be able to handle the puck at top speed," Selanne said. "Otherwise, there would be a lot of speedskaters in this sport. I've always found it a challenge to handle speed, with

whatever I do. You have to handle the car with lots of speed and you have to handle the puck with lots of speed."

Jari Kurri was the first of the great Finnish players and he made the Top 50 as the No. 50 player. Kurri was a hero for Selanne growing up in Helsinki and there's little doubt in Page's mind that Selanne can be Kurri's equal.

"To me, Selanne can be as good as

149

got to shoot five-hole, right for the middle of the net.' Then he scored a few goals five-hole and he had a big smile. Now, he's a 40- or 50-goal-scorer."

As for Sundin, now 27, there was an off-ice breakthrough in his game last season which coincided with his being named Maple Leaf captain. He took on his responsibilities well and became a good leader, who bought into the team's strategy, with no complaints–even though it had a negative effect on his personal numbers (33 goals and 74 points in 82 games).

Nowadays, he gets the classic compliment from coaches; Sundin is regarded as a low-maintenance player. The Leafs excused him from many practices, but he wouldn't stay away because of the message it might send to teammates–that there is a double-standard for stars and grunts.

Sundin is neither a pure playmaker nor a pure goalscorer, he is a hybrid, doing a little of each. He isn't Mario Lemieux with the puck, although physically, he resembles Lemieux in many respects. Sundin's best work happens after he gathers the puck up in the neutral zone and carries it in the zone.

Sundin has a signature move, putting the puck into a defenseman's skates and then shooting through his legs. He can grind like an NHLer, especially on the boards, but he has European-type skills.

He works the give-and-go well and defends the puck well. He can carry a defenseman on his back and make a play the way Lemieux did. No. 66 skated better, faster and with a more powerful stride; Sundin takes short choppy steps, but he finds a way of getting there nonetheless.

Don't be surprised if both Sundin and Selanne find a way of getting there; that is, to earn a berth among the greats of the game by the time the fullness of their NHL careers is realized.

Kurri," Page said. "The same thing that happened to Kurri has to happen to Teemu. Kurri played with Wayne Gretzky and for a long time, he was just an afterthought. Eventually, people realized how good he really was–that he could shoot off the pass and that he was among the best defensive players in the league. The same thing can happen to Selanne. As soon as he gets closer to winning the Stanley Cup, they'll be saying the same things about him."

Sundin had a similar challenge to Selanne in Toronto last season. After playing with a strong supporting cast in his early days with Quebec, he has been isolated with the Maple Leafs, a Picasso on a team of house painters. Teams put five players on the ice to stop Sundin, on the grounds that if you shut him down, you shut down the Maple Leafs.

"He's a completely different player," Page said. "He's a team guy, a class guy–quiet in a Dale Hawerchuk sort of way. People forget, Sundin never scored more than 10 goals in Sweden. When he first came over, he never shot the puck. If the goalie blocked the net, he just passed the puck. We kept saying, 'Mats, you've

The Fab Five of Paul Kariya, Martin Brodeur, Bryan Berard, Peter Forsberg and Keith Tkachuk represent a quintet of young players who have shown all the signs of one day challenging for a place among the best ever to play in the NHL.

Steve Babineau/SA

aul Kariya played fewer than 100 NHL games over the past two seasons, which is what makes what he did in those games so exceptional. In 91 games, Kariya scored 130 points, which works out to 1.43 per game. You don't have to be Einstein to understand how exceptional that is in the scoring-challenged NHL. The only player who came close to duplicating those numbers over the past two years was Jaromir Jagr, who recorded 1.41 points per game.

Defensemen and goaltenders were not able to stop Kariya—only high sticks, pulled muscles and contract squabbles did. Kariya is known more for what he didn't do than what he did the past two years. The Vancouver native played in only 22 games for the Mighty Ducks of Anaheim. His absence from the 1996 World Cup and 1998 Olympics robbed Canada of its most skilled player.

The mark of Kariya's game is his speed, or more precisely, his instant acceleration. There are a lot of fast skaters in the NHL that never pull away from anybody. Kariya beats you in a hurry. There is a myth, too, that Kariya is all raw talent. On the contrary, said his former coach, Pierre Page. No one works harder at his craft than Kariya.

"He is always trying to make himself better," Page said. "Most days, he's at the rink by 8 a.m. to work on something. There is no more dedicated player in the league than him."

Kariya, 24, took up juggling to improve his eye-hand coordination and it helped him become a magician on the ice. He started his NHL life as a playmaker and evolved into a goal-scorer by painstakingly working on his shot.

He has won the Hobey Baker award as the top U.S. college player, made two first team NHL all-star squads, earned two Lady Byng Trophies, plus an Olympic silver medal and a gold at the World Championship.

Martin Brodeur is an amiable, unflappable 26-year-old that graduated from the Quebec goaltending factory spawned by Patrick Roy and, in only five full seasons, has installed himself as Roy's heir apparent.

He is the son of Denis Brodeur, goaltender for Canada's 1956 Olympic team and photographer for *Les Glorieux*, which is why Martin's boyhood home featured a photographic record of all the goaltending greats

Goalie Martin Brodeur

who played for the Montreal Canadiens. In time, Brodeur may find himself in that illustrious company.

In his second year, he won a Stanley Cup. His 1.88 goals-against average in 1996-97 was the lowest in almost 30 years. His 43 wins for the New Jersey Devils in 1997-98 was the third-highest single-season total registered by an NHL goalie and

Brodeur was on pace to challenge the record set by Bernie Parent (47) in 1973-74.

He is the prototypical modern goaltender. He covers everything. He isn't a flopper. He's rarely out of position. His size, his ability to play upwards of 70 games a season and the league's ever-increasing emphasis on defense suggest that some of hockey's most enduring records—say Terry Sawchuk's 447 goaltender wins—may eventually be within his grasp.

He is the first Bryan Berard, not the next Paul Coffey, and that is how it should be. And yet, in watching Berard play, you can't help but be startled by parallels to Coffey, the highest-scoring defenseman in NHL history.

Berard sees the play unfold, relying on instinct to find and then gobble up the open ice that makes him one of the few young defensemen who can change the direction of a game.

Defenseman Bryan Berard

New York Islanders' GM/coach Mike Milbury believes Berard can be the No. 1 defenseman on a Stanley Cup team, which is why he made the trade with Ottawa in January, 1996, to acquire his rights—this before Berard had played a single NHL game.

Berard is a work in progress, playing a position that is the hardest to learn as a

youngster. Playing forward or goal is frequently all about instinct. Playing defense involves a lot of thinking.

Berard scored 48 points as a 19-year-old in 1996-97 to win the Calder Trophy and he was the youngest player chosen to the American Olympic team in 1998.

He has the size—6-foot-1, 190 pounds—to defend the goal to complement his offensive skills. It's just a matter of harnessing it into a complete package.

Brian Winkler/BBS

155

Rocky Widner

Center Peter Forsberg

That Peter Forsberg is so well-schooled in all aspects of his game should come as no surprise to anyone familiar with his schooling. As part of his formal education, Forsberg attended a special hockey academy–known as a *gymnasium*–in his hometown of Ornskoldsvik, Sweden. Three times a week, instead of math classes or biology or English as a second language, Forsberg went to hockey school, where he learned to skate, stick-handle, pass and–most importantly, in his mind–to compete.

In Forsberg's draft year, little separated him from another Ornskoldsvik teenager, Markus Naslund. They were always on different teams in practice and Forsberg said: "I wouldn't accept losing to his team and he wouldn't accept losing to my team, so it was like war every practice."

War can be hell, but it also developed an edge to Forsberg's game that sets the Colorado Avalanche center apart from most other superstar scorers. When opponents push, Forsberg pushes back–and then adds a whack for good measure. His singleminded devotion towards winning enabled Forsberg to complete a unique trifecta–a World Championship in 1992, an Olympic gold medal in 1994 and a Stanley Cup in 1996–all before his 23rd birthday.

There was a time when Forsberg, now 25, was just one of the eight players and/or draft choices traded to Quebec in the Eric Lindros deal from Philadelphia. In time, Forsberg has become Lindros' equal or, perhaps, superior.

Sweden didn't get past the quarter-finals of the 1998 Olympics, but Forsberg will always be remembered for scoring the famous shootout goal against Canada in 1994's gold medal game, a moment that was immortalized on a Swedish stamp and will live on as one of the seminal moments in international hockey history. In Sweden, it may even be on the curriculum.

Keith Tkachuk of the Phoenix Coyotes was not the first player to join the NHL's unofficial 50-200 club, but he may be the most accomplished member. To qualify, a candidate needs to demonstrate enough scoring to score 50 goals without giving any ground on the ice, so he can spend 200 or more penalty minutes in the penalty box.

The meek need not apply.

Kevin Stevens did it first, then Gary Roberts, then Brendan Shanahan and now

Left Winger Keith Tkachuk

Tkachuk. Club meetings could be held in a phone booth, except with this group, in those cramped quarters, somebody would get hurt. The essence of Tkachuk, 26, is that he combines a boyish enthusiasm for hockey with a mannish mean streak.

Tkachuk, the son of a Boston firefighter, was influenced by the Bruins' Cam Neely, who combined power and skill as well as anyone from his generation.

Tkachuk is unique in that he can play it both ways–tough, as a power forward; and skilled, with the ability to beat a defense-man 1-on-1.

Once upon a time, his Jets' teammates dubbed Tkachuk with the nickname 'Meat,' after the untamed, unsophisticated Tim Robbins character in the movie *Bull Durham*.

Like 'Meat,' it didn't take Tkachuk long to turn immense potential into the real deal.

Hockey Hall of Fame

BENCH STRENGTH
From top to bottom, The Hockey News list of the Top 100 players in NHL history is full of all-time greats–including No. 96-ranked Babe Pratt.

ACKNOWLEDGEMENTS

Thanks to the many people who contributed to this book.
Before: Ken Campbell and The Top 50 Selection Committee whose thoughtful choices made possible everything that followed.
During: Sheldon Coles, Lance Neale, and Mike Ulmer who put it all together.
After: Frank Selke, Jr. and Jason Paul who worked overtime to make it a success.